INDUSTRIAL EDUCATION FACILITIES

INDUSTRIAL EDUCATION FACILITIES

A handbook for organization and management

ROBERT D. BROWN
Northern Illinois University

ALLYN AND BACON, INC.
Boston   London   Sydney

Copyright © 1979 by Allyn and Bacon, Inc., 470 Atlantic Avenue, Boston, Massachusetts 02210. All rights reserved. No part of the material protected by this copyright notice may be reproduced or utilized in any form or by any means, electronic or mechanical, including photocopying, recording, or by any information storage and retrieval system, without permission from the copyright owner.

Previous edition published under the title *Industrial Arts Laboratory Planning and Administration*. Copyright © 1969 by Allyn and Bacon, Inc.

Library of Congress Cataloging in Publication Data

Brown, Robert Dean.
   Industrial education facilities.

   Bibliography: p.
   Includes index.
   1. School shops. I. Title.
TT170.B76   658'.91'6071273   78-10736
ISBN 0-205-06171-0

Printed in the United States of America.

To Jan Evan Brown
July the 14th, 1962—November the 19th, 1964

Contents

Foreword   xi

Preface   xiii

1   INDUSTRIAL EDUCATION IN TRANSITION   1

     Introduction   1   The Goals of Industrial Arts   7
     Vocational-technical Education Programs   15
     The Need for Skillful Laboratory Planning   17
     For Further Reading   19

2   THE FACILITIES PLANNING PROCEDURE   21

     Introduction   21   The Industrial Teacher—A Vital
     Planning Resource   22   A General Procedure for
     Planning Industrial Education Facilities   24
     Evaluation and Redesign of Existing Industrial
     Education Facilities   32   For Further Reading   34

3 LEGISLATIVE SAFETY AND HEALTH STANDARDS 37

Introduction 37 Development of Safety and Health Standards 41 OSHA Standards Requiring Employee Training 43 Employer Responsibilities and Rights 44 Employee Responsibilities and Rights 46 Record Keeping and Reporting 48 Enforcement of OSHA Standards, Rules, and Regulations 50 On-site Inspection 53 OSHA–School Relationships 55 Sources of Help in Understanding OSHA 57 For Further Reading 57

4 LABORATORY SPACE AND DESIGN CONSIDERATIONS 59

Introduction 59 Laboratory Location 60 Size of the Main Work Area of a Laboratory 62 Shapes and Proportions of the Main Work Area 68 Auxiliary Areas 69 For Further Reading 91

5 STRUCTURAL TECHNIQUES AND MATERIALS 93

Introduction 93 Building Construction 93 Walls 95 Partitions 99 Roofs 103 Ceilings 105 Floors 108 For Further Reading 116

6 THE VISUAL ENVIRONMENT 117

Introduction 117 Color 117 Lighting 130 For Further Reading 143

7 THE AUDITORY ENVIRONMENT 145

Introduction 145 The Nature of Sound 146 Control of Noise Generation 147 Noise Transmission 154 For Further Reading 157

8 THE AIR ENVIRONMENT 159

Introduction 159 Mechanical Ventilation 160 Heating 162 Air Conditioning 166 Exhaust Systems 168 For Further Reading 182

CONTENTS ix

9 UTILITY SERVICE SYSTEMS 185

Introduction 185 Electricity 187 Water 195
Gas 199 Compressed Air 204 For Further
Reading 220

10 ACQUISITION OF EQUIPMENT, MATERIALS, AND
CONTRACTUAL SERVICES 223

Introduction 223 Equipment Selection 225
Materials Selection 237 Selection of Contractual
Services 240 Development of Purchase Requests
242 For Further Reading 244

11 PRINCIPLES OF LABORATORY ORGANIZATION 245

Introduction 245 Industrial Education Wing
Design 245 Laboratory Design 248 Conclusion 271 For Further Reading 272

12 ADMINISTRATION OF PROGRAMS AND FACILITIES 273

Introduction 273 Selection, Organization, and Improvement of Course Content 274 Acquisition of
Instructional Media 276 Utilization of External
Resources 278 Promotion of Laboratory
Safety 279 Development of a Public Relations
Program 285 Design of Evening Programs 287
Maintenance of Records 289 Operation of a Personnel System 296 Provision of Laboratory Maintenance Services 297 Issuance of Materials and
Equipment 300 Preparation of Budgets 304
For Further Reading 305

Appendixes 307

Index 315

Foreword

The ability to plan and redesign facilities for effective instruction in industrial education has never been more crucial than it is today. Shifting population patterns, changing emphases in programs, and increased participation in the educative process by all age groups have made evaluation and improvement of facilities a continuing need. School districts in some regions are growing and need new facilities; other districts require new facilities because of changes in programs; and all districts must meet the challenge of providing flexible facilities for rapidly changing conditions. These are the issues that Dr. Brown addresses in his book; furthermore, they are issues for which every industrial educator must be able to provide solutions. The costs of poor planning are manifest in wasted instructional time and generally diminished results of teaching.

Timeliness of subject reflects the importance of this book; but the procedures, examples, and technical data it provides are the components that industrial educators will find most immediately useful. The author carries the reader very skillfully through the planning process and into the technical data from which decisions will be made. The teacher or educational planner who has studied these materials will never be at a loss in a planning situation. He or she will be able to guide study committees and make valuable contributions to the work of the architect. And in everyday laboratory management, the teacher will benefit from the straightforward advice about equipment and process organization.

Dr. Brown has amassed the most current information in the field from a wide variety of sources. These sources have been carefully documented for the reader to check, if further information is desired. Moreover, the thoroughness of his search is reflected by the depth of treatment of the topics covered in *Industrial Education Facilities*. This book is a fine contribution to the literature of the profession and will have a substantial impact on facilities planning in industrial education.

ROBERT E. WOOLDRIDGE, Ed. D.
Professor of Industrial Education
Northern Arizona University
Flagstaff, Arizona

Preface

Those who teach industrial subjects, whether as industrial arts teachers or as vocational-technical teachers, require many kinds of professional abilities. These abilities must include skill in planning and administering laboratory facilities because the quality of a program often is related directly to the quality of the laboratory in which it is presented.

This book has been primarily written for teachers and for those preparing to teach. It should also be of use to school administrators and supervisors, governing boards, architects, and others who share the task of planning educational facilities. My hope is that it will be instrumental in improving the designs of the many laboratories for industrial education that will be created in the years to come.

Industrial Education Facilities deals with ideas, principles, techniques, information, and starting points, rather than with "canned" solutions to planning problems. Various types of plans are included as a means of illustrating important points and presenting alternatives. Information that is essential in making decisions and solving problems constitutes the major content of the book, but readers must ultimately reach their own conclusions.

It is evident that many of the nation's facilities for industrial education fall far short of design excellence and therefore must eventually be replaced or reconstructed. The cost of doing this will be high, but it can be minimized by competent design work and good construction. Shortages of critical materials, including fuels, make it necessary that we build to meet the needs of a future that will be much less tolerant of error.

I am greatly indebted to the following companies for providing illustrations and information:

A A Wire Products Company
A A F, Inc.
Air-Loc Products
Armco Steel
Armstrong Cork Company
Bradley Corporation
Robert J. Brady Company
Brodhead Garrett Co.
Bruning Division, Addressograph Multigraph
Champion Pneumatic Machinery Co., Inc.
Clausing Corporation, Machine Tool Group
Eastman Kodak Company
Joy Manufacturing Company
Oliver Machinery Company
OSHA
Owens/Corning Fiberglas
PPG Industries
Proto Tools
H. H. Robertson Company
Rockwell International, Power Tool Division
San Diego State University, Department of Industrial Studies
Span-Deck, Inc.
The Wiremold Company
Steel Joist Institute
Torit Division, Donaldson Company, Inc.
Victor Equipment Company

INDUSTRIAL EDUCATION FACILITIES

1
Industrial Education in Transition

INTRODUCTION

Since the first human appeared on earth, the world's population has been accumulating a heritage of tool and material usage. Every generation has been faced with the same problems of enhancing its heritage and transmitting it to succeeding generations.

For thousands of years, the chief method of transmittal was an informal process of imitation that included a small amount of person-to-person teaching. In the main, the young people in a culture acquired fundamental skills and knowledge by observing their elders at work, imitating them, and receiving such instruction as the elders were willing to give. This process can have merit where relatively small, homogeneous groups are involved; and it is still used by primitive peoples living in the twentieth century. But it has never resulted in rapid technological progress.

A successful means of providing instruction in the fundamental crafts came into existence many centuries ago with the development of the first formal apprenticeship system. Under that system, a young boy who wanted to learn a trade could do so if his parents apprenticed him to a master craftsman who would teach him the trade and provide much of the rest of his education and upbringing. In return, the master craftsman received companionship and derived both a monetary return and leisure time from the labor of his apprentice. After the apprentice had learned his trade, he assumed journeyman status by moving on to full-time, gainful employment for a time before establishing his own business.

The apprenticeship system was effective and superior to the imitative system in most ways, but neither system met the tremendous demands for skilled workers generated by rapidly increasing populations and mounting aspirations. As people came more and more to covet the better life that their intelligence told them could be created from raw materials of the land

Figure 1.1 *Design and drawing are fundamental to most industrial education activities.* (Bruning Division, Addressograph Multigraph)

INTRODUCTION

and sea, they began to understand that the skilled workers needed to produce vast quantities of consumer goods would have to be educated in comparatively large groups by means of formal teaching methods.

Instruction in handwork in scattered European common schools probably began with the addition of sketching and elementary forms of instrumental drawing to traditional programs. During the fourteenth through the nineteenth centuries such instruction spread slowly but fairly steadily. Work with metals and wood was introduced, and the movement was given considerable impetus by the writings and teachings of noted European educators such as Rousseau, Pestalozzi, von Fellenberg, Cygnaeus, Salomon, Goetze, Kerschensteiner, and Della Vos.

Major centers of education in handwork appeared in England, Switzerland, Finland, Sweden, Denmark, Germany, and Russia. Interestingly, along with attempts to teach trades using formal classroom methods spread the concept of handwork as an essential part of general education. More and more people accepted the idea that handwork was advantageous in improving students' strength and coordination, illuminating academic lessons, satisfying creative urges, and serving as a forerunner to education for gainful employment.

Efforts to include handwork in school programs in the United States began in the early nineteenth century. Progress was more rapid than in Europe, because much of what had been learned by European educational leaders could be utilized. The accomplishments of Pestalozzi and von Fellenberg in their schools in Switzerland, Salomon in his Swedish *sloyd* school, Goetze and Kerschensteiner in their manual training programs in Germany, Della Vos in his Imperial Technical School in Moscow, and others were, at times, very influential.

Forces that were instrumental in placing handwork in educational programs on both continents were similar. They included the belief that academic lessons could be made more understandable by introducing concrete applications of principles, the knowledge that many general education values were inherent in handwork, and a conviction on the part of many industrialists that by teaching handwork schools could help to produce large numbers of skilled workers.

Counterpressures were similar, also. They were generated by persons who thought that school programs should be entirely academic in nature and that the inclusion of handwork would degrade educational standards. They believed the intellectual challenge of handwork to be slight. Such views, of course, did not take into account the many creative professions, such as portrait painting and surgery, in which handwork has always been a key ingredient. Opponents, therefore, were extremely shortsighted. There is certainly evidence that the person who, for example, has become a competent draftsman has furthered his or her education no less than a student of French and that accomplishment in the one discipline does not preclude interest and ability in the other.

Many of the early programs of shopwork in the United States, beginning with the Mechanics Institute Movement around 1820, had trade training objectives. One such program was developed by the Worcester County Free Institute of Industrial Science (later the Worcester Polytechnic Institute) in Worcester, Massachusetts, which was established as an engineering training institution in 1868. Its curriculum included a great deal of instruction in the use of tools and materials, offered as trade training so that graduates could support themselves while striving through practical experience to become engineers.[1]

In 1872, Calvin M. Woodward of Washington University in St. Louis, Missouri, organized the first courses in shopwork for his engineering students. The purpose of the shopwork, which was taught by the university carpenter, was to enable students to make wood models that would assist them in visualizing three-dimensional forms.

Woodward did not view shopwork as an engineering subject, per se, and there is no evidence that he used it to acquaint his students with industrial practices. He spoke of the practical values of shopwork as a means of preparing students to work at a variety of trades. He realized, too, that the lack of skill in using tools and materials among his engineering students was very likely typical of the nation's population. Woodward was aware that most people found tool and material usage to be an essential part of their nonvocational lives. Consequently, he began to think, write, and speak about the general education values of shopwork.

Woodward's developing philosophy led directly to the establishment of the St. Louis Manual Training School, which had both trade training and general education goals. The school represented a firm step in the direction of the many fine industrial arts and vocational-technical programs in existence today.[2]

John D. Runkle, president of the Massachusetts Institute of Technology in the late 1800s, also concluded that it was desirable to provide shopwork for engineering students. He organized courses in much the same way as Woodward and eventually formed the opinion that shop instruction was needed by most boys as preparation for entrance into trades and/or as a part of their general education.[3] By the beginning of the twentieth century, numerous other educators believed that the teaching of shopwork in secondary schools was justified by its many and evident values.

---

[1] Based on Charles A. Bennett, *A History of Manual and Industrial Education 1870 to 1917* (Peoria, Ill.: Chas. A. Bennett Co., 1937), chap. 9.
[2] Ibid.
[3] Ibid.

INTRODUCTION

For the first seventy years of its existence, shopwork in the United States was called "manual training." The name was probably borrowed from Germany. In any case, it was descriptive of what went on in most school shops. The work *was* manual and it was training. The emphasis was on learning to perform certain operations in drawing, woodwork, and metalwork. These operations were considered to represent elements of trades and were taught as such.

For the most part, manual training was gradually added to the curricula of existing secondary schools throughout the United States, although a number of manual training high schools were built in the late 1800s and early 1900s. In academic high schools, the teaching of manual training usually began in unused basement rooms. Teachers were recruited from the ranks of local craftsmen and from school custodial staffs. A program designed to prepare teachers of shopwork began at what is now Teachers College, Columbia University, in the last decade of the nineteenth century.

Eventually, leaders of the manual training movement realized that manual training courses would be attractive to most secondary school students and would have maximum value only if they were not taught solely as vocational courses. It also became obvious that inclusion of experiences in general education would depend on careful selection of course content and skillful teaching.

After 1945, there was a steady movement toward courses that encouraged experimentation with design, equipment, materials, and processes. The name "industrial arts" gained universal acceptance, and the field was expanded to include studies of such other basic industries as electricity/electronics, graphic arts, automotive technology, and crafts. In time, crafts courses became broad experiences that encompassed silversmithing and other art metal activities, lapidary, leatherwork, weaving, ceramics, wood sculpture, and creative work with plastics. Thus, craftwork became an important means of achieving the overall objectives of industrial arts, since it provides many avenues of expression and serves as a source of inspiration for the more formal and technical industrial arts areas.

Industrial arts facilities were, and are, called "shops," although the more inclusive term "laboratory" has found increased use. It is now generally recognized that industrial arts courses should stress experiments in design and studies of form and function, as well as the productive processes of industries.

In 1957, most Americans were unhappily surprised to learn that the Soviet Union had become the first nation to place a man-made satellite in orbit around the earth. Predictably, public school programs received a great deal of criticism for the United States' educational shortcomings, many of which proved to be largely fanciful. The notion that it was educationally respectable to use hands only to hold books had not yet been put to rest.

Subsequently, the movement to make industrial arts courses more academic gained a certain amount of momentum. However, most industrial arts teachers believed that academizing courses to the point where manipulative skills, related technical information, and creative expression were only incidental would negate the most important reasons for including industrial arts in secondary school programs. At the same time, teachers were motivated to evaluate programs and courses and many improvements were made. The most significant advance, perhaps, was the widespread adoption of more eclectic approaches to course organization. Useful as it had been in the development of vocational courses, the trade and job analysis technique had done a great deal of harm to industrial arts by causing courses to be rigidly structured, unimaginative experiences that were often almost devoid of real interest.

At the present time, the field of industrial arts is well developed and widely accepted. Industrial arts is firmly established as a subject matter area at the junior high school level. It is considered to have general educational value and is often a required subject, at least for boys, in grades seven and eight. Industrial arts is universally offered as an elective subject for both boys and girls in grades nine, ten, eleven, and twelve. It is less well defined as an area of study in kindergarten and the six elementary grades. Confusion exists concerning the distinction between art and industrial arts, although they tend to emphasize different tools, materials, and processes. The term "activity work" has been applied to both and seems to be a useful name.

Nearly three hundred colleges and universities have industrial education departments, which prepare teachers in adequate numbers (Fig. 1.2); many departments offer graduate programs at the master's degree, sixth-year, and doctoral levels. At the baccalaureate level, industrial arts teachers are most often educated as generalists with one or two technical areas of concentration. There is, however, a noticeable trend toward specialization, particularly through teaching experience and at the senior high school level.

Industries have been interested in producing pieces of equipment that are appropriate for industrial arts classes, and the result is a wealth of sturdy, well-designed equipment available at reasonable prices. In some cases, units of industrial equipment have been modified for school use. In other instances, wholly new designs have been created. Materials, too, have been produced in abundance by manufacturers and vendors to help teachers bridge the gap between industrial arts laboratories and the industries they illustrate.

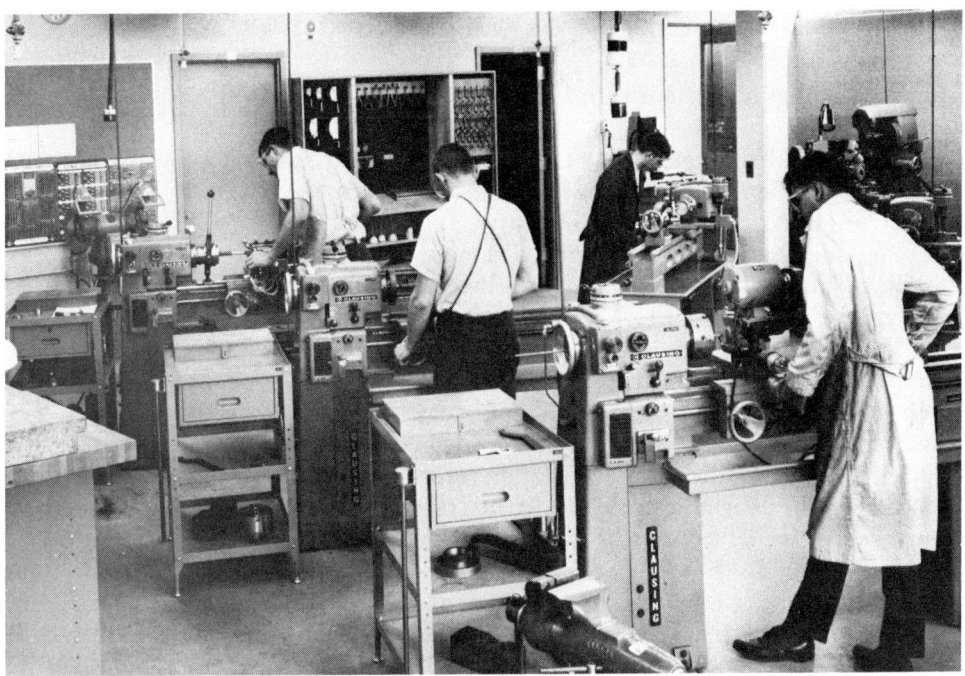

Figure 1.2 *Industrial arts teachers are educated in modern laboratories.* (Clausing Corporation, Machine Tool Group)

THE GOALS OF INDUSTRIAL ARTS

Industrial arts course content can be identified and presented in a number of ways. It is possible to base courses on manufacturing and trade practices, project-centered individual creativity, research and development techniques, or a conceptual approach that stresses common conversion methods — such as shaping, turning, forming, casting, and extruding — that are individually applicable to many materials. There is no evidence that one approach is superior to all others. But there is a substantial body of opinion against the practice of tying courses to trade and job analyses that perpetuate the use of exercises (even in the form of supposedly useful projects) to teach many operations.

At present, the most promising courses stress individual and group creativity with tools, materials, and processes. Certainly, no industrial arts course should ignore current manufacturing techniques, trade practices, action research methods, and conversion processes, but any course of study must treat the student as the key element since students' reactions to what is studied are of major importance. If each individual can be led to develop a strong enough interest in one (or more) of the class activities to continue the activity outside of class, an important goal has been reached.

If not, the most significant and exciting potentiality of the course has been lost.

Industrial arts students should learn to express ideas and translate them into patterns of materials that meet design requirements concerning form, function, constructability, and artistic expression. This kind of a problem-solving approach typifies American industry at its best. It can result in the acquisition of many skills and much technical information, as well as the development of a real interest in creating useful things.

A course that provides the freedom of action essential to creativity tends to emphasize significant activities, not assigned projects. Within each activity, students are encouraged to design and create according to their interests, while the teacher provides the instruction (including a study of the elements of design) upon which their efforts must be based. To illustrate, ceramic slip casting is an important activity in many crafts courses. Where slip casting is included, each student should design and construct at least one pattern, prepare a casting, and complete the processes of bisque firing, decoration, glaze application, and glost firing. The *kind* of piece produced is unimportant, but it must be defensible from the standpoints of design and craftsmanship.

It is apparent that this approach is a demanding one, because it requires the teacher to analyze the available content and make value judgments concerning the relative merit of each activity that *could* be carried on in a course of limited duration. It necessitates evaluation of student work on the same bases that industrial products are evaluated. The reward is that it breathes life into industrial arts courses.

Individual industrial arts courses should exhibit considerable diversity of approach, since there is no best way of achieving course objectives. Standardization of content, teaching methods, and student activities blocks avenues of improvement and can result in mediocrity. Society's only important requirement is that industrial arts courses help meet the goals of secondary education. Throughout the nation, industrial arts teachers and students must make strong, purposeful efforts to achieve commonly accepted educational objectives. *How* they do it is relatively unimportant.

Industrial arts programs contribute to four closely related areas of secondary education: general education, education for self-realization, prevocational education, and preprofessional education. *General education* can be defined as education that is needed by everyone. It is instrumental in enabling all individuals to understand many of the facets of their environment and to function successfully on a nonvocational basis in that environment. *Education for self-realization* aims at meeting nonvocational needs of relatively small groups of students. It provides opportunities for students to pursue individual interests and develop special abilities.

Prevocational education is designed to prepare students to profit from vocational programs undertaken at the senior high school and post–high school levels. It gives students a start toward eventual employment in specific occupations. *Preprofessional education* provides career guidance and the foundations for professional programs undertaken at the college level.

In 1918, the U.S. Bureau of Education published a bulletin entitled *Cardinal Principles of Secondary Education*. That bulletin set forth seven general objectives, which have become known as the seven Cardinal Principles.[4] They are:

1. Health
2. Command of fundamental processes
3. Worthy home membership
4. Vocation
5. Civic education
6. Worthy use of leisure
7. Ethical character

Subsequently written sets of objectives[5] differ in wording but not, essentially, with respect to content. Thus the Cardinal Principles remain a respected listing of the goals of secondary education, as well as a fine statement of educational philosophy. None of the Cardinal Principles has become unimportant or even less important with the passage of time.

If the role of industrial arts is to be defined, answers to the following questions must be available:

1. What *unique* contributions can industrial arts courses make to the achievement of the Cardinal Principles or some other equally good set of objectives of secondary education?
2. What objectives must be included in a set that specifies the responsibilities of industrial arts in secondary education?

It is not a purpose of this chapter to present a complete list of the contributions of industrial arts. The discussion that follows is only illustra-

---

[4]U. S. Bureau of Education, *Cardinal Principles of Secondary Education*, Bulletin No. 35, 1918, p. 11.

[5]Two additional formulations of educational objectives have been well received. One is a statement by the Educational Policies Commission in *The Purpose of Education in American Democracy* (Washington, D. C.: National Education Association, 1938). Another such statement was developed by an organization of secondary school principals. It is "The Imperative Needs of Youth," *Bulletin of the National Association of Secondary School Principals*, 31 (March 1944):1–144.

10   INDUSTRIAL EDUCATION IN TRANSITION

tive and can be greatly expanded. It is, in fact, the duty and opportunity of the field of industrial arts to develop such a list, since an industrial arts course can be fairly appraised only on the basis of the contributions it makes to meeting the overall goals of a school. This is not a new proposition, but it is one that has great significance because it sets the same standard of evaluation for an industrial arts course as for any other kind of course. Unfortunately, this is *not* the basis upon which industrial arts

Figure 1.3 *Industrial education students acquire safe work habits.* (Oliver Machinery Company)

teachers have usually tried to justify their teachings. The profession should move rapidly in this direction.

Health

Most people use tools and materials throughout their lives. Deterioration of physical and mental health can result from accidents that cripple or maim. Therefore, safety must be considered essential in maintaining good health. Industrial arts is the only school subject in which hand-tool and machine safety can be properly taught (Fig. 1.3).

Certain aspects of cleanliness, such as good housekeeping, clean hands, and the habit of promptly caring for minor injuries, can be effectively taught in industrial arts classes.

Creative activities are known to be beneficial to mental health. They occupy the mind, reduce tensions, and provide important successes.

Increased physical strength can result from certain industrial arts activities. Most activities help students develop better coordination.

Command of fundamental processes

In essence, literacy is the ability to read and write. It is the most fundamental area of learning included in programs of formal education. But literacy always exists in degree and there is no such thing as a perfectly literate individual. Literacy level is determined by the number of words a person is able to read, understand, spell, pronounce, and use correctly. Judged by that standard, each of us is substantially illiterate.

Industrial arts students can raise their literacy levels by taking command of hundreds of words that pertain to equipment, materials, processes, and industries. Words such as kerf, axonometric, capacitor, quoin, fid, extrusion, pinion, and tappet assume real meaning when students learn them in contexts of use.

Students in industrial arts classes also learn to apply mathematical principles. They make a great variety of calculations while solving design and measurement problems in such courses as architectural drawing, machine metals, and automotive technology.

Many industrial arts activities require applications of scientific principles in ways that expand students' understanding of the physical world. An automobile power-steering system, for example, provides an excellent illustration of the application of principles of fluid power transmission.

Accurate and constructive thinking is another fundamental process that can be developed in industrial arts classes. There is little doubt that this is one of the results of a course that stresses design.

Worthy home membership

A person who is a worthy home member possesses many abilities. Among them are competence in maintaining an automobile, yard tools, recreational equipment, and the home and its furnishings. The person who allows pieces of family property to deteriorate wastes family income, lessens the satisfaction the family derives from its purchases, and exposes members of the family to the dangers of using unsafe equipment. At the very least, everyone needs information that permits purchasing necessary maintenance services at reasonable cost. Usually, the bulk of the maintenance work around a home is handled by the two adult members of a family and only certain specialized services are purchased. Interior and exterior house painting, lawn mower repair, boat maintenance, recreation room construction, and automobile ignition-system service are a few examples of the many tasks performed by family members. Much of what is done has recreational value and offers the satisfaction that derives from performing useful work.

Obtaining maximum value in return for each expenditure of family income is another important part of worthy home membership. This ability entails skill in recognizing sound construction techniques, quality workmanship, appropriate materials, and good function and appearance.

Industrial arts, unlike other areas of the secondary school program, can give students the skills, knowledge, and understandings they need to perform well in these and other aspects of family living.

Vocation

The secondary school program exists, in part, to help students choose their future occupations. It is vital that they have concrete experiences in areas of potential interest, since merely acquiring information about certain occupations is seldom enough to enable them to make wise choices.

Industrial arts courses can make it possible for students to explore a wide variety of occupations, such as architecture, automotive service, electrical engineering, drafting, and photography. Students who are considering careers in architecture, for example, can learn much about the work of the architect and about their own related interests and abilities by completing a course in architectural drawing and home planning. In the classroom, they will obtain drafting skills and technical knowledge that will be helpful in a study of architecture in college. No other area of secondary education can make these and numerous other important contributions to students' vocational success.

Students in industrial arts classes can acquire habits of self-discipline, accuracy, perseverance, and neatness that are necessary in any occupation.

Civic education

As a portion of its service, the secondary school aims at teaching each student how to take an active part in the public affairs of the community, state, and nation. Industrial arts courses have a part to play in this effort, since they are well able to increase students' social consciousness and their desire to contribute to significant civic undertakings. Industrial arts classes and clubs have produced play equipment for needy children, built furniture for schools and youth centers, organized programs designed to diagnose safety defects in automobiles, and conducted numerous community beautification projects.

Worthy use of leisure

Leisure time is comparatively abundant in the United States today. Moreover, it is probable that the amount of time per week that each wage earner must devote to earning a living will decrease. At the same time, it is clear that leisure can be used in ways that are destructive to both individuals and society. Thus one of the most serious problems facing the nation is that of finding acceptable outlets for energies that need no longer be expended in employment.

There are, of course, numerous worthwhile avocational activities, and industrial arts courses can teach students to carry on many of them. By their very nature, people are tool and material users. Ample evidence of the widespread interest in craftwork is documented in the success of *Popular Science, Popular Photography,* and other periodicals that collectively cover most phases of equipment and material usage. Yearly sales of equipment and materials for avocational use total many millions of dollars.

It seems likely that as the United States progresses toward more or less complete industrial automation with its regrettable tendency to make robots of workers, industrial arts will become increasingly important as a humanizing force in society. Creative activities will disappear from jobs, but the need to create will remain strong in most people and it will be satisfied during leisure hours or not at all. Our schools' duty to teach students to work imaginatively with equipment and materials has been recognized and expressed in statements of the objectives of education. Consequently, industrial arts will become more and more significant as a means of teaching people to be creative.

Avocational interests and abilities will not be well taught if they are viewed as by-products of industrial arts courses. With proper selection of course content and intelligent course organization, industrial arts can superbly prepare students to engage in many kinds of creative leisure time activities and can be justified in a program of secondary education on this basis alone, if necessary.

Ethical character

One manifestation of ethical character is respect for public and private property. This area of learning has increased in importance as the population of the United States has grown. Many social agencies are greatly concerned with it.

Industrial arts classes involve students in the use of more public property than they will use in any other subject matter area. They work with pieces of equipment that are small and large, inexpensive and costly, crude and precise, and delicate and strong. Micrometers, drafting machines, leather-carving tools, engine test equipment, exposure meters, table saws, hammers, and ceramic kilns are representative of the items used.

Students also use and have access to many kinds of materials, some of which are very expensive. Opportunities for waste, damage, and pilferage are endless. Consequently students must act responsibly, as they are being taught to do in industrial arts laboratories all over the nation. Students quickly learn that abusing equipment and wasting materials lead to operating problems, safety hazards, increased costs, and interruptions in class activities.

With respect to other facets of the objective of ethical character, industrial arts has obligations similar to those of other instructional areas. It is in a position to make important contributions.

Objectives set forth for industrial arts must give evidence of dedication to all phases of secondary education. Each objective should express a unique contribution to the achievement of one or more goals of secondary education. Further, it must represent a contribution that industrial arts, in fact, can make with the equipment, materials, laboratories, teaching talent, and student abilities that are available.

The following objectives can be justified on all of the suggested bases. They are teacher objectives, stated in terms of desired student behavior.

TO DEVELOP IN EACH STUDENT:
1. The ability to make skillful use of a variety of materials and pieces of equipment that are common to selected industries, vocations, and professions
2. A fund of technical information concerning equipment, materials, processes, and applications of scientific principles
3. An understanding of the importance of safety and the habit of observing the best safety practices at all times
4. The ability to produce and interpret fundamental types of drawings
5. An interest in creative work and the ability to solve design problems
6. The ability to evaluate consumer products accurately with regard to quality of design and workmanship
7. Skill in maintaining consumer products
8. An interest in and the ability to carry on creative leisure-time activities
9. An understanding of the workings of basic industries, especially their design and productive functions
10. A knowledge of the requirements of and opportunities provided by a variety of important vocations and professions
11. An understanding of his or her interests and abilities as they relate to specific occupations

Collectively these objectives specify the commitment of industrial arts to secondary education and they define industrial arts, since any instructional area is precisely what its objectives say it will do. The objectives make it evident that industrial arts is not an area of study that encompasses everything known to man and that it is not the answer to all educational problems. But it *can* achieve a number of important objectives and this is the task upon which it must concentrate.

VOCATIONAL-TECHNICAL EDUCATION PROGRAMS

The idea that high school graduates should possess salable skills and knowledge, in other words, that they should be occupationally competent, is widely accepted. This principle does not mean, of course, that the choice of a life career must necessarily be made prior to graduation, although some students do so. What it *does* mean is that every graduate should be prepared to take part in the world of work, either permanently or during a period of further education. The self-confidence that stems from being able to earn a living is invaluable to anyone, and the nation's work force can be greatly improved by the addition of skilled teenagers. During the nearly six decades since the formulation of the Cardinal Principles of secondary education, the belief has been growing that occupational education should be available at public expense to those who want it and can profit from it.

Occupational education encompasses *all* programs aimed at preparing students for gainful employment. The range of existing programs is very broad and includes such diverse areas of study as meat cutting and industrial sewing.

Vocational-technical education programs are a vital part of occupational education. The general program titles under which vocational-technical courses are grouped include drafting, metals, transportation, electricity/electronics, graphics, woods, building construction, and refrigeration.

A widespread, comprehensive system of vocational-technical education has been developed to give substance to the notion that occupational competence is important. The system comprises senior high school vocational-technical programs in the eleventh and twelfth grades; area vocational schools, usually at the twelfth grade level; and such post–high school institutions as technical institutes and community colleges. Collectively these programs provide education in all vocational-technical areas. Many individual programs offer work in a variety of technical fields.

The objectives of vocational-technical education are fewer and more direct and therefore are easier to set forth than the objectives of industrial arts. Consequently, the nature of vocational-technical education is more readily understood than the concept of industrial arts. There may be some confusion concerning the role of industrial arts in our system of public education, but the role of vocational-technical education is abundantly clear.

Essentially, vocational-technical education has three purposes. They are: (1) to provide career guidance in a variety of technical occupations, such as drafting and automotive service; (2) to give students exploratory experiences in technical occupations; and (3) to enable each student to acquire entry-level skills and knowledge in a specific technical field.

The objectives of vocational-technical *courses* are similarly concrete and should be stated in behavioral terms. Each objective must be directly related to some aspect of a student's performance in a technical occupation.

Vocational-technical education is a dynamic, ever-changing segment of the educational enterprise. Courses should reflect industrial practices and standards to the greatest extent possible so that the skills and knowledge acquired will be readily marketable.

Laboratory facilities for vocational-technical courses must provide the best possible match with industrial equipment, materials, work practices, and standards. Courses cannot be conducted with maximum effectiveness unless the laboratories in which they are taught permit preparing students for existing conditions ranging from rudimentary to outstanding.

THE NEED FOR SKILLFUL LABORATORY PLANNING

Three types of laboratories have been developed for industrial arts and vocational-technical classes. They are the unit laboratory, the general unit laboratory, and the general laboratory.

A unit laboratory makes it possible to provide relatively great depth of experience within some part of a technical area. Consequently it is a useful, even essential type of facility for certain highly specialized vocational-technical courses, such as welding, automatic transmission service, and photography. However, the unit laboratory is the least useful

Figure 1.4 *Photography is an important part of any graphic arts program.* (Eastman Kodak Company)

of the three types for achieving the objectives of industrial arts. It does not permit giving students enough breadth of experience, unless several unit laboratories are provided for each technical area included in a program so that classes can be rotated from one laboratory to another during each school term. But such a solution is needlessly expensive, and it tends to be self-defeating. Lack of instructional time almost always prevents exploitation of the potential of a unit laboratory since it provides considerably more capacity than can or should be utilized in a nonvocational course.

A general unit laboratory is larger and much more comprehensive than a unit laboratory. It is planned and equipped so that most of the activities found in a technical area can be performed in reasonable depth. A general graphic arts laboratory is an example of a general unit laboratory (Fig. 1.4). It permits work in letterpress printing, offset printing, photography, block printing, silk screen printing, bookbinding, gold stamping, airbrush illustration, and other important types of reproduction.

The general unit laboratory is an excellent facility for certain vocational-technical courses, such as drafting, automotive technology, and woods technology. It is easily the best choice for industrial arts programs at both the junior high school and senior high school levels. Exploratory experiences can be provided by a program in which students are rotated from one general unit laboratory to another during a school term. Each general unit laboratory also makes in-depth work possible in semester and year courses.

A general laboratory is designed for broad, exploratory work in several industrial arts areas. It is more useful at the junior high school level than it is at the senior high school level because courses taught there cannot include much depth of experience.

A general laboratory should contain the basic equipment of three or more industrial arts areas. A typical combination is drawing, woods, metals, and electricity/electronics; but patterns that include graphic arts, automotive technology, and crafts can be equally good. A comprehensive crafts laboratory that provides equipment for wood sculpture, wood lamination, leatherwork, art metalwork, jewelry casting, lapidary, ceramics, and work with plastics is essentially an excellent general laboratory, too.

It is not wise to have more than five areas in a general laboratory, unless the laboratory is quite large and an unusually versatile teacher (or a team of teachers) can be employed. If too many areas are included and/or a teacher of average competence is in charge, the danger is that the instruction will be superficial in all but one or two areas.

A course taught in a general laboratory can be organized so that the entire class rotates from area to area at predetermined times. More commonly the class would be divided into smaller groups that would begin work in different areas and rotate in the same manner. An advantage of the latter plan is that the quantity of equipment purchased for each of the several areas can be much smaller. In addition, students receive inspiration from the varied activity that constantly takes place. A disadvantage is that the teacher will not be able to concentrate his or her efforts on one area at a time and, as a result, may be less effective. More reteaching will be necessary because of the longer periods of time between presentation and application. A major goal of both plans is to enable students to undertake creative work that cuts across area lines.

Valid industrial arts and vocational-technical programs are made possible by skillful teachers, effective selection and organization of course materials, and well-designed laboratories. In a very real sense, anyone who plans a laboratory plans the future of a program, because the link between laboratory planning and the achievement of objectives is a direct one.

Laboratory planning is a continual search for better solutions to the problem of constructing physical settings conducive to first-rate programs. It is the concrete expression of a philosophy, since all desires, ideas, and understandings concerning industrial arts and vocational-technical education are manifest in the facilities.

FOR FURTHER READING

American Council on Industrial Arts Teacher Education. *A Guide to the Planning of Industrial Arts Facilities*. 24th yearbook. Bloomington, Ill.: McKnight Publishing Co., 1975.

American Council on Industrial Arts Teacher Education. *Planning Industrial Arts Facilities*. 8th yearbook. Bloomington, Ill.: McKnight Publishing Co., 1959.

Barlow, Melvin L. *History of Industrial Education in the United States*. Peoria, Ill.: Chas. A. Bennett Co., 1967.

Bennett, Charles A. *A History of Manual and Industrial Education Up to 1870*. Peoria, Ill.: Chas. A. Bennett Co., 1926.

Bennett, Charles A. *A History of Manual and Industrial Education 1870 to 1937*. Peoria, Ill.: Chas. A. Bennett Co., 1937.

Campbell, Edward A. "Let's Plan for the Future." *Industrial Arts and Vocational Education*, March 1965, p. 42.

Ericson, Emanuel E., and Andrews, R. *Teaching Industrial Education: Principles and Practices*. Peoria, Ill.: Chas. A. Bennett Co., 1976.

Finsterbach, Fred C., and McNeice, William C. *Creative Facilities Planning for Occupational Education*. Berkeley Heights, N. J.: Educaré Associates, 1969.

Schmitt, Marshall L., and Taylor, James L. *Planning and Designing Functional Facilities for Industrial Arts Education*. Washington, D. C.: U. S. Department of Health, Education, and Welfare, 1968.

2
The Facilities Planning Procedure

INTRODUCTION

If the appearance of a school is to express its function and if the school is to serve its purpose, it must be carefully designed and constructed. Only adept blending of materials, equipment, technical processes, and skills can produce structures that satisfy our many educational building requirements (Fig. 2.1).

Good design is based on knowledge of the uses to which a school building will be put so that it can be planned to fulfill specific needs. In short, answers to the following questions should be obtained before the architects begin work:

1. What does this community, this state, this nation require in the proposed facility?
2. What do the instructors need in order to teach effectively?

School planning should be chiefly an objective procedure. An architect's emotional involvement with his or her design represents a measure of dedication that is deeply rooted in personal philosophy, and it

Figure 2.1 *A well-designed school building is functional in appearance.*

can add immeasurably to the completed work. Nevertheless, it is not wise to allow intangible factors — for example, appearance and the desire to utilize unusually expensive construction materials — to assume undue importance. Many of an architect's decisions must be tempered by opinions of professional educators.

A number of people — among them governing board members, school administrators, teachers, interested and informed lay members of a community, and specialists in architecture, law, and finance — can contribute to the creation of public school buildings. The most important task confronting the person charged with providing the overall leadership (usually the school's chief administrative officer) is to enlist the help of capable people of all kinds. Ultimately, good design will be the result of a *coordinated* effort by all who take part in planning a facility. Each person must be able to contribute to the limit of his or her ability within an effectively structured and articulated planning procedure. The results of inadequate planning procedures are manifest in the many marginally useful facilities that have been constructed in the past.

THE INDUSTRIAL TEACHER — A VITAL PLANNING RESOURCE

Any architect can put together a school of rooms. Upon completion, it may prove to be a handsome, well-built structure constructed of appropriate materials and filled with quality equipment. It may even be a success from the standpoint of public acceptance. But whether or not it is well designed for teaching and learning is another matter. The degree to which each part of the structure is able to serve its educational purpose will determine whether the community has purchased a real school or just another building that will be used for educational purposes.

Nontechnical areas of a school's curriculum are not especially demanding with respect to facilities, but they can be better taught in rooms specifically designed for them. Subjects such as chemistry, physics, industrial education, music, and home economics, on the other hand, *are* demanding, and planning their facilities requires a much greater understanding of content and methods than most architects possess. Therefore, the design of any school can be greatly improved by bringing teachers' professional knowledge to bear on the problem.

For the most part, industrial arts and vocational-technical teachers are well educated in their professions. Many, perhaps most, have earned one or more graduate degrees. Often even the beginning teacher has a good knowledge of educational philosophy, pedagogy, course content, and facilities planning. These teachers have much to contribute to the design of new facilities and the redesign of outmoded structures.

A school district that wants to include industrial education in the curricula of its schools or add new industrial education areas to existing programs will find it profitable to employ one teacher for each new technical area and assign to him or her the task of designing that laboratory. Teachers with such assignments will not conduct classes immediately, but the investment in their services will be worthwhile.

Industrial teachers already employed by a district should have reduced teaching loads and/or reimbursed vacation assignments, as necessary, to enable them to participate in the solution of planning problems. The expense to the district will be far lower in the end than the cost of building facilities that are not really well suited to the task of educating students. Teachers' salaries represent an immediate financial burden that can be met through normal budgeting procedures. The costs of poorly planned facilities will plague the district for many decades. Even though these costs cannot be accurately expressed in dollars, they exist and are substantial.

The referendum on a proposal to construct new laboratory facilities should not be held until the appropriate sizes and basic shapes of all rooms to be included in each laboratory complex have been determined. Moreover, voters should not be forced to wonder about the potential effectiveness of what has been planned. It must be made clear that the sizes and shapes of rooms are directly related to educational needs. Therefore a scale drawing of each laboratory complex, showing the placement of all equipment, should be prepared. The architect cannot afford to devote this much time to a proposal that may be rejected by the voters, and in any event, he or she is not competent to plan every type of laboratory. The school system *must* use its teachers for this task and publicize the resulting designs as widely as possible.

A GENERAL PROCEDURE FOR PLANNING INDUSTRIAL EDUCATION FACILITIES

There are three fundamental areas of facilities planning: physical plant, equipment selection, and equipment organization. If industrial education laboratories are to permit valid education programs, the original planning in these areas must be good. In addition, subsequent program evaluation and laboratory redesign should be continuous.

There is an effective procedure that enables an industrial designer to identify a human need, develop a product capable of meeting that need, and be reasonably sure the product will be marketable. Van Doren[1] sketches the procedure in bold, clear strokes. The planning of new industrial education facilities is also a design procedure, and it is similar to the one followed by industrial designers.

The industrial education laboratory planning procedure has two distinct parts. First, a proposal is prepared for referendum, and second, the approved proposal is translated into working drawings and the construction and equipping of the facility are completed. Many of an industrial teacher's contributions are made prior to the referendum. Thereafter the teacher should function mainly in an advisory capacity, although minor problems of redesign — especially during the time in which pieces of equipment are installed on the floors and walls — will occupy some of his or her time. Thus the planning procedure can be outlined as follows:

Part One
  Phase 1 — compilation of design criteria
  Phase 2 — completion of the initial design of the building, wing, or area and each laboratory complex
  Phase 3 — transmittal of information to the architectural firm
  Phase 4 — preparation of preliminary building layouts

[1]Harold Van Doren, *Industrial Design* (New York: McGraw-Hill, 1954), pp. 35–83, 207–70, 329–37.

REFERENDUM

Part Two
    Phase 1 — completion of the work of design and construction
    Phase 2 — acquisition of equipment, materials, and contractual services
    Phase 3 — installation of equipment
    Phase 4 — completion of repairs and modifications

Part one should begin well in advance of the selection of the architectural firm so that phases 1 and 2 can be completed and the resulting information made available to the architects when the preliminary discussions are held.

PART ONE, PHASE 1

During this portion of the planning procedure fundamental decisions concerning curriculum are made. The nature of the industrial education program to be carried on in the new facility should be described in easily understood terms. Many members of the community may take part in this activity, but the leadership must come from teachers of industrial arts or vocational-technical education.

To begin with, the overall objectives of the school's industrial education program must be set forth. Each objective, of course, will relate to one or more of the broad purposes of the school. Everyone involved in drafting the objectives should be convinced that the completed set represents realistic goals that will mean significant educational gains for students. Each objective should be one to which the school can commit itself without reservation.

Next, the separate industrial education areas to be included in the program and the type(s) of laboratories to be constructed should be identified. If all of the basic areas — woods, metals, drafting, building construction, electricity/electronics, automotive technology, refrigeration, crafts, and graphics — cannot be included, those believed to be the most helpful in meeting the objectives should be chosen. In some cases, it is worthwhile to add a general laboratory to a series of general unit laboratories so that students will be able to do at least some work in all areas.

Finally, the activities that will be carried on in each laboratory should be listed, since this information will eventually be used in preparing lists of necessary equipment and materials. Graphics, for example, can include many reproduction activities, each having special equipment and material requirements. The decision as to *which* activities will be taught must be based on estimates of the relative value of each in helping to achieve course objectives.

Special kinds of instruction that are not parts of the regular industrial education program but that the school may want to offer on occasion, must be identified if this instruction will take place in industrial education laboratories. Offerings such as short-term courses for local industries, adult avocational classes, and in-service courses for faculty members may require space, equipment, and supplies that ordinarily would not be provided.

Limitations that cannot be overcome (for example, lack of land) and the economic structure of the community must be kept in mind when new facilities are planned. The anticipated rate and type of growth of the community will also influence the program and laboratory designs. However, financial considerations should not be allowed to affect decisions unnecessarily. Most communities can afford whatever they consider important, and school facilities are underbuilt more often than they are overbuilt.

The total load on the proposed facility should be determined in part one, phase 1. It is necessary to know how many separate classes will be taught per day in each laboratory, how many times each class will meet per week, what the maximum size of each class will be, and the ages, grade levels, and sex of students who will be enrolled in the various classes. Obtaining valid solutions to many of the basic planning problems depends upon having such information available, and records that trace the growth of the community and school system are essential to an accurate prediction of load.

Those who engage in planning industrial education facilities should be familiar with the building codes of their communities and states. Preparing a checklist of code standards can save a great deal of design time.

Planning information compiled at the state level can be helpful. Some state departments of vocational-technical education have been active in developing realistic design and construction standards and making data available to those who need it.

It can be worthwhile for facilities planners to visit industrial education laboratories believed to be well designed. Such laboratories usually possess a variety of interesting and valuable design features. Photographs should be taken for later reference and to assist in making decisions.

The information and other assistance that college and university industrial education departments (both in and out of state) can give should not be overlooked. Most institutions of higher education are guided by the assumptions that they exist to provide instruction, increase knowledge in a variety of fields, and contribute to the dissemination of knowledge by engaging in consulting activities. Of course, it is not wise to submit a planning problem to a college department and ask for a *complete* solution. Industrial education departments usually do not have the resources to give this kind of help on a wide scale. For the most part, planning problems should be solved by those who will use the facilities.

PART ONE, PHASE 2

This phase is the creative portion of the planning procedure, during which the designs of industrial education laboratories and a wing, building, or area to house them are brought to completion. Information compiled in part one, phase 1 will determine the direction of the design effort. The school's industrial education faculty should be responsible for completing the task.

The design process utilizes expressions of educational philosophy, descriptive statements, lists of equipment, photographs, sketches, models, and scale drawings. The intent is to provide the architects with an accurate floor plan of each laboratory, as well as a drawing that shows the spatial relationships of the laboratories to each other.

Each floor plan should show the placement of all pieces of equipment in main work areas and auxiliary areas. Types and sizes of equipment, directions of machine feed, names of rooms, and other details should also be indicated.

Written statements accompanying the drawings should explain, supplement, and justify the design work. These statements may specify flooring materials, partition construction, color schemes, types of windows, vertical placement of windows, lighting systems, utility service systems, exhaust systems, and acoustical treatments. In addition, they should present reasons for doing what has been done. For example, the rationale for a specific amount of floor space in the main work area should be based on information gathered from a variety of informed sources *and* on a well-designed floor plan. To the greatest extent possible, evidence should be incontestable. Each written statement is as important as the list of specifications that accompanies the working drawings of a house. It should be carefully drafted and have the approval of school administrative officers and members of the governing board.

Separate lists of the equipment and contractual services needed by each laboratory should be available so that architects can calculate building costs. The quantity, unit price, and total price of each item should be listed.

Successful completion of part one, phase 2 is critically important in planning a valid industrial education facility because it provides the best possible defense against unreasonable reductions in the size, comprehensiveness, convenience, and durability of each laboratory. Industrial arts teachers do not desire to gain overly large facilities at the expense of other areas of the school program; neither do they want to lose laboratory space unnecessarily. There is little effective defense against cutting the size of an empty room because it does not reflect its educational purpose. It is much more difficult to justify taking floor space away from a fully planned laboratory because it is obvious that it would damage the program. Compromises may become necessary, but they must always be made with full knowledge of their effects on programs.

PART ONE, PHASE 3

Turning over initial designs and all supplementary information to the architects should take place at a meeting of the architects, school administrative officers, industrial teachers, industrial education supervisors (local and state), and representatives of the school board. At the meeting, the architects' questions should be answered, and they should be familiarized with the educational philosophy, program, and data underlying the materials presented. Then the architects can proceed with their part of the design function: blending individual laboratory designs into a building that facilitates teaching and learning and meets the community's needs for durability and aesthetic quality. It is not acceptable that the architects, through their building design, influence course content and teaching method. Their attention should be focused on structure and appearance.

PART ONE, PHASE 4

In this part of the planning process, the architects incorporate the various laboratory designs into the total school design. Industrial teachers should serve in an advisory capacity so that necessary changes in room sizes and other design modifications will do the least amount of harm to the program. Even small changes can be immensely damaging if they curtail the scope of the work that can be carried on. For example, reducing the size of a project storage room can significantly influence the breadth and depth of a general woods program by limiting the size of projects that students could undertake. Many students who would be interested in and fully capable of completing large projects would not be able to do so because such projects could not be stored.

Other modifications can be equally detrimental to the program and/or inimical to laboratory safety, administrative efficiency, and aesthetic design. Additional examples could be provided, but it is evident that vigilance during this part of the planning process is necessary to prevent partial invalidation of the original design. If teachers are fully informed as the work progresses, it may even be possible to make design changes that will lead to improved programs.

PART TWO, PHASE 1

This portion of the planning process should begin soon after residents of a school district have voted favorably in a referendum. Generally speaking, an affirmative vote reflects acceptance of the proposal, including approval of the projected structure, equipment, and financial arrangements. The architects prepare working drawings of the buildings; a general contractor and subcontractors in excavation, masonry, structural steel, electrical, plumbing, heating and air conditioning, decorating, and other areas are selected; the building is constructed; and the landscaping is completed.

During phase 1, industrial teachers should again serve as consultants. As the architects transform preliminary layouts to working drawings of each part of the school, many problems will arise. Substantial revisions in the designs of individual instructional areas may be necessary in order to solve some of these problems.

The architects must work within the framework of a budget that, in most cases, is limited by law. If labor, equipment, and materials costs are not stable, financially dictated cutbacks can be troublesome. There is a noticeable tendency in such cases to reduce costs by decreasing the size of laboratories and classrooms. But, in fact, money should be saved by eliminating unnecessarily expensive building shapes, costly but not always more serviceable building materials, and design features (such as large foyers) that do not directly contribute to classroom instruction.

Cutbacks in the size, number, and variety of rooms should be only a last resort, since space is critically important to any educational program.

Lack of floor space for instructional purposes will handicap a school's program more than any other factor, and this deficiency is the most expensive to correct.

PART TWO, PHASE 2

This is the portion of the planning process during which industrial teachers compile the remaining information needed to prepare purchase requests for equipment, materials, and contractual services. Much information concerning types and quantities of equipment will have been gathered in part one, phase 2. Current list prices, catalog numbers, model numbers, and specifications regarding construction materials, finishes, options, workmanship, and delivery remain to be determined so that bids can be obtained, dealers chosen, and orders placed.

Budget systems vary, but their basic features are often similar. Equipment usually includes hand tools, machines, laboratory furniture, attachments of various kinds, and instructional media. Most pieces of equipment are assigned to permanent locations and listed in inventories. However, many items such as twist drills and table saw blades are consumed through use; therefore it is not desirable to carry them on inventory. The usual solution is to select a dollar value to serve as an arbitrary dividing line between permanent equipment and items that, by virtue of being consumable, are really materials. Even so, it is necessary to build flexibility into a budget system, because certain items (such as a twelve-volt storage battery) may cost enough to be considered permanent equipment, which they are not.

Many budget systems have two categories of materials: (1) resale items that students will purchase and that must be carried on inventory and (2) consumable items that may be used for all legitimate educational purposes and are not inventoried.

Contractual services are needed in organizing laboratories, keeping them in good repair, and performing a number of redesign tasks. Normally such services are supplied by specialists not in the permanent employ of the school, although industrial teachers can be hired occasionally to complete certain jobs during vacation periods.

When purchase requests are prepared, it may be desirable to revise equipment and materials lists. Improved designs, new products, and new materials appear on the market from time to time and should be substituted for items originally specified, if doing so will improve the program. Dealers' discounts and price reductions may permit some increases in quantities and/or the addition of items cut from the budget because of an anticipated lack of funds. Unfortunately, the reverse is more often true. It is helpful if teachers have opportunities to redraft their requests within moderation during this phase of the planning process, because hindsight is a valuable adjunct to foresight.

PART TWO, PHASE 3

The work of this part of the planning process should be organized to promote efficient handling of equipment and materials as they arrive. The date of completion of the facility and its transfer from the general contractor to the school district should be scheduled as early as possible in the spring of the year, because the tasks of organizing equipment and "shaking down" the laboratories are time-consuming.

The efficient school district hires teachers who will have laboratory responsibilities to work through the vacation period preceding the school term during which the facilities will be used for the first time. If necessary, professional labor should prepare a laboratory for service, but the help of teachers in planning and directing the work of equipment organization, performing some of it, and checking the operation of each piece of equipment is invaluable. Inevitably, adjustments to equipment, small construction jobs, and storage, classification, and coding tasks arise and must be completed in order to ensure smoothly running laboratories. Many of them can best be handled by industrial teachers. As is true in any industrial design situation, some of the brilliance of the planning can be lost through faulty execution.

PART TWO, PHASE 4

This is the final portion of the planning process. The word "final" is used in a relative sense, since laboratory development never ceases. In most cases, part two, phase 4 will terminate some time during the first year or two that industrial education laboratories are in use, whenever warranty repairs are finished and as warranties expire. Warranty service necessitated by faulty materials and workmanship should be completed as rapidly as possible in order to avoid undue class disruption. It is scarcely necessary to add that this work should be scheduled for Saturdays and other times when classes are not in session. The school's industrial teachers are the ones who must detect defects in equipment and materials and make sure that the terms of agreements between the school district and contractors and suppliers have been fully satisfied.

Minor modifications in industrial education laboratories may become necessary during phase 4, and it is good administrative practice to provide a contingency fund for this purpose. However, proposed alterations should be carefully scrutinized because of the high cost of doing work not covered by the original contract. It may be found that such work can be performed as well, and at less cost, by the school's maintenance staff and/or industrial education faculty.

Periodic revisions in the physical plant and equipment inventory are both unavoidable and desirable. They should be financed by normal budgetary procedures from year to year so that the industrial education program can be an ever-improving one.

EVALUATION AND REDESIGN OF EXISTING INDUSTRIAL EDUCATION FACILITIES

Periodically industries find it desirable to modernize or replace pieces of income-producing property. Tax advantages and prestige are motivating factors in some cases, but the need for competitive facilities in a changing world is the most important consideration. School districts should adopt the same policy. Buildings and equipment do not remain indefinitely capable of yielding a satisfactory educational return, and it makes little sense to educate students in a school world that is unlike the world in which they will live and work. The author's experience of seeing a new vocational architectural drawing laboratory equipped with T-squares and triangles needs no comment.

Problems of redesign vary greatly. They range from simple reorganization of equipment to complete laboratory renovation. A substantial part of the procedure for planning new facilities applies in redesign situations, but certain differences in approach are necessitated by the following factors:

1. Redesign problems are often less involved than original design problems due to limitations imposed by existing structures and by equipment that cannot be replaced. However, these limitations may also prove to be inimical to satisfactory solutions.
2. Reconstruction may not require a referendum. Sometimes financing can be handled through customary budget procedures applied over a span of several years.
3. The services of an architect may not be required.

The improvement of an existing facility must begin with a thorough understanding of what a school district's industrial education courses have been and a clear view of what they should be. No educational field can attempt to do tomorrow's job with yesterday's courses and hope to remain in business very long. Thus the starting point for redesign is the same as it is for planning new facilities — the program.

Second, it is necessary to make an accurate appraisal of the physical condition of a facility in order to suggest worthwhile modifications. Specifically the exact condition of the floors, ceilings, walls, partitions, windows, doors, storage facilities, equipment, and lighting, heating, ventilation, dust collection, and utility service systems must be known. The *validity* of the facility must also be determined. It is difficult to overemphasize this last point, because the difference between a mediocre laboratory complex and a superb one is often attributable to ostensibly minor differences in design. For example, the condition of the paint on walls and partitions may be good, but the color scheme may be psychologically

Figure 2.2 *Sample checklist for evaluating industrial education facilities.*

LABORATORY EVALUATION FORM

SCHOOL ______________ LABORATORY ______________

EVALUATOR'S NAME ______________ DATE ______________

ITEM	CONDITION					DESIGN					COMMENT	ACTION
	EX.	GD.	AV.	FR.	PR.	EX.	GD.	AV.	FR.	PR.		
EQUIPMENT												
LIGHTING												
ACOUSTICS												

unsound. Similarly, a machine may be well constructed and in good operating condition, but its capacity may be inadequate.

A comprehensive checklist will simplify the task of appraisal. To be of value, checklists must contain an ample amount of space for use in explaining the ratings. A checklist should also provide space for recommendations to improve or replace each item listed. As an example, it is not enough merely to rate a lighting system as poor. The rating should be accompanied by data indicating the intensity of illumination on work surfaces and by specific recommendations for changes in luminaires (lighting fixtures), luminaire placement, switch placement, circuitry, local lighting, and the level of general illumination.

There is no best form for a checklist. Everyone who has the responsibility of evaluating a facility should develop an instrument that fits the conditions at hand. The partially completed checklist shown in Fig. 2.2 is intended to serve as a starting point.

Once a facility has been evaluated, a summarizing report written, and the recommendations accepted by the governing board, the process of redesign is much the same as the procedure for planning new facilities. The report will serve as a statement of design criteria. In minor redesign problems, phases 3 and 4 of part one can be eliminated. A general contractor should be selected and the work of renovating, equipping, and checking completed. More comprehensive redesign and reconstruction projects require the services of architects and may necessitate the expenditure of more money than can be allocated from yearly budgets. They should be handled in the manner suggested in the procedure for planning new facilities.

In both situations, industrial teachers should play leading roles as designers and consultants. Provisions for them to do so should be made in their teaching schedules and, if necessary, in their salaries.

Reconstruction, no less than new construction, is time-consuming. Therefore part one of the planning procedure should begin early enough to allow ample time for design, construction, acquisition of equipment and materials, and installation and testing of equipment.

FOR FURTHER READING

Alger, Leon, and Dowling, John. "Shop and Facility Planning." *School Shop*, November 1975, p. 32.

American Council on Industrial Arts Teacher Education. *A Guide to the Planning of Industrial Arts Facilities*. 24th yearbook. Bloomington, Ill.: McKnight Publishing Co., 1975.

Campbell, Edward A. "Advice on Planning New Shops and Laboratories." *Industrial Education*, March 1975, p. 33.

Campbell, Edward A. "Let's Plan First Class Facilities." *Industrial Education*, March 1974, p. 32.

Finsterbach, Fred C., and McNeice, William C. *Creative Facilities Planning for Occupational Education*. Berkeley Heights, N. J.: Educaré Associates, 1969.

Gillespie, Paul R. "Planning a Lab?" *Industrial Education*, March 1974, p. 50.

Jones, Richard A. "Eight Guidelines for Planning a Vocational Technical Education School." *American Vocational Journal*, January 1969, p. 36.

Leu, Donald J. *Planning Educational Facilities*. New York: Center for Applied Research in Education, 1965.

Mahal, L. Kenneth, and Olson, Ray E. "Architects' Approach to Vocational School Planning." *American Vocational Journal*, January 1969, p. 31.

Midjaas, Carl L. "Decision Matrix for Vo-Ed Programs." *School Shop*, April 1976, p. 48.

Nerden, Joseph T. "A Q & A Session for Facility Planners." *School Shop*, April 1976, p. 46.

Oregon State Department of Education, Division of Community Colleges and Vocational Education. *Guide to Planning Industrial Arts Laboratory Facilities*. Salem, Ore., 1968.

Russo, Michael. "Concepts and Procedures for Systematic Planning." *American Vocational Journal*, January 1969, p. 23.

Schmitt, Marshall L., and Taylor, James L. *Planning and Designing Functional Facilities for Industrial Arts Education*. Washington, D. C: U. S. Department of Health, Education, and Welfare, 1968.

Steeb, Ralph, and Hurst, Marshall. "Evaluating Your Industrial Arts — Procedures and Guidelines." *Industrial Arts and Vocational Education*, February 1968, p. 20.

Sumption, Merle R., and Landes, Jack L. *Planning Functional School Buildings*. New York: Harper, 1957.

Wilber, Gordon O., and Pendered, Norman C. *Industrial Arts in General Education*. Scranton, Pa.: International Textbook Co., 1967.

3

Legislative Safety and Health Standards

INTRODUCTION

The industrial revolution began in the United States in the early years of the nineteenth century. Since that time, manufacturing has grown rapidly to form a vast industrial complex with a mushrooming urban population.

Great productive capacity and the demand for manufactured goods generated by emphasis on the individual as consumer led manufacturers to concentrate on output at the expense of other considerations. Two of the results were predictable and perhaps inevitable: bad working conditions and a steadily deteriorating environment. Employers assumed that wages provided adequate compensation for injuries and job-related illnesses and that the environment had an infinite capacity to absorb damage.

Gradually it became evident that industrial safety and health conditions had to be improved. Consequently, in 1914, the U. S. Public Health Service was expanded to include the Office of Industrial Hygiene and Sanitation. The primary purpose of that office was to encourage and conduct research designed to identify work hazards and to suggest ways of eliminating them. After 1930, the medical field began to emphasize preventive medicine as well as corrective procedures. The preventive medicine concept is simple: what does not occur need not be treated. General acceptance of this concept has led to mandatory physical examinations for industrial workers; control of occupational diseases, such as silicosis and lead poisoning; machinery guards; and improved general work environments.

The Walsh-Healey Act of 1936 (Public Service Contracts Act) and supplementary acts of 1958, 1965, and 1969 were intended to promote occupational safety and health. The Walsh-Healey Act provided that any agency of the U. S. Government contracting for materials costing more than $10,000 had to stipulate in the contract that "no part of such contract will be performed nor will any of the materials, supplies, articles, or equipment be manufactured or fabricated in any plants, factories, buildings, or surroundings which are unsanitary or hazardous or dangerous to the health and safety of employees engaged in the performance of said contract." It also stipulated that meeting the safety, sanitary, and factory laws of the state in which the materials were produced would constitute satisfactory compliance with the law. Unfortunately this provision proved to be a significant weakness, because only California, Illinois, Massachusetts, New York, Ohio, and Pennsylvania had state regulatory personnel capable of enforcing their laws. Moreover, only about forty federal inspectors were available to assist state personnel.

Other long-standing problems have been a general lack of expertise in recognizing occupational diseases and the haphazard ways in which these diseases have been reported to regulatory personnel. Employers have seldom been able to employ enough professionally trained people to do a good job of monitoring environmental problems and the symptoms of work-related illnesses. Until 1970, reports on these diseases were required only in California and there was little legal incentive to improve the situation.

The *annual* work-related death and disability record in United States workplaces in 1970 included approximately 14,000 employee deaths, 2 million injuries of varying seriousness, and 300,000 new cases of occupational illness. Strikes consumed only about one-tenth as many employee days as accidents and illness. Thus it was evident that comprehensive federal legislation that could be enforced would be needed to provide American workers with adequate safety and health protection while at work.

To correct the situation, Congress passed Public Law 91-596, *Occupational Safety and Health Act* (OSHA), in 1970 and President Nixon signed it into law. OSHA is administered by the Occupational Safety and Health Administration of the U. S. Department of Labor. The OSHA Office of

Figure 3.1 *Industries must provide safe workplaces.* (OSHA)

Training and Education provides training courses and teaching materials to help employers comply with the law.

Fundamentally, OSHA is responsible for developing occupational safety and health standards that are legally enforceable. The act covers much of the United States civilian labor force by requiring that employers having one or more employees provide safe and healthful working conditions (Fig. 3.1). Work-related hazards are to be abated as rapidly as possible, and new or improved safety and health programs are to be established.

OSHA outlines separate, but closely related, responsibilities and rights for both employers and employees. Employee safety and health are recognized as public problems rather than private or individual concerns. All standards promulgated by OSHA become explicit public policy. Record-keeping and reporting procedures have been set up to monitor job-related injuries and illnesses. States are encouraged to develop and enforce their own safety and health programs, but these programs must be at least as stringent as OSHA if they are to be approved.

Four groups of workers are not covered by OSHA. They are: self-employed persons, workers on family-owned and -operated farms, employees already protected by other federal agencies under other federal laws, and employees of state and local governments. OSHA monitors workplaces protected by other federal agencies under other federal laws to make sure that their work environments meet the standards promulgated for private employers. States desiring OSHA approval of their occupational safety and health programs must also cover their own employees in ways that match or exceed OSHA standards for private industry.

A number of definitions are incorporated in Public Law 91-596 in order to foster understanding of the act. They include the following:

1. *Secretary* — Secretary of Labor
2. *Commission* — Occupational Safety and Health Review Commission
3. *Commerce* — trade, traffic, commerce, transportation, or communication among the several states or between a state and any place outside thereof or within the District of Columbia or a possession of the United States (other than the Trust Territory of the Pacific Islands) or between points in the same state but through a point outside thereof
4. *Person* — one or more individuals, partnerships, associations, corporations, business trusts, legal representatives, or any organized group of persons
5. *Employer* — a person engaged in a business affecting com-

merce who has employees but does not include the United States or any state or political subdivision of a state

6. *Employee* — a person who is employed by one whose business affects commerce
7. *State* — a state of the United States, the District of Columbia, Puerto Rico, the Virgin Islands, American Samoa, Guam, and the Trust Territory of the Pacific Islands
8. *Occupational safety and health standard* — a standard that requires conditions or the adoption or use of one or more practices, means, methods, operations, or processes reasonably necessary or appropriate to provide safe or healthful employment and places of employment
9. *National consensus standard* — any occupational safety and health standard or modification thereof that (1) has been adopted and promulgated by a nationally recognized standards-producing organization under procedures whereby it can be determined by the Secretary that persons interested and affected by the scope or provisions of the standard have reached substantial agreement on its adoption, (2) was formulated in a manner that afforded an opportunity for diverse views to be considered, and (3) has been designated as such a standard by the Secretary, after consultation with other appropriate federal agencies
10. *Established federal standards* — any operative occupational safety and health standard established by any agency of the United States and presently in effect or contained in any act of Congress in force on the date of enactment of this act
11. *Committee* — National Advisory Committee on Occupational Safety and Health established under this act
12. *Director* — Director of the National Institute for Occupational Safety and Health
13. *Institute* — National Institute for Occupational Safety and Health established under this act
14. *Workmen's Compensation Commission* — the National Commission on State Workmen's Compensation Laws established under this act

DEVELOPMENT OF SAFETY AND HEALTH STANDARDS

Developing safety and health standards to protect workers in some 5 million covered workplaces is a task that must be completed over a period of many years. Moreover standards often require interpretation, as well as the addition of methods and procedures that make them effective in individual situations. Where standards are not yet available, employers must operate in accordance with the *intent* of the general duty clause of OSHA. They must, according to the act, provide "employment and a place of employment which are free from recognized hazards that are causing or are likely to cause death or serious physical harm to employees."

Recommendations for standards may be submitted to OSHA by employers or employees, developed by OSHA, or submitted by the National Institute for Occupational Safety and Health (NIOSH). NIOSH was established by OSHA as an agency of the Department of Health, Education, and Welfare (HEW). The basic purpose of NIOSH is to generate and carry on research related to various safety and health problems (including concomitant psychological conditions), provide technical assistance to OSHA, and recommend standards for adoption. NIOSH was also created to develop the basic research needed to prepare standards covering such potentially harmful substances as asbestos, vinyl chloride, and known carcinogens (cancer-producing materials).

There are four general categories of occupational safety and health standards: general industry, maritime, construction, and agriculture. If OSHA decides that a standard is needed, an advisory committee can be asked to make specific recommendations. For example, the National Advisory Committee on Occupational Safety and Health (NACOSH) may be asked for advice. This is the committee that advises the Secretaries of Labor and HEW on the administration of OSHA. A standard proposed for the construction industry would probably be referred to the Advisory Committee on Construction Safety and Health for study and recommendations. Similarly the Standards Advisory Committee on Agriculture usually would be called on to consider a standard proposed for agriculture. If necessary, a proposed standard can be referred to an ad hoc committee appointed by the Secretary of Labor at the request of OSHA. By law, the life of an ad hoc committee is limited to 270 days.

Any standard that OSHA considers adopting, amending, or deleting must be published in the *Federal Register*. Once a description of the proposed action has been published, members of the public have a stated time (as long as sixty days) to respond to it. The response may take any of a number of forms, including a request for modification, a request for additional information, support for the proposal, or a request that the proposal be eliminated. Hearings on the proposal may also be requested, and if hearings are called for, OSHA must schedule them. The times and places of hearings are published in the *Federal Register*.

OSHA must publish its decision, as well as the complete language of an adopted standard, an addition to a standard, or the elimination of a standard in the *Federal Register*. The notice must include the date on which a new or modified standard will take effect. Copies of OSHA standards are available from the nearest OSHA area office. The *Federal Register* is another excellent source of information on standards. It is always up-to-date, since all OSHA actions are published in it as they are taken. Many public libraries subscribe to the *Federal Register*, or it is available from the Superintendent of Documents, U. S. Government Printing Office, Washington, D. C. 20402. The OSHA Subscription Service (also available from the Superintendent of Documents) makes all changes available in looseleaf form.

OSHA STANDARDS REQUIRING EMPLOYEE TRAINING

A number of OSHA standards require that employees be trained to recognize hazards of various kinds; to understand the purposes and practices of medical surveillance programs, including self-examination procedures; to understand decontamination purposes and procedures; to take part in emergency procedures; to render appropriate first aid; and to operate certain pieces of equipment.

Safety and health training requirements have been developed for general industry employment, maritime employment, the construction industry, and agriculture. It is assumed that adequate training will help prevent accidents and health problems that can occur even where employers are in compliance with existing standards.

General industry standards (part 1910 of the Code of Federal Regulations [CFR]) that require training employees in safety and health practices include the following:

1. Occupational health and environmental control
2. Hazardous materials
3. Personal protective equipment
4. General environmental controls
5. Medical services and first aid
6. Fire protection
7. Materials handling and storage
8. Machine operation and machine guarding
9. Welding, cutting, and brazing
10. Special industries

Maritime employees who are injured while working within the federal maritime jurisdiction on navigable waters of the United States can claim compensation under the terms of the Longshoremen's and Harbor Workers' Compensation Act. The act mandates that employers provide safeguards and safety equipment for employees and maintain reasonably hazard-free working conditions. OSHA maritime standards require employers to train workers engaged in shipbuilding, ship repairing, and ship demolition. These standards cover:

1. Welding, cutting, and heating
2. General working conditions
3. Tools and related equipment
4. Personal protective equipment

Part 1926 of CFR contains OSHA training standards for construction industries. These standards were promulgated by the Secretary of Labor in section 107 of the Contract Work Hours and Safety Standards Act (Construction Safety Act). Employers are required to train workers in the following general areas:

1. General safety and health provisions
2. Occupational health and environmental controls
3. Personal protective and life-saving equipment
4. Fire protection and prevention
5. Welding and cutting
6. Tunnels and shafts, caissons, cofferdams, and compressed air
7. Blasting and use of explosives

Occupational safety and health training standards for agriculture are listed in part 1928 of CFR. The standards require that employees operating agricultural tractors be given specific operating instructions (listed in the standard) designed to prevent roll-over injuries.

EMPLOYER RESPONSIBILITIES AND RIGHTS

OSHA regulations carefully spell out employer responsibilities and rights so that all covered employers will understand how the act affects them. In general, every employer is required to take certain actions that will help to create a hazard-free workplace and is granted a number of rights intended to facilitate compliance with the act. In short, responsibilities and rights are carefully coordinated to generate respect for

EMPLOYER RESPONSIBILITIES AND RIGHTS

OSHA and encourage observance of the law. Employer responsibilities comprise the following:

1. Provide a safe work environment and comply with all OSHA standards, rules, and regulations
2. Make sure that all employees are fully informed of their OSHA responsibilities and rights
3. Use color codes, posters, labels, and signs to warn employees of potential hazards
4. Require employees to follow good safety and health practices
5. Provide all medical examinations required by OSHA
6. Report in the manner specified by OSHA
7. Maintain records required by OSHA
8. Cooperate with OSHA compliance officers
9. Permit employees to exercise their OSHA rights without discrimination
10. Promptly eliminate cited violations of OSHA standards

Employer rights assist employers in bringing their establishments into compliance and provide protection against governmental harassment. Every employer is entitled to:

1. Request advice from and off-site consultations with OSHA officials
2. Take an active part in the job safety and health program of the appropriate industry association
3. Demand proper identification of OSHA compliance officers
4. Demand the reasons for an inspection
5. Schedule an opening and closing conference with a compliance officer
6. File a *Notice of Contest*, if appropriate, with the nearest OSHA area office; this action must be taken within fifteen working days of the issuance of a citation
7. Apply to OSHA for a temporary variance from a standard
8. Apply to OSHA for a permanent variance from a standard
9. Help develop occupational safety and health standards by assisting the OSHA Standards Advisory Committee and by working with other organizations devoted to job safety
10. Secure a long-term loan through the Small Business Administration (available only to small business employers)
11. The privilege of confidentiality of trade secrets noted by an OSHA compliance officer during an inspection

EMPLOYEE RESPONSIBILITIES AND RIGHTS

Employee responsibilities require workers to perform and conduct themselves in ways that make it possible to achieve the objectives of OSHA. Employees must comply with OSHA standards and make every reasonable effort to avoid safety and health hazards (Fig. 3.2). Specifically, employees are required by the act to:

1. Keep informed of all applicable OSHA standards, rules, and regulations
2. Comply with all applicable OSHA standards, rules, and regulations
3. Follow all employer safety and health rules
4. Report hazardous conditions to their immediate supervisors
5. Report job-related injuries and illnesses to their employers and obtain medical treatment for such injuries and illnesses
6. Cooperate with OSHA compliance officers
7. Exercise all OSHA rights in a responsible manner

Employee rights define the legal entitlement of employees to work in places that are free of safety and health hazards. According to the act, every employee shall have the right to:

1. Review any OSHA standard, rule, or regulation
2. Obtain information from his or her employer concerning (1) safety and health hazards present in the workplace, (2) precautions to be taken, and (3) procedures to be followed in case of accident or exposure to a toxic substance
3. Request an OSHA inspection
4. Confidentiality when a complaint is made
5. Information from OSHA about the action taken on a complaint
6. Complain to OSHA about harassment, demotion, discharge, or any other penalty resulting from an exercise of rights granted by the act. Such a complaint must be filed within thirty days of the incident, and OSHA must take action on the complaint within ninety days of the filing
7. Have an authorized employee representative from the workplace accompany the OSHA compliance officer during an inspection
8. Respond to questions asked by a compliance officer
9. Observe measurements of hazardous substances by a compliance officer and have access to records of data obtained

EMPLOYEE RESPONSIBILITIES AND RIGHTS

10. Participate in a closing conference with the compliance officer who has conducted an investigation
11. Request information from NIOSH concerning any substance in the workplace that has potential toxic effects in the con-

Figure 3.2 *Safety on the construction site benefits employers and employees.* (Rockwell International, Power Tool Division)

centration used. The employee's name shall be withheld from the employer when such a request is made

12. Object to the length of the abatement period allowed by a citation. Any complaint must be submitted to the OSHA area director within fifteen working days of the issuance of the citation
13. Receive notification whenever the employer applies for a variance hearing
14. Appeal the decision handed down following a variance hearing
15. Submit information to OSHA concerning the issuance, modification, or revocation of a standard and request a public hearing on it

RECORD KEEPING AND REPORTING

Anyone who employs more than ten people must maintain a running record of job-related injuries and illnesses as they occur. Employers of fewer than ten employees are required to keep records only if chosen by the Bureau of Labor Statistics to take part in one of the Bureau's periodic statistical surveys of occupational injuries and illnesses.

An *occupational injury* is defined as a cut, fracture, sprain, or amputation caused by a work-related accident. Similarly, an *occupational illness* is any abnormal condition resulting from exposure to environmental conditions in the workplace. Inhalation, ingestion, or direct contact with a toxic substance can result in an occupational illness.

OSHA requires a record of all occupational injuries and illnesses that result in death, loss of workdays, loss of consciousness, restriction of the physical mobility of an employee, transfer of an employee to another job, or medical treatment other than routine first aid. If death results from an accident in the workplace or if five or more employees are hospitalized because of an accident, OSHA must be notified within forty-eight hours of the incident.

Employers must maintain records for all work establishments, including plants, business offices, construction sites, and others. A work establishment is defined by the act as a single physical plant location where business is conducted or where services are performed. Two types of records must be kept on a calendar-year basis:

1. OSHA No. 100 is the *Log of Occupational Injuries and Illnesses.* Each separate incident must be recorded on this form within six working days of the time the employer is informed

of it. Information to be recorded includes the injured person's name, occupation, and department; date of occurrence; nature of the incident; number of workdays lost; and an indication of whether or not transfer or termination was required.
2. OSHA No. 101 is a supplementary record that contains essentially the same information as OSHA No. 100.

An employer who prefers to use record-keeping forms other than the two listed may apply to the Regional Director of the Bureau of Labor Statistics for permission to do so. The petition for a record-keeping variance should describe and justify the proposed alternative system of records. A copy of the petition must be given to the employees' authorized representative, and it must be posted in a conspicuous location in the workplace. Employees have ten days from the date of notification in which to file a response.

To keep employees properly informed about OSHA and about the company's safety and health records, every employer must post the following notices in a prominent location in the workplace:

1. OSHA No. 2203 (job safety and health protection) informs workers of their responsibilities and rights under the act. Copies of the act and this poster must be given to all employees requesting them.
2. OSHA No. 102 (summary of occupational injuries and illnesses) is the annual summary. It must be posted by January 31 of each year. It summarizes job-related injuries and illnesses for the preceding year. OSHA No. 102 must remain posted for at least thirty days.
3. Summaries of petitions for variances from standards and record-keeping variances.
4. Copies of OSHA citations for violations of standards must remain posted for three days or until the violation is corrected, whichever is longer.

When an OSHA standard is being prepared, it may be necessary for NIOSH to carry on research aimed at measuring employee exposure to harmful substances. If this is the case, employees or authorized employee representatives have the right to be present when readings are taken and are entitled to access to any records made. Every employee shall also have access to his or her own examination records and must be notified if the exposure level has exceeded the level to be set by the standard. In addition, employees must be informed of corrective measures that are being taken.

ENFORCEMENT OF OSHA STANDARDS, RULES, AND REGULATIONS

Compliance officers, including safety experts and industrial hygienists, have been recruited from a number of sources and trained by OSHA to evaluate safety and health hazards in the nation's covered workplaces. An on-site inspection by a compliance officer is usually the first step taken to induce an employer to meet OSHA standards. The compliance officer will utilize personal observations, consultations with employers and employees, examinations of records, instrument readings, and photographs to determine whether or not standards are being violated (Fig. 3.3). All findings must be reported to the OSHA area director, who may issue a citation. The compliance officer may also issue a citation, if the situation is ominous enough to justify a telephone conference with the area director and if the area director approves the citation.

Four types of citations can be issued. In a given situation, the one used will depend on the seriousness of the violation. The four types are as follows:

1. *De minimus* — A violation that represents no direct or immediate threat to job safety and/or health. A notice is issued to the employer.
2. *Nonserious violation* — A violation that *does* pose a direct or immediate threat to job safety and/or health but is not likely to lead to death or serious injury. Penalties range up to $1000 per day.
3. *Serious violation* — A violation that includes the strong probability that death or substantial bodily harm will result from conditions in the workplace and that the employer is aware or should be aware of the situation. Penalties of up to $1000 per day are mandatory.
4. *Imminent danger* — A violation that carries reasonable certainty that hazards likely to cause death or serious injury exist in the workplace. Further, it is probable that normal enforcement procedures will not eliminate the hazards before death or injury results. If the employer refuses to remove employees from the danger area and abate the hazards at once, OSHA will take immediate action in Federal District Court to force compliance.

Falsification of records, applications, or reports can result in a $10,000 fine and a six-month jail sentence for an employer. Assaulting, opposing, intimidating, or interfering with a compliance officer is punishable by a

Figure 3.3 *OSHA inspections identify health and safety hazards.* (OSHA)

fine of up to $5000 and a jail sentence of up to three years. Willful or repeated violation of an OSHA standard carries a fine of up to $10,000 per violation. If death results from a violation and the employer is subsequently convicted of willful violation, the penalty is a fine of up to $10,000 and/or up to six months in jail. A second conviction will double the penalty.

Both employers and employees may appeal an OSHA decision to issue a citation or not to issue one. The appeal submitted by an employer is called a "Notice of Contest." Such an appeal must be filed with the OSHA area director, who will forward it to the Occupational Safety and Health Review Commission. OSHRC is an independent body not under the control of the U. S. Department of Labor. An unfavorable ruling by OSHRC may be appealed to the U. S. Circuit Court of Appeals.

Small business employers who are financially unable to comply with either OSHA standards or state safety and health standards can apply to the Small Business Administration for a long term loan. Money borrowed may be used only for bringing the establishment into compliance.

States are encouraged by OSHA to develop their own occupational safety and health programs. These programs must be at least as stringent as OSHA to gain credit for complying with OSHA standards, rules, and regulations. Approved state programs can be funded by OSHA up to a maximum of fifty per cent of operating cost.

Any permanent standard adopted by OSHA can be appealed to the U. S. Circuit Court of Appeals, as long as the appeal is filed within sixty days of publication in the *Federal Register*. The standard will remain in effect during an appeal, unless the Circuit Court orders a stay of enforcement.

If OSHA decides that serious danger exists in a workplace due to exposure to a toxic substance or some new kind of hazard, a temporary emergency standard, effective immediately, can be adopted. This type of standard must also be published in the *Federal Register*. It serves as a proposed permanent standard and is subject to the normal adoption procedure. The final ruling on it must be made within six months of publication.

An employer may apply to OSHA for variances from standards if immediate compliance is not possible or if it can be demonstrated that protection already provided is at least equal to that required by OSHA. No variance can be made retroactive; that is, an employer cannot avoid being penalized for a citation by submitting an application for a variance. After receiving an application for a temporary or permanent variance, OSHA can grant an interim order permitting operation under existing conditions until a variance decision can be reached.

A temporary variance can be granted to an employer who cannot comply with a standard by the date on which it becomes effective. However, inability to comply must be due to lack of materials, equipment, or personnel or to new construction or alterations that cannot be completed by that date. Moreover, the employer must show that a sincere effort to comply is being made and that acceptable temporary protection is being provided for employees. If necessary, a temporary variance can be renewed, but it cannot remain in effect longer than two years.

A permanent variance can be obtained by an employer who can prove that the company's practices, operations, and conditions provide as safe and healthful a work environment as the one required by OSHA.

A variance can also be granted to permit an employer to participate in a program designed to evaluate a new occupational safety or health procedure. However, the evaluation procedure must be approved by the Secretary of Labor or the Secretary of Health, Education, and Welfare.

The Secretary of Labor can approve a variance if it can be shown that compliance would be harmful to the national defense program.

ON-SITE INSPECTION

OSHA is authorized by the act to conduct on-site inspections in covered work establishments. After a compliance officer has presented the proper credentials, he or she is entitled to immediate admission to an establishment, provided the request to enter is made at a reasonable time. During normal work hours is a reasonable time to conduct an inspection. All parts of the workplace are to be open to inspection, and the compliance officer can privately question the employer, owner, operator, or agent, as well as the employees. If an employer refuses to admit a compliance officer or interferes with an inspection, OSHA can take legal action to force cooperation.

Inspections are conducted without advance notice, except in unusual circumstances. It is, in fact, illegal for *anyone* to warn an employer that an OSHA inspection is to be made. Advance notice can be given by OSHA only if:

1. An imminent danger situation requiring immediate abatement may exist
2. The inspection must take place outside of working hours
3. Special preparations must be made for the inspection
4. It is necessary to ensure that the employer, employee representative, or other personnel will be present
5. The OSHA area director decides that advance notice will permit a more effective inspection

An employer receiving advance notice of an inspection is responsible for informing employees or the employee representative of the impending visit.

Because a large number of workplaces remain to be checked for compliance with the act, OSHA has set up a series of inspection priorities. They are:

1. *Imminent Danger* (top priority)
   This priority covers situations in which serious physical harm, temporary or permanent disablement, and health hazards, injuries, or illnesses that are difficult to diagnose are likely to result from conditions in the workplace.

Employees (or an employee representative) detecting a possible imminent danger situation must immediately inform the employer. If no action is taken to abate the hazard(s), the nearest OSHA office must be notified and requested to inspect the workplace. Names of those making the request will be kept confidential.

The OSHA area director will evaluate the complaint and, if it seems justified, notify the OSHA regional administrator and regional legal counsel. At the same time, a compliance officer will be assigned to conduct an immediate on-site inspection.

In the event that the inspection discloses an imminent danger situation, the compliance officer will ask the employer for immediate abatement of the hazard and will direct that the employees be removed from the danger area. Before leaving the workplace, the compliance officer will inform the employees of the danger. If the employer refuses to eliminate the hazard, OSHA will take legal action in Federal District Court to force compliance.

Employees found to be working in an imminent danger situation may legally leave the job only if (1) the employer has been asked to abate the hazard and has not done so AND (2) the danger is so great that normal enforcement procedures will not eliminate it quickly enough AND (3) there is real danger of death or substantial physical harm AND (4) there is no reasonable alternative to a walkout.

2. *Catastrophes and Fatal Accidents* (second priority)
Catastrophes, deaths, and accidents requiring hospitalization of five or more employees are to be reported to OSHA within forty-eight hours of occurrence. OSHA will assign a compliance officer to conduct an inspection of the workplace.

3. *Valid Employee Complaints* (third priority)
If an employee believes that a standard has been violated or that dangerous or unhealthful conditions exist, he or she can request OSHA to make an inspection. OSHA will inform the complainant as to the action taken.

4. *Special Emphasis Programs* (fourth priority)
From time to time, OSHA will schedule inspections of specific industries, occupations, or substances believed to be unusually hazardous.

5. *Random Inspections* (fifth priority)
These are routine inspections of workplaces believed to be potentially hazardous.

6. *Reinspections*
Establishments cited for serious violations of standards will be reinspected to ensure that the hazards have been eliminated.

OSHA–SCHOOL RELATIONSHIPS

Public schools are not covered by OSHA because they are units of state or local governments. It is possible, of course, that state and local governments will be required to comply with OSHA standards, rules, and regulations in the future. Therefore some states are taking steps to bring their schools into compliance with the act. There is little doubt that compliance can result in safer school environments, which are certainly desirable. However, limited budgets will force most school districts to move slowly. Since federal inspections would ordinarily be necessary to ensure that schools met OSHA requirements, special provisions for preserving state and local autonomy in school matters would be needed. A state could accomplish that by developing its own OSHA-approved occupational safety and health program and financing it with little or no federal assistance. With minimum state guidance, compliance could be enforced by local governing boards.

Areas of operation in which school districts and governing boards can and should voluntarily attempt to comply with OSHA standards include the following:

1. *Hand-tool, machine, and equipment safety* — The design and physical condition of every item included in an industrial education laboratory must be good. Substandard items should be renovated or replaced by pieces known to be well designed and constructed.
2. *Safety in working with hazardous materials* — Exposure to hazardous materials must be minimized and, if necessary, eliminated. Appropriate protective equipment, such as paint masks, should be available and its use enforced.
3. *Training in safety and health requirements* — Teachers, students, and civil service employees should be taught to recognize work hazards and potentially dangerous environmental conditions.
4. *Fire protection* — All necessary fire protection devices and services, including fire extinguishers, sprinkler systems, and fire department assistance, should be available.
5. *Physical plant design* — The physical plant in which an

industrial education program is carried on must be planned so that it is free of safety and health hazards. Key design features of such a structure include adequate space, proper storage of materials, a good arrangement of rooms, and an effective organization of equipment.

6. *Physical plant condition* — The floors, walls, partitions, ceilings, windows, doors, and other parts of a laboratory must be kept in good repair. An industrial education building, wing, or area should also be well maintained.
7. *Air environment* — Students and teachers must be able to work in air that is clean, fresh, safe, and comfortable. Effective heating, air conditioning, mechanical ventilation, and exhaust systems are necessary.
8. *Visual environment* — Natural and artificial lighting systems must be properly designed and maintained so that people working in a laboratory can see clearly and comfortably.
9. *Auditory environment* — Sound intensities in industrial education laboratories must be kept below the level at which hearing can be damaged. Noise transmitted from a laboratory to other parts of the school must also be strictly controlled.
10. *Utility service systems* — Electrical, water, gas, and compressed air systems must be planned and constructed so that hazards related to the use of these utilities are minimal. Good system maintenance is essential.
11. *Housekeeping* — Laboratories must be kept clean and in good order at all times. Adequate storage of materials, especially waste products, is of major importance to laboratory safety.
12. *Sanitary facilities* — Drinking fountains, wash facilities, and restrooms must be well designed, in good operating condition, and cleaned regularly.
13. *First aid and emergency procedures* — Teachers, students, and civil service employees should be trained in basic first aid and emergency procedures.
14. *Class discipline* — Laboratory work environments must be free of hazards that stem from poor class discipline.

Industrial education teachers have done a remarkably good job of maintaining safe and healthful working conditions in their laboratories. For far longer than OSHA has been in existence, teachers have understood that safety and effective learning go hand in hand. The fine accident records in industrial education laboratories throughout the nation clearly indicate an emphasis on safety. It is interesting to note that these records have often been achieved in spite of school districts' unwillingness to spend money on such things as good lighting, dust collection systems, and adequate laboratory space.

SOURCES OF HELP IN UNDERSTANDING OSHA

The nearest OSHA area office is a good place to start developing an understanding of OSHA. Copies of Public Law 91-596, as well as pamphlets and fact sheets that explain the law, can be obtained at the area offices. OSHA officials are available at these offices to answer questions, discuss the law, and schedule presentations to interested groups of people.

Subscriptions to the *OSHA Subscription Service* and OSHA's monthly publication, *Job Safety*, furnish up-to-date information on the act and its many provisions. A subscription to the *Federal Register* is recommended for anyone who must comply with OSHA standards.

The OSHA Training Institute, 10600 Higgins Road, Rosemont, Illinois 60018, offers free certification programs designed to prepare for compliance with parts 1926 and 1910 of the act. The National Technical Information Service, U. S. Department of Commerce, Springfield, Virginia 22151, also can provide instructional materials dealing with OSHA. Other instructional materials that are useful in teaching courses can be obtained from the National Audiovisual Center (GSA), Washington, D. C. 20409 and from the Superintendent of Documents.

Much additional information relating to occupational safety and health standards has been developed by the National Safety Council, the National Fire Protection Association, Underwriters' Laboratories, Inc., the American Society of Safety Engineers, and the American National Standards Institute. Any of these organizations can provide help with specific problems.

FOR FURTHER READING

Campbell, Edward A. "Design Safety into Your Shops and Labs." *Industrial Education*, March 1976, p. 30.

Johnston, Wallace L. "OSHA: What It Is — How to Do It." *School Shop*, February 1975.

Sawyer, David E. "What You Should Know About the Law and Liability." *Industrial Education*, March 1974, p. 66.

U. S. Congress. *Occupational Safety and Health Act of 1970*. Public Law 91-596. 91st Congress, 1970.

U. S. Department of Labor, Occupational Safety and Health Administration. *All About OSHA*. OSHA 2056. Washington, D. C., 1976.

U. S. Department of Labor, Occupational Safety and Health Administration. *General Industry.* OSHA 2206. Washington, D. C., 1976.

U. S. Department of Labor, Occupational Safety and Health Administration. *Training Requirements of OSHA Standards.* OSHA 2254. Washington, D. C., 1976.

Witte, Carl W. "Would This Safety Program Work for You?" *Industrial Education,* March 1975, p. 64.

Wolff, Charles S. "After 5 Years: OSHA and the School Shop." *School Shop,* April 1976, p. 66.

4
Laboratory Space and Design Considerations

INTRODUCTION

The term *physical plant* refers to the portion of an educational facility that is planned by a staff of architects and built by a general contractor and subcontractors. This includes the building itself, all utility service systems, and equipment — such as chalkboards, bulletin boards, book shelves, display cases, and student lockers — that is more or less permanently attached to the basic structure.

The acquisition, arrangement, installation, and storage of equipment and materials are not considered to be elements of physical plant planning. For the most part, they are not direct concerns of either architects or contractors. They relate to physical plant planning only insofar as they affect total building costs, room sizes and shapes, the design of utility service systems, and structural characteristics of buildings.

An industrial teacher will not be assigned the task of designing the structure of the part of a school that houses industrial education laboratories. Nor will a teacher be called upon to write technical specifications for an air conditioning system, a heating plant, or an acoustical treatment. However, he or she must be familiar enough with the various aspects of physical plant planning to be able to express the requirements of a given teaching area and evaluate designs and workmanship. It is necessary, for example, to have a working knowledge of one or more comprehensive color systems so that recommendations for laboratory color schemes can be made. Similarly, a teacher should know enough about the physical and aesthetic characteristics of materials, such as those available for surfacing floors, to be able to judge their usefulness in the various industrial education laboratories.

Eleven subtopics of physical plant planning can be set forth. They are: (1) laboratory location, (2) laboratory main work area size, (3) main work area shapes and proportions, (4) auxiliary areas, (5) walls, partitions, and ceilings, (6) floors, (7) the use of color, (8) lighting, (9) acoustics, (10) the air environment, and (11) utility service systems. The first four of these subtopics are discussed in this chapter. The others are explored in Chapters 5 through 9.

LABORATORY LOCATION

If several areas of industrial education are included in a school's curriculum, the laboratories serving these areas should be grouped to facilitate interarea work and to achieve architectural efficiency. The major means of obtaining effective groupings are the separate building concept, the building wing plan, and building area design.

Undeniably, an industrial education building that is separate from a main school building offers advantages. Such an arrangement can be very efficient with respect to design, and it can provide an ideal pattern of laboratories. A service drive for delivery of equipment and supplies and a parking lot are easy to plan for a separate building. Problems of noise transmission to other parts of the school are avoided, and laboratories are readily accessible for use by evening classes. The separate building concept also makes it possible to set up a good system for disposing of waste products.

At the high school level, a separate industrial education building should be connected to the main school building by a hard-surfaced walkway. Walkways should be covered to protect students from the sun and rain in climates that are warm or moderate. Enclosed, heated walkways are essential in geographic areas having a cold winter season.

Walkways, of course, add to construction costs as do the additional wall required by a separate building, longer heating and air conditioning runs, and longer sewer, water, and gas lines. Unit heating and air conditioning systems may reduce the extra costs somewhat.

Aesthetically a price must be paid for housing industrial education laboratories in their own building, unless the entire school is designed as a campus of separate buildings to accommodate the different programs. It is not always possible to achieve an integrated design if there is one large main building and a much smaller one for industrial education. And walkways, whether enclosed or not, are not necessarily things of beauty.

The heaviest cost, however, is a philosophical one. Locating these laboratories in a separate building can have the effect of setting the program apart, both physically and philosophically, from other parts of the school curriculum. Industrial education may seem to be a discipline that caters mainly to the special vocational or avocational needs of a comparatively small group of students, whereas a substantial portion of the worth of the program is its contribution to the general education of boys and girls at all grade levels.

Building wing design provides suitable isolation while avoiding most of the drawbacks of a separate building. Laboratories can be effectively grouped, and the architectural validity of a wing can be as great as the abilities of the architect permit. The means for effective noise control are inherent in the basic design. Service drives and parking facilities are not difficult to plan.

There is no serious philosophical objection to building wing design. A certain physical separation exists, but other curriculum areas, such as music, physical education, and the sciences, also find building wings effective in meeting their needs. The land area devoted to a wing (or separate industrial education building) should be large enough to permit expansion of the facility.

Finally, a school's industrial education laboratories can be grouped in one area of the school if the location of the area is carefully chosen and if sufficient space can be provided. Such an area must be relatively free of noise from external sources and located so that noise created in the laboratories will not disturb other classes.

Any area allocated for industrial education laboratories must be continuous. It should not be divided into two or more smaller areas by corridors or other kinds of facilities. The area must be large enough to house all necessary laboratories, classrooms, and special-purpose rooms, and it should have direct access, if necessary, to a service drive and a parking lot. In addition, it should not be located adjacent to a noise producer — such as a railroad right-of-way, heavily traveled street, gymnasium, band room, or playground.

Multistory buildings do not provide the most effective housing for industrial education laboratories. Floors above ground level are more difficult to supply with equipment and materials. Teacher-student movements between laboratories that are on different levels are considerably less efficient, and noise problems can be both numerous and troublesome to solve.

It is possible, of course, to reduce the amount of land needed for a school by constructing a building having more than one story. But the resultant monetary saving will be offset, at least partially, by the costs of the necessarily greater foundation and structural strength of such a building.

If multistory building design is unavoidable in a given situation, heavy laboratories and those having the highest noise levels should be located on the first floor. Except for technical drawing, it is difficult to suggest a laboratory that can operate as well on an upper story as it can at ground level. Electronics, crafts, and graphic arts laboratories are the next best choices for placement on upper stories.

Laboratories should not be located below grade level, unless the building is well sealed and air conditioned. Dust that seeps in from outside and humidity can be all but insurmountable problems without perfect window sealing and temperature and humidity control.

On balance, schools that are fortunate enough to have several areas of industrial education included in their curricular offerings usually find the single-story building wing to be the best choice. It has more advantages and fewer limitations than any other design.

In the northern hemisphere, the windows of a laboratory's main work area should face north in order to minimize the sun's glare and heat. The second best direction is south, although during winter months glare can be moderately disadvantageous with south-facing windows. Windows should not face east or west. Several methods, almost all expensive and none entirely satisfactory, can be employed to reduce the detrimental effects of each of the four exposures.

SIZE OF THE MAIN WORK AREA OF A LABORATORY

A complete laboratory complex consists of a main work area and one or more auxiliary areas. The size of the main work area is determined by two factors: the type of technical area to be housed and maximum class enrollment. The floor area value (expressed as a certain number of square feet per student) that is appropriate to the first factor multiplied by maximum class enrollment gives a total area within which it is always possible to achieve a valid arrangement of equipment.

Floor area values have been derived from experience and from research. Experimentation with laboratory designs of all kinds has provided a valuable means of testing biases acquired through experience. Experimental layouts utilizing actual equipment sizes and the known space needs of the human anatomy have yielded a great deal of information concerning main work area sizes. Consequently it is possible to express these sizes in terms of the number of square feet of floor space required per student in each type of laboratory.

Industrial arts laboratories can be categorized as "heavy" (in need of relatively more floor space) or "light" (in need of relatively less floor space). Auxiliary areas influence this categorization only to the extent that heavy laboratories tend to include more of them. The sizes of auxiliary areas remain fairly constant from one type of laboratory to another.

Heavy laboratories employ heavy, bulky equipment. This group includes woods, metals, graphic arts, automotive, and general laboratories. Electricity/electronics, crafts, and drawing laboratories are the light ones. Their equipment and the activities that take place in them require less floor space.

The sizes recommended for the main work areas of industrial arts laboratories at the junior and senior high school levels are given in Table 4.1. It is important to emphasize that these values represent *starting* points for design and that, at times, they may require modification to accommodate student activities and equipment purchases. Of real impor-

Figure 4.1 *Drawing laboratory work station—minimum size.*

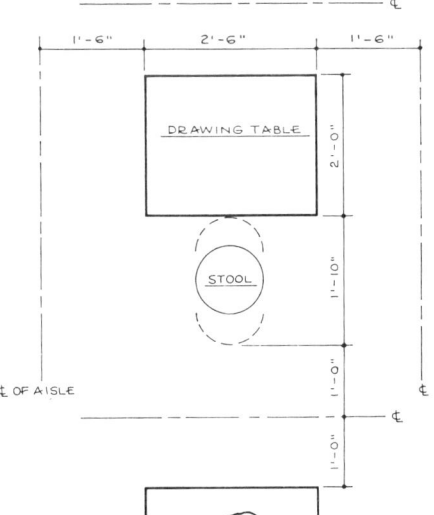

64 LABORATORY SPACE AND DESIGN CONSIDERATIONS

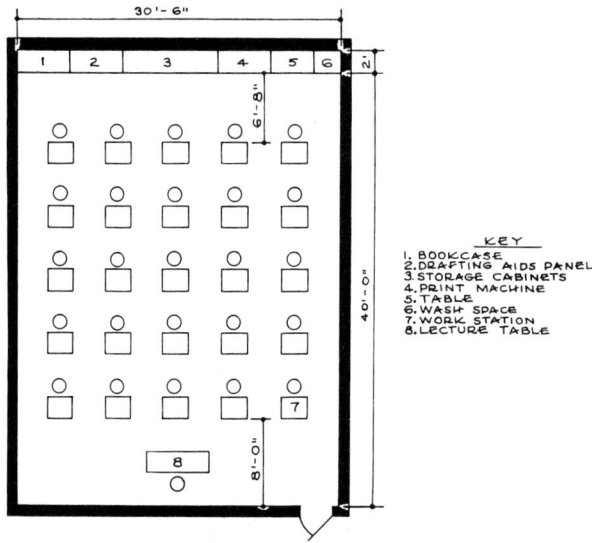

Figure 4.2 *Drawing laboratory with "minimum" space rating.*

Figure 4.3 *Drawing laboratory work station—excellent size.*

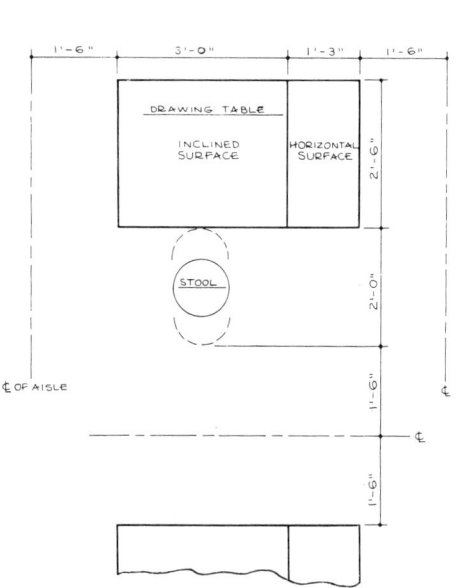

tance is the fact that the given sizes establish guidelines within which valid facilities can be designed. It is not inaccurate to say that these guidelines *will* produce valid facilities to the extent that validity is dependent on size.

Laboratories that are significantly smaller than the recommended minimums probably will not permit truly good industrial arts programs. Those that are larger than the recommended maximums might well waste floor space. The first is vastly the greater of these two errors.

A minimum size work station for a drawing room is presented in Fig. 4.1. Three-feet-wide traffic lanes exist on both sides of the drawing table. A two-foot space in front of the table and behind it allows a teacher to move across the room as he or she works with students. The drawing surface is adequate, but the table does not have a horizontal surface that can be used to hold books and drawing equipment during work periods. A total of thirty-two square feet of floor space is needed for this arrangement. Multiplying this number by the maximum number of students who will be in class and increasing the total area by a space large enough to provide side, front, and rear traffic lanes and to house essential pieces of drawing room equipment gives the total size of the room.

Fig. 4.2 shows an efficient drawing room organized in the resulting 1281-square-foot area. The per-student square footage is approximately 51. The drawing program permitted by this facility would be limited by lack of space to make large layouts and to comfortably do the three-dimensional work (model making) that is helpful in design courses. All auxiliary areas are necessarily small. Nevertheless, a good drawing program could be carried on.

A very effective work station is shown in Fig. 4.3. This plan also utilizes three-foot traffic lane widths at the sides of the drawing table, but it provides three feet of space between the front edge of the table and the stool in front of it in order to make lateral traffic lane widths more comfortable. The drawing surface is adequate for large drawings, and the horizontal surface offers storage space for reference materials and equipment. This arrangement requires fifty-four square feet of floor space and allows a complete drawing program to be offered. A drawing room design that incorporates twenty-five of these work stations is presented in Fig. 4.4. The room is planned so that work in design, including three-dimensional representations, can be a part of the drawing program. Very large layouts could be produced and printed, and many of the basic techniques of technical illustration could be taught. Slightly less than 93 square feet of floor space per student is provided. The total square footage is 2320.

A complete general woods laboratory that is rated "excellent" with

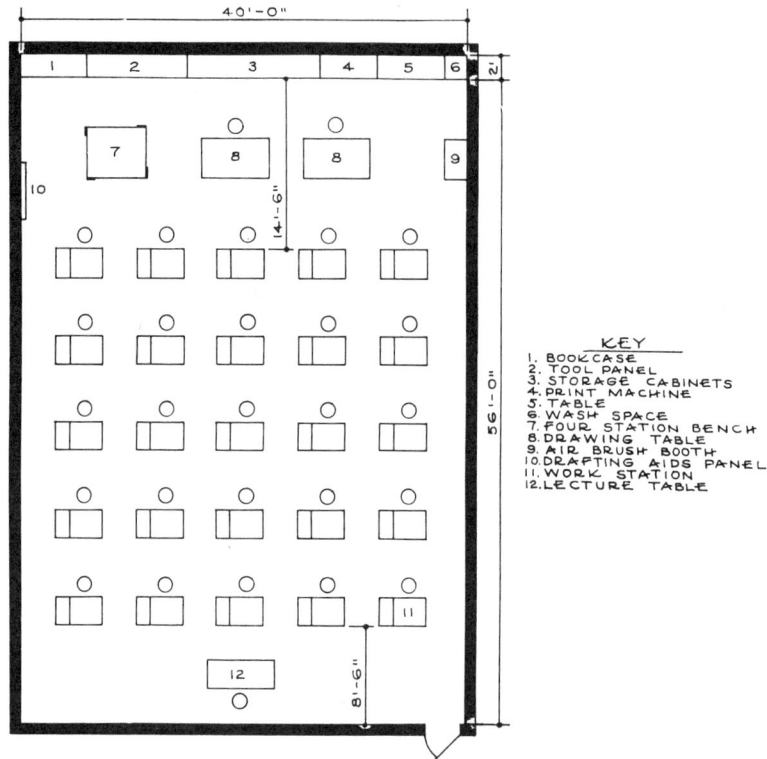

Figure 4.4 *Drawing laboratory with "excellent" space rating.*

regard to main work area space, is shown in Fig. 11.4. The main work area encompasses 2675 square feet of floor space. Based on a maximum class size of twenty-four, the per-student floor area is somewhat greater than 111 square feet. This drawing illustrates the planning of a heavy laboratory within the framework of space recommendations contained in Table 4.1.

Laboratories designed for vocational-technical classes should be larger than industrial arts laboratories. Vocational-technical classes tend to be smaller than industrial arts classes, but because much greater duplication of certain work stations is necessary and more comprehensive projects are undertaken, floor space requirements are quite high. Light vocational-technical laboratories should be given approximately 100 square feet of floor space per student. Heavy laboratories can often make good use of twice this amount.

Balconies that provide work space are not recommended for industrial education laboratories. They require teachers to supervise on two

Table 4.1 FLOOR AREA VALUES FOR MAIN WORK AREAS

Space Rating	Sq. Ft. Per Student (Main Work Area)	Total Sq. Ft. (Class Size of 24)
Light Laboratories — Drawing, Crafts, Electricity/ Electronics		
Minimum	50	1200
Good	70	1680
Excellent	90	2160
Heavy Laboratories — Woods, Metals, Graphic Arts, Automotive, General		
Minimum	90	2160
Good	100	2400
Excellent	110	2640

levels and can cause serious deficiencies in supervision and safety standards. Balconies intended for use as classrooms or for storage are not as objectionable, although the attendant stairways are often hazardous, as well as inconvenient. Stairs to balconies also consume valuable main floor space and can make good equipment organization less easy to achieve.

A work station is defined as any equipped place where a student can pursue some phase of a class activity. Wood lathes, vises on benches, drawing tables, hydraulic hoists, paint spray booths, potters' wheels, and engine analyzers are examples of typical work stations. It is usually necessary to provide *more* work stations than there will be students in class at any one time. Having an extra number will avoid unnecessary restriction of activities and the waste of a student's time that occurs when he or she must wait to use equipment. Overcapacity is, thus, inherent in good laboratory design. Three techniques are used to provide it: equipment choices that accurately reflect program needs, duplication of pieces of equipment known to be in greater-than-average demand during class sessions, and the provision of pieces of equipment that enrich class activities.

The amount of overcapacity that is desirable varies with the type of laboratory. Generally, light laboratories, especially drawing rooms, require less overcapacity than heavy laboratories. Obviously, an adequate drawing program can be carried on in a room where the number of work stations matches the number of students in class. The best drawing laboratories, however, are those in which substantial breadth and depth of experience can be gained by students. They contain at least one-third more work stations than students. The number of work stations in a drawing laboratory can be increased by the addition of large drafting tables intended for special problems work and/or by the inclusion of pieces of special equipment (such as print machines and air brush installations) that add important dimensions to courses.

The general woods laboratory shown in Fig. 11.4 is planned for a maximum class size of twenty-four students. It has fifty-six separate work stations, or thirty-two more work stations than students. This amount of overcapacity is appropriate. Well-designed industrial education laboratories should have enough work stations for 133 to 250 per cent of maximum class size. Space recommendations made in Table 4.1 are adequate to provide overcapacity in this range.

A generous amount of floor space is essential to valid laboratory design. Where enough space has been provided, the possibilities for good organization and management are unlimited. An inadequate amount of floor space always precludes excellence.

SHAPES AND PROPORTIONS OF THE MAIN WORK AREA

The shape of a main work area has much to do with equipment organization, laboratory administration, safety, utilization of natural light, and acoustical design. Consequently it must be carefully planned. A teacher should be able to give close supervision to an entire main work area from any point in the room. L-shapes, T-shapes, and other nonrectangular shapes can weaken class control by reducing visibility. These designs have an adverse effect on safety, also, because the teacher may not see unsafe acts. The only fully effective shape is a rectangular one. Placement of auxiliary areas must not be allowed to destroy rectangularity of the main work area.

A laboratory width of less than thirty-five feet usually makes it difficult to achieve good equipment organization. Quite often, an inadequate width precludes maintaining four-foot traffic lanes that run lengthwise. Also, a narrow laboratory requires too great a longitudinal spread of equipment to permit really efficient movement of people and materials. Where the width of a main work area is not sufficient, the length must be excessive.

A relatively long, narrow laboratory has two other potential disadvantages. It can hamper teacher efforts to provide effective class supervision, and it can exhibit unfortunate acoustical characteristics. A teacher who is at one end of a very long laboratory is too far away from activity going on at the other end to be able to move quickly from one end to the other in case of emergency. Finally, noise can reverberate badly in a laboratory that is too long and narrow.

No one ratio of width to length is best. The easiest and most effective way of creating a useful main work area is to begin with an arbitrarily selected laboratory width of at least thirty-five feet — preferably forty feet or more — and combine it with a length that is sufficient to yield the desired number of square feet of floor space per student. The resulting dimensions may be adjusted to accommodate the best possible organization of equipment.

AUXILIARY AREAS

An auxiliary area is a relatively small part of a laboratory complex. It is highly specialized with respect to purpose and equipment, because it is intended to supplement the capabilities of the main work area and may or may not be housed in a separate room. More often than not, an auxiliary area is designed to accommodate a small group of students. Its size depends on its purpose and on the estimated intensity of use it will get.

The importance of auxiliary areas should not be underestimated. A program can function without them but never with maximum effectiveness. Therefore it is necessary to plan auxiliary areas as carefully as main work areas. Thirteen basic types of auxiliary areas can be identified. They are:

1. Design center
2. Class area
3. Teacher's office
4. Laboratory library
5. Demonstration area
6. Display facilities
7. Student locker area
8. Project storage room
9. Materials storage room
10. Equipment storage room
11. Project assembly area
12. Toilet/lavatory room
13. Wash area

The finishing room, the darkroom, and the materials testing center have been purposely omitted from this list, although they are often considered to be auxiliary areas. In reality, they make it possible to carry on major course activities and must be considered to be parts of main work area planning problems. They are, in effect, minilaboratories.

A well-designed laboratory complex includes many of the types of auxiliary areas listed. Some areas can be combined for purposes of economy or to improve an overall laboratory design. It is not difficult, for example, to plan a single room that will serve as a classroom, design center, and library. Such a room might also include certain display facilities.

The following discussion is intended to develop an understanding of the design needs of each of the auxiliary areas. Requirements that are common to all — for example, good lighting, proper flooring, adequate ventilation, and accurate temperature and humidity control — are discussed in subsequent chapters.

Design center

Project design has never received the emphasis that it deserves or that it seems destined to get. A student who has completed one or more industrial education courses should be at least moderately proficient as a designer. If class activities lead in this direction and facilities are adequate, students can become competent designers.

A design center should permit a student to engage in many of the activities carried on by an industrial designer. It should provide comfortable seating for reading and reflection; a variety of reference materials; bulletin board space; facilities for sketching and drawing (including a chalkboard); many kinds of materials; equipment for making models of clay, paper, wood, plastic, plaster of Paris, and other materials; and a generous amount of storage space.

A design center should be enclosed to exclude noise and dust produced in the main work area. The enclosure should be constructed of a transparent material from forty-two inches above floor level to the ceiling so that the teacher can supervise without having to be in the room.

In a practical sense, electricity/electronics and drawing laboratories *are* design centers. Consequently, enclosed areas for design are not usually required in these laboratories. What is necessary in both cases is enough floor space and equipment to permit the full spectrum of design activity. An automotive laboratory has little or no need of a design center unless chassis and body construction are to be undertaken.

The amount of floor space consumed by a design center is approximately equivalent to the area of a light laboratory, that is, fifty to ninety square feet per student. The total floor area can be considered satisfactory if 25 per cent of a class can work in a design center at the same time.

Class area

With the exception of drawing, every laboratory has need of a class area. The technical content of all industrial education courses increases year by year, and while hands-on experiences are of key importance, most teachers find it necessary to include significant amounts of nonlaboratory activity in their courses in order to achieve their objectives.

A class area need not be enclosed to be effective, although in many instances an enclosed area is best. The major advantages of an open class area are the ease of laboratory redesign it permits, greater flexibility of operation, and the initial saving of money required to construct an enclosure. A class*room*, on the other hand, offers much more freedom from noise and dust. It can be designed to serve additionally as a teacher's office and laboratory library, is easier to darken when projected visuals are to be used, and permits better seating.

A class area should be large enough for an entire class to be seated at the same time. Provision of forty square feet of floor space per student helps to ensure good seating, adequate traffic lane widths, and space for a demonstration table, a chalkboard, bulletin boards, projection equipment, and storage devices for reference materials and classroom equipment. If the area is enclosed, the enclosure should be transparent above the forty-two-inch level. It is necessary to be able to darken all class areas quickly and effectively.

The seating in a class area should be comfortable, easy to maintain, and placed to facilitate both seeing and hearing. Each seat should be equipped with a writing surface and book storage space. According to Dale,[1] the first lateral row of seats should be placed at least two screen widths away from a projection screen. The last row should be no more than six screen widths from the screen. All seats should be located within an area that extends thirty degrees on each side of the center line of a beaded screen. (The use of a matte screen or lenticular screen enlarges the angle considerably.) Each seat should command a good view of the demonstration table and should be within easy range of the teacher's voice. Stepped seating (each succeeding lateral row on a higher level, beginning with the second row from the front) may be a good solution in some cases, although it is a permanent arrangement that lacks flexibility.

The area around a demonstration table must permit an entire class to stand close to the table. The table top should be large enough to contain all equipment needed for the most extensive demonstration planned, and the base of the table should have locking storage space for demonstration equipment. In some laboratories, sinks, hot and cold water, electrical service, and gas should be provided at the table.

[1]Edgar Dale, *Audio-Visual Methods in Teaching*, rev. ed. (New York: Dryden Press, 1954), p. 222.

A contemporary class area requires a generous amount of chalkboard space. The chalkboard should be placed at the front of the area where it is easy to see. It should face the source of any natural light that enters the room, since light falling obliquely on a chalkboard can make information written on it all but unreadable for students seated on the far side of the room near the front.

A lighting system should be built in along the top edge of the chalkboard; fluorescent strip lighting can be very effective. All light-emitting surfaces should be shielded from students' eyes. The light control switch should be conveniently located. The chalk tray should be thirty-eight inches above floor level, and the top of the board should be eighty inches high in order to provide forty-two inches of vertical board space. Chalkboard length should be no less than two-thirds the width of the class area.

A good grade of slate, properly surfaced to provide enough "tooth" for the chalk and to facilitate cleaning, is the best chalkboard material available. Slate is more expensive than synthetic or composition materials, but it provides an infinitely better writing surface and is far more durable. There is little evidence to suggest that colors other than black are more restful to students' eyes. Nor is there evidence that other colors offer better contrast with white or yellow chalk.

Certain display materials (bulletin board wax; fonts of large letters, numbers, and symbols; and dry cell-powered, low rpm motors, etc.) should be available in a class area.

Finally, a class area, like any other place where students and teachers work, should possess certain standard items of equipment, including an electric wall clock, a waste basket, and a pencil sharpener.

Teacher's office

Every teacher needs a place in which to prepare class materials, evaluate student work, confer with students, write, and do professional reading. Wherever possible, a teacher should have a private office. No more than two teachers should be assigned to a single office. Office efficiency drops markedly when an office must be shared. One hundred forty square feet is the minimum amount of floor space needed to house one teacher in reasonable comfort. An office intended for two teachers should include at least 200 square feet of floor space.

An industrial teacher's office may be situated in a laboratory or in an office block in an industrial education wing, building, or area. Location in a laboratory has the advantage of housing a teacher close to the place of

AUXILIARY AREAS

teaching. It has the disadvantages of consuming laboratory floor area, reducing a teacher's privacy, and complicating the task of laboratory design. It also gives rise to administrative problems when a teacher is transferred from one laboratory to another, when one teacher teaches in two or more laboratories, and when several teachers teach in the same laboratory. These problems cannot often be solved without disadvantage to someone.

Offices in laboratories should be centrally located, preferably along the ends of main work areas. They should be separated by transparent partitions from all areas in which students work so that teachers can maintain visual contact with their classes whenever they find it necessary to be in their offices during class periods. No office should be designed to serve as a passageway between adjacent laboratories or from one part of a laboratory to another. An office must be as soundproof and dustproof as is economically possible.

An office located in an office block can also place an instructor close to his or her laboratory, and it avoids the administrative problems noted. Of course, the block should be situated so that it is approximately equidistant from all laboratories in the group. The office block plan has the additional advantage of making possible the inclusion of a teachers' conference room and lounge, rest rooms, an office supply room, a display case, and other needed rooms or areas.

From the foregoing discussion, it seems evident that grouping industrial teachers' offices in a central office block is clearly the better solution. The costs of both plans are similar because both consume the same amount of floor area.

It is important that an office be fully equipped for professional work. The following basic pieces of equipment belong in a one-teacher office:

1. Desk with file drawer and lock
2. Swivel-type armchair
3. Flexible-arm fluorescent desk lamp
4. Enclosed bookcase with lock
5. Side chair
6. Wardrobe-type storage cabinet with lock
7. Four-drawer filing cabinet with lock
8. Drafting table with flexible-arm fluorescent desk lamp
9. Drafting chair
10. Drafting machine
11. Office electric typewriter
12. Typing table
13. Typing chair

74 LABORATORY SPACE AND DESIGN CONSIDERATIONS

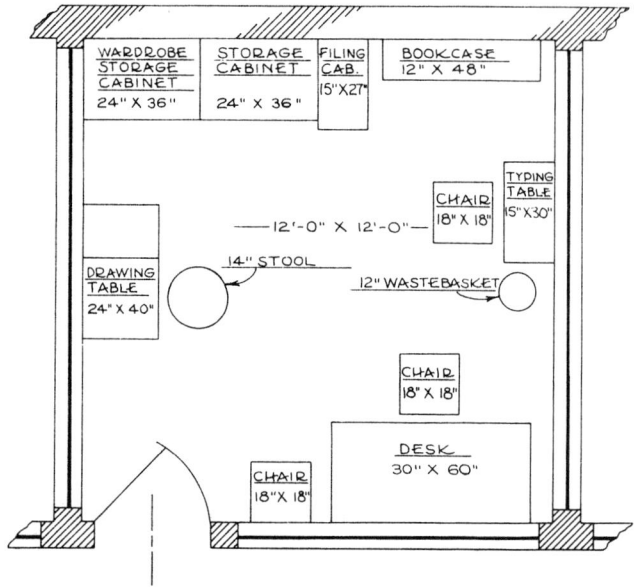

Figure 4.5 *Industrial education teacher's office.*

14. Electric wall clock
15. Pencil sharpener
16. Telephone
17. Desk calendar (memo type)
18. Transparent tape dispenser
19. Stapler

Top-quality steel office equipment is the most economical and satisfactory over a long period of time.

An effective arrangement of equipment in a one-teacher office is shown in Fig. 4.5. This office is designed for placement in a laboratory. Without the glass partitions, the same design would lend itself well to location in an office block.

Laboratory library

A well-stocked library is needed to support design, research, and construction activities, and it is often desirable to combine it with a class area and/or design center. The equipment needs of a library include shelves, a filing cabinet, vertical book holders, a card file, chairs, and tables. Steel furniture is recommended. Seating capacity should be great enough to accommodate at least one-fourth of a class at the same time. A well-planned library will utilize approximately twenty-five square feet of floor space per student.

A library should contain a substantial number of reference books of various kinds, as well as periodical literature and manufacturers' literature in the technical area it serves. Textbooks that are loaned to students for entire school terms can be stored in a laboratory library between terms and during terms when they are not in use.

Demonstration area

A demonstration area is a place in the main work area of a laboratory where members of a class can be brought together for relatively short presentations. A chalkboard that contains fifteen or more square feet of writing space is its principal instructional medium. While it is often well to equip a demonstration area with a fixed chalkboard, a portable board can be a useful substitute. The floor space must be large enough for an entire class to stand or sit for short periods of time. Folding steel chairs (preferably with tablet arms) provide convenient seating. If such seats are used, a storage rack must be provided nearby.

A demonstration area that encompasses a bench area or a portion of it makes it possible for students to sit on bench tops or stand during presentations and enables the instructor to use the benches and bench equipment. A major advantage of this arrangement is that the floor area and chalkboard serve another (and primary) purpose: students use both during activity periods. The disadvantage is that the space must often be cleared of student work and waste materials before it can be used by the teacher.

Display facilities

An industrial education department presents displays from time to time to accomplish six broad objectives:

1. To develop students' understanding of the total industrial education program
2. To present information about industry to industrial education students
3. To develop in teachers, school administrators, students *not*

taking industrial courses, parents, and other interested persons an understanding of the industrial education program
4. To acquaint such persons with certain industrial materials, equipment, processes, techniques, and problems
5. To assist in making maximum use of the motivating power of student work and to provide sources of ideas
6. To give recognition for student work that is well done

The two types of display facilities that are used most frequently are the bulletin board and the display case. A bulletin board is primarily suitable for displaying graphic materials, although many items having limited depth and weight can be shown to advantage. A display case permits the display of graphic materials and three-dimensional pieces of various sizes.

Several large bulletin boards should be present in every laboratory complex. They should be installed in design centers, class areas, libraries, main work areas, and corridors in places where students cannot very well avoid seeing them. One excellent location is on the latch side of a door leading *from* an area in which students work. Individual lighting adds greatly to the visibility and attractiveness of a bulletin board.

A number of synthetic and natural materials that are not damaged by pins and thumbtacks can be used for surfacing bulletin boards. Neutral but attractive colors should be chosen so that attention is not drawn from materials displayed. These colors should be low in chroma (intensity) and of medium value (neither very light nor very dark). A small amount of texture can add appreciably to the attractiveness of a bulletin board surface and help to provide the nonglare surface that is desirable.

A bulletin board frame should be narrow and unobtrusive, yet it should give the appearance of good quality and expert workmanship. Hardwood with a natural finish is always appropriate, as is extruded aluminum. Frames should be set level with bulletin board surfaces so that displayed materials can, if necessary, overlap the edges.

The size of a bulletin board depends on the amount of wall space available and the needs of the program it will serve. As is true of a chalkboard, the lower edge should be approximately thirty-eight inches above the floor and the top edge eighty inches high. A board that is forty-two inches high and sixty-eight inches wide has an especially pleasing balance of height to width of about 1 to 1.6. Bulletin boards can be wider, of course, but the recommended heights of the upper and lower edges should be maintained so that all areas of a board can be easily reached.

A portable bulletin board can be useful in a laboratory or corridor.

Floor models and table models, which are inexpensive to construct or purchase, are effective for making announcements, displaying materials during demonstrations, and serving other display purposes.

Every laboratory should have its own display case. In addition, each industrial education building, wing, or area needs a large, centrally located case that is available to all faculty members. Such a case can be used to present comprehensive displays, as well as displays having general significance within the field of industrial education.

The functional and aesthetic qualities that a display case must possess are similar to those of a bulletin board, since the basic purposes of the two media are the same. A display case can be constructed so that it is loaded from the front, the rear, or either side. A front-loading case is the easiest to use, especially if one person is arranging a display, because the emerging display is viewed from the position of the audience.

Security and utility are related problems that are difficult to solve satisfactorily in a front-loading display case. Front-loading cases are often equipped with bypass glass doors, and although fairly good locks for bypass doors are available, their use exacts its price. The resulting center division presents a serious visual obstruction as does the lock itself, however small. Moreover, bypass doors make loading difficult. Visually, it is better to use a single panel plate glass door equipped with a continuous hinge on one side and a lock on the opposite side. The glass panel must be framed to permit installation of the lock and hinge. Because of the relatively heavy weight of this kind of door and the attendant strain it can put on the frame and hinge, it should not be used in the construction of unusually large display cases.

A rear-loading display case has the inherent design advantage of an unobstructed view and excellent security. Rear doors need not detract from the appearance of the background. The single fault of a rear-loading case, and it is a serious one, is that the arrangement of a display is made more difficult by the necessity of organizing it from the rear.

A side-loading display case can be recommended only as a last resort. It has no advantages over the other types, and arranging displays in it is inordinately difficult.

It is often desirable to construct a display case so that it projects through a partition that separates a laboratory from a corridor. Since many partitions are not thick enough to provide sufficient depth for a display case, it may be necessary to extend such a case into the laboratory and/or corridor. The result, unfortunately, can be the creation of a safety hazard. Consequently, each extension should be no greater than six to eight inches and the case should be recessed completely, if possible.

An adjustable and removable divider that can be installed parallel to a partition and used to separate the front and rear sections of a through-the-partition display case is a useful accessory. It should be thin, strong, and opaque. Such a divider permits the simultaneous presentation of two displays — one to viewers in the corridor and a second to students in the laboratory. It also prevents passersby from using the case as a means of seeing into the laboratory.

Certain design features are essential in display cases if they are to be of maximum use to teachers. First of all, they must be large enough to display objects produced in industrial education classes and in local industries and shallow enough to facilitate the arrangement of displays. Height-width, depth-width, and depth-height proportions should be good.

Construction materials used in display cases must be durable and attractive and the colors interesting but not overpowering. Adjustable, removable shelving is necessary to lend versatility. Every display case should be equipped with a lighting system that can produce effects ranging from complete diffusion to one or more spots of light and from low to high intensity. Several conveniently placed electrical outlets should be provided. The outlets should be well hidden from view. Mechanical ventilation is advisable to prevent heat and humidity from damaging displayed items. A good ventilation system keeps air moving into and out of a display case at a rate that does not cause graphic materials and light objects to flutter. It should be noiseless in operation, highly durable, and either invisible or unobtrusive.

A display case should occupy a position that will be highly visible to the persons at whom displays will be aimed. Junctions of corridors are among the most effective locations.

In the northern hemisphere, an exterior case must not face east or west. North is the best direction. South is permissible if the case can be shielded from the oblique rays of the sun. An exterior case must be kept from freezing in a cold climate. It must also be well insulated and equipped with insulating glass to prevent frosting.

There are many variations of the two basic types of display facilities. All must meet the design criteria set forth, if they are to be truly useful.

Student locker area

It is desirable to provide a minimum of two cubic feet of locker space for every student who takes a laboratory class other than one in drawing. Laboratory aprons, parts of unfinished projects, personal tools, plans, references, and small quantities of construction materials are among the items that students must store between class periods. The total

Figure 4.6 *This four-place work bench has cabinet base lockers.* (Terry Green, Brodhead-Garrett Company)

number of lockers needed in a given situation depends on the maximum number of students to be enrolled in any class and the number of separate classes that will use the laboratory. For example, if a metals laboratory can serve twenty-four students and maximum utilization will be five separate classes per week, including evening students, 120 or more student lockers will be required. A few additional lockers should be included to meet the needs of the teacher, the occasional extra student, and the student whose work necessitates additional locker space. All lockers should be located within the laboratory complex.

The two general types of lockers suitable for industrial education laboratories are the cabinet base type used to support a bench top and the standard tiered wall locker. Many modifications of each type exist so that specific needs can be met. Cabinet base lockers, for example, are available in a variety of sizes of modular units that can be assembled in the manner of building blocks to satisfy almost any requirement (Fig. 4.6).

Congestion at the beginning and end of a class period can be minimized if lockers are scattered throughout a laboratory instead of being concentrated in one area. Scattered lockers, however, can be detrimental to other aspects of laboratory design. The most practical solution, therefore, is to divide the lockers into two or possibly three groups near the main door so that students can enter the laboratory and walk to their lockers in smaller groups. Placement of cabinet base lockers is not a difficult problem. Once bench top locations have been determined, the bases follow naturally. Wall lockers, however, *can* be difficult to place because they must compete for space with machinery, tool panels, chalkboards, display cases, bulletin boards, transparent partitions, windows, and doors.

Wall lockers should be recessed, if possible. If they cannot be recessed, they should be legless, and the bottom tier should rest on a low base that extends slightly in front of the lockers and provides full support. Locker units on legs can be troublesome because the legs create areas that trap waste materials and are difficult to clean. Legs are also less desirable from the standpoint of appearance.

Each locker unit must be securely fastened to the wall behind it. The top tier of lockers should be equipped with sloping tops so that dust can be easily removed and so that the tops do not become storage spaces for scraps of materials and miscellaneous pieces of equipment. Unrecessed wall lockers should always extend from one wall or partition to another or from doors to walls, partitions, or other doors so that they do not create corners and recesses that are impossible to utilize and difficult to clean.

Top tiers of lockers should extend no more than seventy-two inches above floor level. Higher lockers can become the cause of injuries due to falls. Even lockers at the seventy-two-inch level will be out of the comfortable reach of a few students.

Figure 4.7 *Steel wall lockers are available in several sizes.* (Armstrong Cork Company)

Steel is a far better locker construction material than wood. Steel is durable and fireproof, and the fits of component parts are not affected by moisture in the air. Steel lockers, of course, require the protection of a good finish. Sides, backs, tops, and bottoms of lockers should be fabricated of twenty-four-gauge or thicker sheet steel, and doors should be at least sixteen-gauge in thickness. Fasteners used for assembly and major pieces of hardware, such as locks and door handles, should be rustproofed with a metallic plating or constructed of a noncorroding metal or alloy.

Lockers can be purchased with drawers, baskets, or hinged doors. Doors are the most common type of closure and are probably the most suitable for laboratory use. Lockers should be ventilated in order to prevent the formation of rust and to eliminate concentrations of humidity and odors. Perforated and louvered doors are available. Of the two, the louvered door is visually the better choice; but both ventilate adequately.

Lockers can be ordered with either padlock hasps or built-in door locks. Every unit should be equipped with a high-quality lock that will withstand long, hard service. Padlocks and built-in locks are equally satisfactory with regard to security and convenience of operation. Both are available as key locks, combination locks, and master-keyed combination locks. Padlocks can be lost, however, so built-in locks are somewhat the better choice. The inconvenience caused by lost keys and keys that are locked in lockers is eliminated by the use of combination locks. The built-in, master-keyed combination lock is, perhaps, the best choice of all.

Hinged doors on cabinet base lockers are not customarily equipped with latches, but they are available with spring-loaded hinges that close them automatically and hold them closed. Most wall locker doors *do* have latches. A well-designed, well-constructed latch keeps a door securely closed when it is unlocked, provides two- or three-point latching, and permits prelocking — a situation in which a door that is locked, then closed, will latch in the locked position.

Each wall locker should have a double-pronged ceiling hook and two single-pronged side hooks. A shelf may be desirable. All lockers should have number plates. When lockers are ordered, a single number series should be specified so that no two lockers will have the same number.

Project storage room

Project storage rooms are essential to the effective operation of many industrial education programs. The largest project storage rooms are needed in woods laboratories. Drawing rooms and graphic arts laboratories have relatively modest needs, although as drawing programs increase their emphasis on design, project storage requirements will rise.

Other areas — electricity/electronics, crafts, metals, and automotive technology — have project storage space needs that range from slight to moderate.

A teacher can be handicapped to the point of having to make undesirable changes in course content if a laboratory lacks proper project storage facilities. For example, a student who takes a woods course can complete several projects during the school term. It is likely that some pieces will be large and that more than one will be in progress at the same time. If the laboratory load is assumed to be 120 different students per week, storage space must be provided for at least this many projects. Students' lockers provide some storage space for smaller items, but a pressing need for much additional space in the form of a project storage room always exists.

One alternative to adequate storage space is to curtail the program by discouraging projects that exceed a certain size and by limiting the number of projects undertaken — an obvious disservice to many students. Another alternative is to store projects in corners, traffic lanes, and free floor areas in various parts of the laboratory. The effects of this practice on project security, housekeeping, safety, and efficient operation are obvious.

A project storage room has several essential design features. First, it should store projects of all kinds and minimize the possibility of damage caused by the room or its equipment. Thus, the room must have adequate floor space, as well as a generous amount of shelf space. Shelves should be smooth, free of projections, strongly supported, and well finished. A safe ladder must be available so that projects can be stored on upper shelves.

A woods laboratory that is planned for 120 students per week requires approximately 400 square feet of project storage room floor space and at least 200 linear feet of 36-inch shelving. One effective design is a U-shape in which shelves line three walls of a room, extend to the ceiling from a level that is 36 inches above the floor, and are placed 30 inches apart. Such an arrangement will store all but unusually large pieces. These items can be set on the floor underneath the first level of shelving.

A project storage room should be close to the main work area of a laboratory. It should also be adjacent to the finishing room because the principal lines of movement of semifinished projects are between the main work area, the finishing room, and the project storage room. The door of a project storage room should be equipped with a lock. A single thirty-six-inch door is satisfactory, but if double doors are desirable in a specific situation, each half should be thirty-six inches wide.

As a laboratory course reaches its concluding stages and the accumulation of student work reaches a peak, even a very large project storage room can become overcrowded. At this point, the class area, the design center, and other parts of the laboratory can be used for temporary storage without undue loss of operating efficiency.

AUXILIARY AREAS

Materials storage room

An industrial education laboratory is incomplete without one or two rooms for the storage of bulk quantities of materials. If the course work utilizes chiefly one type of material, a *major* storage room for this material and its chief variations is a necessity. And a *minor* storage room for supporting materials may be equally desirable. Laboratories that should have both kinds of storage rooms include woods, metals, and general. The other industrial education areas either do not place as much emphasis on single types of materials or they make use of materials that are less demanding in their storage space requirements. Consequently, each can be effectively served by a single storage room.

A major storage room should be designed to make receiving and dispensing as easy as possible. It should keep materials secure, orderly, and in good physical condition. Efficient receiving is largely dependent on the distance between a storage room and a door that opens onto a loading dock or service drive. The best design is one in which the room has its own exterior door (preferably double insulating type doors that provide a six-foot opening) so that materials can be unloaded directly into the room and placed in the storage racks.

If it is not possible to provide a major storage room with direct access to the outside, the main work area should have an exterior door located near the door to the storage room. The floor area between the two doors, of course, must be kept clear of permanent installations. An exterior door should be kept locked at all times, but it can serve as an emergency exit, even if located in a storage room.

A storage room door through which materials are dispensed should be adjacent to the machine area of a laboratory. In a woods laboratory, the lumber room door should be near the band saw, planer, jointer, radial arm saw, and table saw. Lumber handling can be greatly facilitated by a partition opening that accommodates a twenty-four-inch roller track. The track should extend from the interior of the lumber room to the radial arm saw and several feet beyond it, and it should be supported at exactly the same level as the saw table. Security can be achieved by equipping the opening with a vertical sliding panel operated from inside the lumber room. The panel should be lockable.

Lumber and metal forms — such as rods, angles, and bands — should be stored on end. Vertical storage keeps these materials, especially lumber, in good condition and provides four other important advantages: ease of classification, convenience of retrieval, full utilization of air space up to ceiling height, and elimination of falling injuries that can occur when the upper levels of horizontal storage racks are unloaded. A vertical storage rack should have a low floor that slopes gently toward a wall or partition.

Dividers may or may not be solid panels — a one-inch pipe framework can serve effectively — and they should be spaced to conform to the requirements of the various types, quantities, and sizes of materials stored.

Sheet materials — such as plywood, hardboard, particle board, acrylic plastic, and galvanized steel — should be stored flat on racks that support them in level positions and classify them according to type and size. All supports must be smooth and free of projections. Unloading should be safe and easy.

Smaller materials such as dowels and welding rod may be stored either flat or on end and should be classified by the storage devices used. A rack of horizontal, semiround shelves constructed of twenty-gauge perforated metal provides excellent storage, and it lacks the one really serious disadvantage of vertical storage — the difficulty of retrieving short lengths.

A major storage room should also make provision for storing and classifying smaller, irregularly shaped pieces of material — the usable scrap. Vertical storage is impractical. Bins can store large quantities of scrap, but they make it difficult to locate usable pieces very far below the top layer. Flat storage on shelves seems to be the most effective solution.

Almost without exception, industrial education laboratories are stocked with a great number of supporting materials for project construction and laboratory maintenance. Included are abrasives, adhesives, fasteners, hardware, finishing materials, solvents, lubricants, fabrics, decorative materials, conductors, insulators, chemicals, fuels, component parts, and base materials such as solder and type metal. Many supporting materials will quickly deteriorate if improperly stored. Therefore it is evident that separate minor storage rooms can be put to good use.

A minor storage room can be equipped with bin, pigeon hole, drawer, cabinet, shelf, rack, tote box, locker, or basket rack storage or any combination of types of storage devices. The tall steel cabinet offers exceptionally fine storage possibilities because of its many options, the ease with which items stored in it can be classified, its flexibility of arrangement, portability, durability, security, low cost, and generally good appearance. Many of these advantages, of course, are possessed by other types of steel storage equipment. On the whole, steel storage devices are more useful than any other kind.

Since students usually do not and should not have open access to materials storage rooms, it is desirable to place small quantities of most materials in main work areas and in other parts of laboratories. For example, small amounts of finishing materials should be kept in a finishing room where they will be available to students. Again, steel storage devices are the best.

Equipment storage room

A fifth type of storage facility needed in many laboratories is the equipment storage room. Its purpose is to store and classify spare parts, pieces of equipment that are seldom used, items of equipment in need of repair, duplicate pieces of equipment that provide overcapacity, and instructional media.

An equipment storage room must possess the same general attributes as other storage facilities, such as an effective security system, efficient dispensing, a location convenient to bench and machine areas, storage devices that classify pieces of equipment and keep them in good condition, and sufficient floor space. The total quantity of equipment stored in any one laboratory can be large — especially if the program has been in operation for a considerable length of time — and the dollar value of such equipment is usually high. Therefore storage space must be provided. A separate room is normally the best solution, but if necessary, equipment can be kept in a room primarily used for minor materials storage.

Industries find it necessary to devote much valuable floor space to the storage of equipment. Proper equipment storage is no less important in an industrial education laboratory.

Project assembly area

Large projects, such as boats, patio and lawn furniture, cabinets for high fidelity sound systems, and rebuilt and customized automobile engines, can have significant educational value for many students and should not be excluded from industrial education courses. These projects require fairly large amounts of floor space where they can be assembled, finished, and, in some cases, tested. Thus, sizable areas of free floor space should be included in all new laboratory facilities and in those that have been redesigned. The temptation to install equipment in these areas must be restrained as the years pass.

A project assembly area should be adjacent to or near the bench area of a laboratory. Bench operations are frequently employed in fitting parts of a project to each other, fastening them, and preparing the piece for finishing. Sometimes it is possible to design a laboratory so that the free floor space in front of a large exterior door can serve as a project assembly area. Auxiliary areas that are little used during the latter stages of courses can also be utilized for the assembly of large projects.

In the woods laboratory shown in Fig. 11.4, a 200 square foot area of free floor space is provided between the bench area and the twelve-inch table saw and gluing bench. An area roughly the same size is located in front of the double door leading to the lumber room. In the final portion of a course when the lectures, demonstrations, and student design work have been completed, armchairs in the class room and design center can be stacked and a large share of the room used for project assembly. A well-equipped bench is available to facilitate students' work. Projects should not be sanded in this room because of the presence of library materials and drafting and projection equipment, but this is a minor limitation. Parts can be prepared for finishing, both before and after assembly, in several places in the main work area.

Toilet and lavatory room

Toilet and lavatory rooms for boys and girls should be provided either as a part of a laboratory complex or very close to it. There are three disadvantages in giving each laboratory its own toilet and lavatory rooms: plumbing costs are increased; the resulting system is less compact and more complex; and more janitorial service is required to maintain adequate standards of sanitation. Even so, convenience and ease of administration make integral toilet and lavatory rooms an attractive option. The most desirable situation exists where each laboratory in an industrial education wing or building has its own toilet and lavatory rooms and two larger, centrally located restrooms exist to serve all laboratories and meet students' out-of-class needs.

An integral toilet and lavatory should be designed to be used by one person at a time. It should have one each of the following items of equipment:

1. toilet
2. urinal (if intended for boys' use)
3. sink (with hot and cold water)
4. large floor drain
5. towel dispenser (paper or linen roll, but preferably linen)
6. powdered or liquid soap dispenser
7. toilet tissue dispenser
8. waste receptacle
9. mechanical ventilation system (activated by the light switch)
10. wall shelf above the sink

Provision of a mirror is optional and possibly not desirable. The door should be equipped with an inside keyless lock that can be opened from the outside with a key if an emergency arises.

AUXILIARY AREAS 87

A central restroom should have the same equipment in sufficient quantity to permit simultaneous use by a maximum of six students. Toilets should be placed in enclosures having inside-locking doors and shelves for books and other items. Again, mirrors may be provided, but breakage can be a serious problem. The door to the corridor should be lockable only with a key and only from the outside. A baffle must be used to conceal the inside of the room when the door is opened.

If integral toilet and lavatory facilities are constructed as single units, they can be used by teachers as well as students. Centrally located restrooms, on the other hand, should *not* be used by both students and faculty members. Separate facilities should be provided.

Fig. 11.1 presents an effective pattern of central restrooms. Separate, easily reached facilities are provided for male students, female students, and faculty members.

Figure 4.8 *Contemporary restroom design.* (Bradley Corporation)

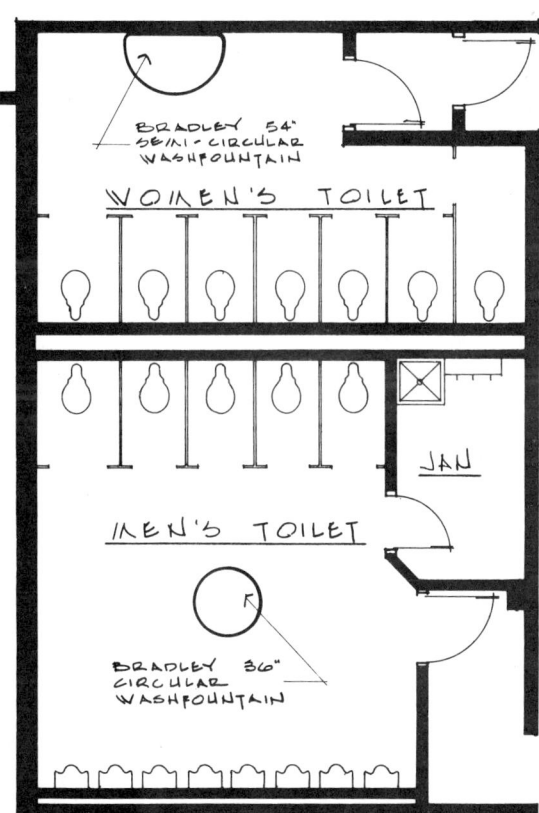

Wash area

Every industrial education laboratory should include one individual wash space for approximately every six students, or four separate spaces for normal classes of 20–24 students. A wash area should be equipped with one or more soap dispensers for powdered or liquid soap (or soap dishes for bar soap), a towel dispenser for paper towels or linen roll towels, and a waste receptacle. A first aid cabinet should be installed on a wall near the sink. It is important that wash accessories of good quality be purchased. Chrome-plated brass and stainless steel are durable basic construction materials. Manufacturers' reputations and guarantees, as well as reports of independent testing companies, should also be used to guide purchases.

A wash area should be located near the bench section of a main work area. It must be isolated from machines and other electrically operated devices and all parts of the electrical distribution system. At the same time, it should be easily accessible to students working in various parts of the laboratory.

Figure 4.9 *Semicircular washfountain construction.* (Bradley Corporation)

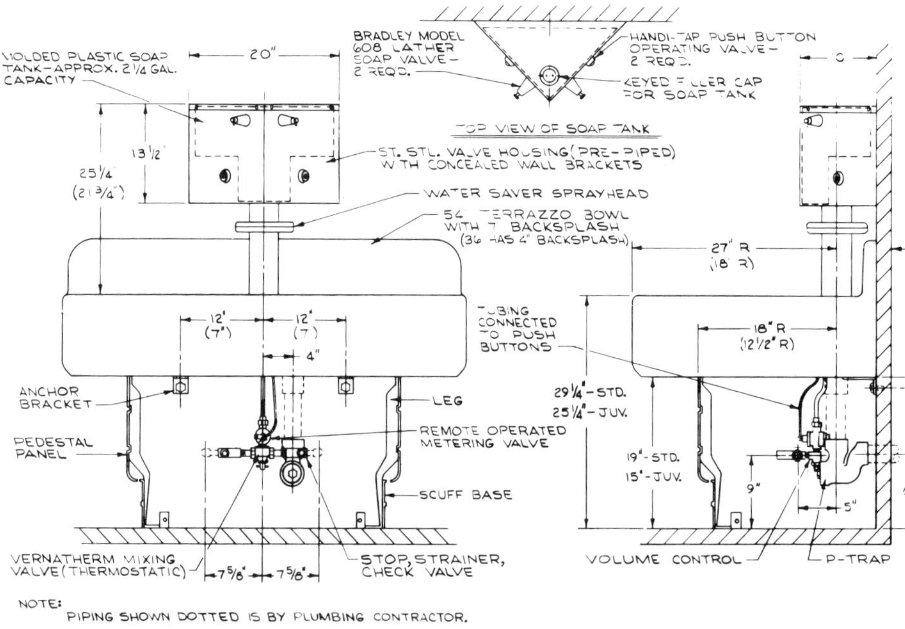

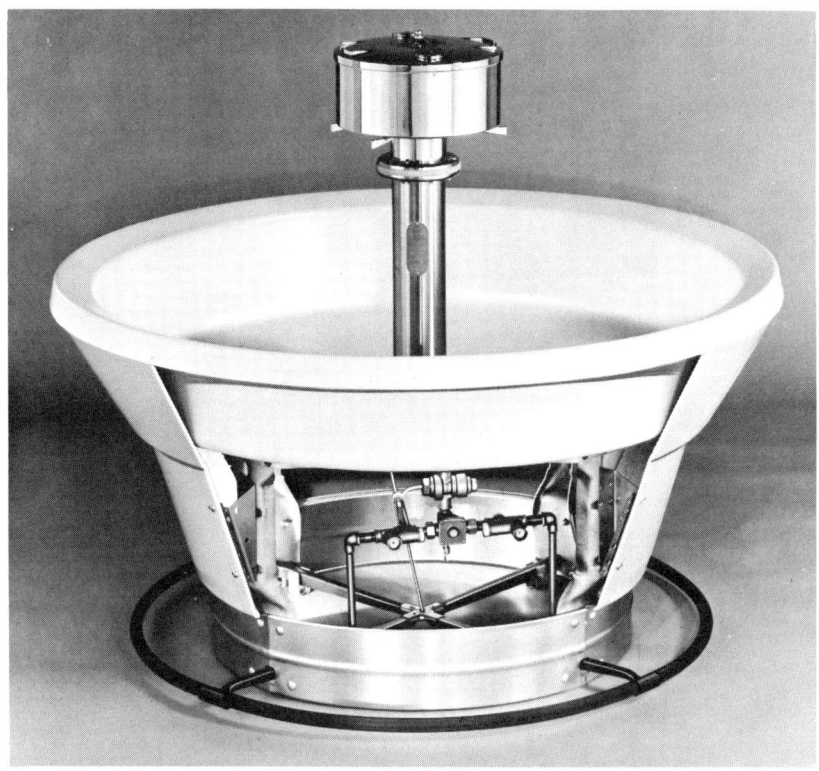

Figure 4.10 *Cutaway view—washfountain pedestal.* (Bradley Corporation)

The two types of wash equipment in common use are the washfountain and the standard wall-hung or counter-mounted bowl. Both types are available in enough sizes, shapes, and colors to meet the needs of any laboratory.

Washfountains are manufactured in circular and semicircular forms. Each type rests on the floor, and neither requires fastening. The basic parts of a washfountain include the pedestal, center supporting tube, bowl, and spray head (Figs. 4.9 and 4.10). A built-in soap dispenser is standard equipment. Hot and cold water are piped into the pedestal where the water temperature can be regulated by a manually operated mixing valve before it is routed through the supporting tube to the spray head. Rate-of-flow is controlled by a foot-operated valve that closes automatically when foot pressure is released. Waste water is piped away through the pedestal. A trap in the drain system eliminates odors.

Washfountain bowls are available in stainless steel, precast marble,

Figure 4.11 *Semicircular washfountains offer excellent services.* (Bradley Corporation)

precast stone, and porcelain-enameled steel. The first three materials are suitable for school use. Porcelain-enameled steel is not recommended because of the possibility of chipping.

The design of the washfountain offers a number of advantages. The most important are its appearance and durability. A contemporary washfountain is pleasing to the eye and efficient looking. It is a long-lasting piece of equipment that is easy to clean and maintain. It requires many less plumbing connections than a bowl designed to serve the same number of simultaneous users. A semicircular washfountain requires less floor space than a circular unit, but the amount of space saved is small.

A washfountain has several significant limitations. To begin with, it is much more expensive than a long, deep, wall-hung bowl capable of serving four persons at a time. A washfountain is inconvenient as a place to fill containers with water, as is sometimes necessary, and it does not facilitate soaking and certain other operations. Finally, it does not offer the ease, or range, of water temperature regulation provided by dual temperature/flow control faucets and, especially, by single-lever faucets.

On balance, however, the washfountain is an important type of wash equipment and well worth consideration whenever a wash area is planned. Of the sizes and types available, the fifty-four-inch diameter, semicircular fountain equipped with a stainless steel, precast stone, or precast marble bowl seems the best choice for most industrial education laboratories. Such a unit offers, for its type, a satisfactory blend of compactness and utility.

Wall-hung and counter-mounted bowls are made of china, porcelain-enameled steel, procelain-enameled cast iron, and stainless steel. Of these materials, only the last two are durable enough for laboratory service.

Bowls can be purchased in regular and deep shapes. They can provide good solutions to wash-facility design problems. Bowls are inexpensive, durable, easy to maintain, and readily available. They make it easy to fill containers and perform soaking operations. Rate of flow and water temperature can be precisely regulated at each faucet. Wall-hung bowls conserve floor space, but counter-mounted bowls consume more floor space than any other type of wash equipment.

A deep bowl that is eighty-four inches long and equipped with four faucets is excellent for use in an industrial education laboratory. Each faucet unit should have a dual temperature/flow control and a swing spout. It should have an aerator to control splashing and a soap dish. The bowl should be constructed of porcelain-enameled cast iron and equipped with a three-inch diameter drain, a drain plug, and a trap.

FOR FURTHER READING

American Council on Industrial Arts Teacher Education. *A Guide to the Planning of Industrial Arts Facilities*. 24th yearbook. Bloomington, Ill.: McKnight Publishing Co., 1975.

American Council on Industrial Arts Teacher Education. *Planning Industrial Arts Facilities*. 8th yearbook. Bloomington, Ill.: McKnight Publishing Co., 1959.

Banerdt, Jack, and Stoehr, Keith M. "Plan for Flexibility and Growth." *American Vocational Journal*, January 1969, p. 25.

Biggam, William R., and Cassetto, James M. "How Big Should a Shop Be?" *Industrial Education*, March 1975, p. 41.

Castaldi, Basil. *Creative Planning of Educational Facilities*. Chicago: Rand McNally, 1969.

Finsterbach, Fred C., and McNeice, William C. *Creative Facilities Planning for Occupational Education*. Berkeley Heights, N. J.: Educaré Associates, 1969.

Oddie, Guy. *School Building Resources and Their Effective Use.* Washington, D. C.: Organization for Economic Cooperation and Development, 1966.

Schmitt, Marshall L., and Taylor, James L. *Planning and Designing Functional Facilities for Industrial Arts Education.* Washington, D. C.: U. S. Department of Health, Education, and Welfare, 1968.

Streichler, Jerry. "New Facility: Program Calls the Tune." *School Shop,* October 1974, p. 66.

Sumption, Merle R., and Landes, Jack L. *Planning Functional School Buildings.* New York: Harper and Brothers, 1957.

Terry, Thomas P., and Hein, James B. "Problems of Teachers Using the Same Shop." *Industrial Education,* March 1974, p. 61.

Wolin, Robert B. "Occupational Center Uses Open Plan Concept." *Industrial Education,* March 1973, p. 46.

Woodruff, Alan P. "Can You Go Cluster in Your Shop?" *School Shop,* April 1976, p. 71.

5

Structural Techniques and Materials

INTRODUCTION

The purpose of facilities planning is the creation of laboratories that make the best instruction possible. To reach this goal, walls, partitions, floors, and ceilings must be designed so that they possess satisfactory functional and aesthetic qualities. Unfortunately, many educational programs have been needlessly handicapped by such defects as poor ceiling treatments and unsatisfactory floors. In order to prevent inadequacies, the industrial teacher must know functional building design and the elements of appearance well enough to be able to judge the validity of architectural plans and, if necessary, suggest improvements.

BUILDING CONSTRUCTION

One of the best basic types of building construction consists of a structural steel frame encased in concrete to shield it from fire. The concrete is cast on site after the frame has been erected. Other types of shielding, such as a sprayed-on coating of mineral fiber, can also be employed. Unshielded frames are widely used, too.

Figure 5.1 *Precast, prestressed concrete sections find increasing use.* (Span-Deck Incorporated)

A structural steel skeleton includes vertical columns; girders, which connect columns; beams, which connect girders; and purlins, which connect beams. Wide flange columns and square tube columns are often used in this type of framing. Girders, beams, and purlins are usually wide flange units. The various parts of a structural steel frame may be bolted together with high tensile strength bolts, or they may be welded.

Another fine type of construction utilizes precast columns and beams — or combined column/beam units — made of prestressed concrete. The concrete is prestressed by steel cables that exert longitudinal compressive stresses to counteract bending stresses. Hydraulic jacks can be used to stretch the cables before the concrete is cast and maintain tension until it has hardened. Releasing the tension causes the cables to apply compressive pressure. Prestressed concrete members can have enormous strength.[1]

A building can also be framed using columns, beams, and purlins built

---

[1] American Council on Industrial Arts Teacher Education, *Planning Industrial Arts Facilities*, 8th yearbook (Bloomington, Ill.: McKnight Publishing Company, 1959), p. 102.

of reinforced concrete. The concrete is cast on site and is strengthened by steel-reinforcing bar assemblies.

Post-and-beam construction combining wood, reinforced concrete, or structural steel posts with laminated wood beams has been a valuable means of framing school buildings. Alternatively, laminated structural arches that eliminate separate posts can be used.

Laminated beams designed to support roof decking are manufactured in a great variety of forms and sizes. They arrive at the construction site ready for installation. Since these beams are spaced relatively far apart, heavy plank decking is used to span the distances between them. In some cases, purlins are used to connect beams and provide additional support for the decking.

WALLS

Walls are upright structural sections that define the perimeter of a building and, together with the roof, enclose the building. In most instances, they are partially supported by the frame. Their outside faces are exposed to the weather. Walls are often load-bearing. They transfer the weight of the roof, roof-mounted equipment, ceilings, and climatic elements (chiefly wind and snow) to the compacted earth or bedrock that supports the foundation.

Figure 5.2 *A cavity wall provides good control of heat loss and heat gain.* (Robert J. Brady Company)

96 STRUCTURAL TECHNIQUES AND MATERIALS

There are many kinds of walls. The type that is used in a given school is determined by the climate; availability of building materials, construction equipment, transportation, and labor; the amount of money that can be spent; the nature of the structure (single- or multiple-story); surrounding architectural styles; professional and lay opinion; and other variables.

A cavity wall is an excellent structure that provides strength and durability, as well as effective control of heat loss and heat gain. Typically it includes a backing wall constructed of 4-inch partition block and a facing wall of 4-inch split block laid with the textured side toward the weather. The two walls are separated by a 2-inch air space that is often filled with 1½-inch rigid polyurethane foam or polystyrene foam insulation boards. Steel wall ties that connect the backing and facing walls pass through the insulation boards and hold them in place.

A composite (faced) wall is similar to a cavity wall, except that it does

Figure 5.3 *Curtain walls can reduce construction time.*

not have an air space. The backing wall is usually constructed of four-inch partition block and faced with brick. The block and brick walls are tied together with steel wall ties placed approximately thirty-two inches apart. The ties are laid across the brick and block in the horizontal mortar joint of every sixth course of brick.

Walls framed of light-gauge steel studs, runner tracks, lintels, bridging, and other parts have become increasingly popular. Steel studs are C-shaped sections that range in depth from three inches to six inches. They are formed of 14–20-gauge sheet steel. The steel may be plain or galvanized, but plain steel must be coated with zinc chromate or some other primer to prevent rust formation.

Steel wall sections are assembled by welding or with self-drilling, self-tapping screws. The inside and outside surfaces of a stud wall are finished with conventional building materials, such as exterior grade plywood sheathing, wood siding, and gypsum board.

The curtain wall represents an interesting architectural technique that has grown in importance because of its versatility and appearance and because it tends to reduce building costs. In essence, a curtain wall is a single-story prefabricated panel (with or without windows) that is designed to fit a bay formed by a structural skeleton. It is bolted in place and made weathertight through the use of gaskets and/or sealers. The term curtain wall has been applied to this type of wall section because the panels are, in a very real sense, hung in place. Modular panels can be joined to form segments of the walls of multistory buildings.

Curtain walls (Fig. 5.3) may be constructed of metal framing and glass so that they are transparent or translucent, or they may utilize solid sheet or sandwich materials, such as insulated porcelain-enameled steel. A curtain wall is not load-bearing; consequently it can be repaired or replaced easily. Its chief advantages are:

1. Rapid installation
2. Uniformity of quality due to the use of sheet materials and mass manufacturing methods
3. Low cost
4. High versatility which permits use in many building designs

The lower interior wall surfaces in laboratories must be dent- and abrasion-resistant, yet easy to clean. Extreme durability need extend only to approximately the forty-two-inch level, however, since most wall damage is sustained below this point.

Smooth, unglazed brick, matte-glazed brick, matte-glazed concrete block, and matte-glazed ceramic tile are good wall-facing materials. Mate-

98   STRUCTURAL TECHNIQUES AND MATERIALS

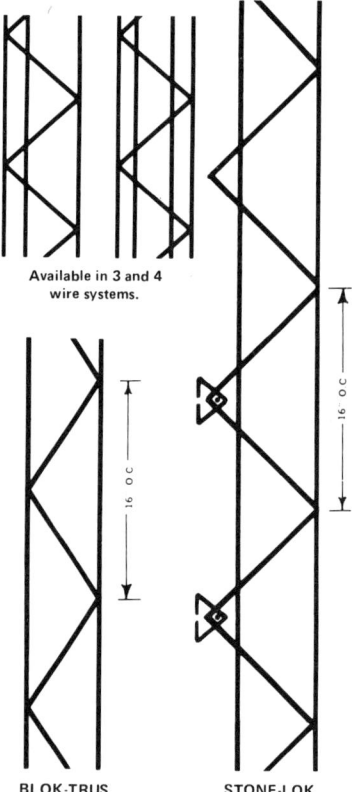

Figure 5.4 *Many types of truss-design masonry wall reinforcement are available.* (AA Wire Products Company)

rials that have gloss surfaces must be avoided. A wall should be surfaced above the forty-two-inch level with a material that absorbs sound well and is easy to maintain. Certain of the acoustical plasters are effective for this purpose.

Unfortunately, compromises must be made in the selection of wall-surfacing materials. Most materials do not rate highly with respect to all of the needed qualities — appearance, strength, surface durability, sound absorption, proper light reflectance, resistance to fire, low electrical and thermal conductance, resistance to cracking, and resistance to decay and attacks by vermin.

Wall space is limited in most laboratories, and it is well to conserve it by placing all windows approximately nine feet above floor level. This practice offers several other important advantages that are discussed in subsequent chapters. Window ledges should slope to discourage their use as storage areas, and they should be surfaced with a smooth material that will minimize dust adherence.

Hinged doors that are set in walls must open *out* to provide efficient exits during fires. Overhead doors are effective for enclosing large openings. They also can serve as emergency exits.

PARTITIONS

Partitions are upright structural sections that are used to divide the floor area of a building into two or more subareas. They are usually attached to, and gain their support from, floors, walls, other partitions, and ceilings. It is essential that partitions be nonload-bearing wherever possible so that building interiors can be conveniently redesigned to meet changing needs. A partition that is properly designed and constructed possesses several qualities, including

1. Good appearance
2. Low construction and erection costs
3. Resistance to fire
4. High sound absorption (low transmission and reflection)
5. Optimum light reflectance
6. Strength, rigidity, and flexibility
7. Surface durability (resistance to chemicals, dents, and abrasion)
8. Low thermal conductance
9. Low electrical conductance
10. Resistance to decay and attacks by vermin

Partitions must be arranged so that they do not break a floor area into subareas that are difficult to administer. This precaution is especially important to the industrial teacher who must supervise a large laboratory complex. Partition surfaces should be constructed in the same way as interior wall surfaces.

The two basic types of partitions are the movable partition and the fixed partition. Movable partitions can be designed as solid or hollowcore panels that slide or as flexible sections that fold and stack in small amounts of space. Folding partitions are usually constructed of plastic-coated fabric or hardwood slats. Neither type of movable partition can be load-bearing. Either can be motor-driven if it is too heavy to be moved comfortably by hand. Both are generally well designed. As yet, however, they have found little application in school laboratory facilities except as fire barriers and as

Figure 5.5 *Horizontal joint reinforcement is essential in block partitions.* (AA Wire Products Company)

temporary dividers. In the case of an audiovisual area, for example, a folding partition can be useful because it avoids the necessity of committing floor space permanently to needs that occur sporadically.

When a folding partition is used to divide a room, an entrance should be provided for each section that the closed partition creates. Lighting systems (including controls and fixtures) and heating and ventilation ducts must be separate. In fact, the total area must be planned as two self-contained facilities. The folding partition must connect to a wall or partition surface on each side of the room. It should not divide a window section.

Fixed partitions are much more common than folding ones. They can be built of many different materials and assembled in a variety of ways. Architects have devoted a great deal of time to improving partition design, and a number of new materials have made this job easier. A consuming clientele that, in the past, has been tolerant of (or resigned to) such partition defects as excessive transmission of noise is no longer as compliant and the demand for improved partitions has led to the development of vastly better products.

Three types of fixed partition that are widely used in the design of school laboratories are the masonry partition, the steel stud partition, and the transparent partition.

A masonry partition is usually constructed of one of the many forms of concrete block. Four-inch partition block and $8 \times 8 \times 16$-inch two-core stretcher block are common partition materials. Solid brick partitions are used less frequently because of cost.

A block partition can be designed as a single-wythe partition, a cavity partition, or a composite partition with brick on one side or both sides.

The surfaces of a concrete block partition can be faced with a number of materials, including plaster, gypsum board, ceramic tile, and sheet vinyl. Glazed block offers a variety of colorful, durable, and easily cleaned surface patterns. In most cases, however, block partitions simply are painted in order to minimize construction costs. Painting is satisfactory if a school district accepts the natural qualities of block and paint and does not insist on greater perfection than is possible.

Cracking can be a serious problem with block partitions. Thus, partitions must be strongly supported by concrete footings or floors. They must also be uniformly loaded and equipped with horizontal joint reinforcement. See Fig. 5.4 for typical joint reinforcement patterns.

The steel stud partition is versatile and possesses the qualities that are essential to good partition design. It is usually less expensive than a masonry partition, yet for the most part it is equally satisfactory. Steel studs have the advantage of being perforated; consequently, electrical conduit and plumbing pipes can be easily installed within the partitions.

Steel studs are produced to close tolerances by rolling, forming, and punching single pieces of sheet steel. They are strong and exceptionally light in weight. Protection against rust is provided by hot-dipped galvanizing or by a sprayed coat of zinc chromate or some other primer.

The air spaces between the studs in a steel stud partition can be filled with a sound-absorbing material; and the surfaces must be finished. A common facing technique is to apply gypsum lath to both sides of a partition, plaster it, and paint the plastered surfaces. However, gypsum board and hardwood paneling are also employed to achieve a variety of effects. Certain facing materials — for example, gypsum board and ceramic tile — can be used in combination.

Transparent partitions should be used to enclose auxiliary areas in which there is student or teacher activity. Design centers, classrooms, teachers' offices, and libraries are examples of such areas. Glass is the material most often used in transparent partitions. It can be framed with aluminum, steel, stainless steel, or hardwood. Metal is preferable because it permits less bulky framing and better visibility.

Glass used in partition construction should be safety plate — either tempered or laminated — because it eliminates distortion and provides the necessary strength, as well as maximum safety. For aesthetic reasons, glass that is reinforced with wire mesh is not recommended, although it is safe and durable.

Tempered plate glass is manufactured by a process that includes heating and sudden cooling in order to leave the outer surfaces in compression and the center section in tension. The result is a glass that is highly resistant to breakage and does not develop dangerous edges and points when it is shattered. Certain sharp impacts can cause it to craze and become opaque, a condition that is intolerable in an automobile windshield but of no consequence in a partition. Tempered plate glass is less expensive than laminated plate glass and less safe.

Laminated plate glass is a sandwich of two layers of polished plate bonded by a layer of tough, transparent plastic resin that has great strength, elasticity, heat resistance, and adhesion. When laminated plate glass is fractured, the glass tends to adhere to the resin, thus reducing hazards created by flying particles.

Acrylic plastic also can be used in transparent partition construction. It has the advantage of high impact, compression, tensile, and flexural strength. It affords excellent light transmission, freedom from distortion, low weight, and low thermal and electrical conductance. But its use in school laboratories has been limited by its cost, relatively low fire resistance, tendency to build charges of static electricity that cause dust and lint particles to adhere, and lack of resistance to scratching.

Glass is often used in the top sections of partitions that separate laboratories from corridors. Its use there can improve general lighting, particularly in corridors; and it can engender a feeling of spaciousness that might otherwise be lacking. Certainly glass helps to provide an attractive, contemporary appearance. To preserve wall space, the transparent part of a partition should begin nine feet above floor level and extend to the ceiling.

In the future, mass produced sheets of homogeneous or sandwich materials, or both, may be widely used in partition construction. The high standards of quality control, high production rates, and low costs made possible by automated manufacture will make them attractive to architects and contractors. It will be possible to cut sheets (or order them produced) to specified sizes and erect them as finished partitions that have all necessary qualities, including fine appearance.

Each enclosed auxiliary area should have one door. Doors in transparent partitions should be transparent above the forty-two-inch level. For fire safety reasons, doors generally should open *out* of areas in which students work. However, doors that open out of auxiliary areas often project into main work areas where they present obvious hazards. A door opened suddenly in someone's path can cause serious injuries. Moreover, a substantial amount of free floor space must be provided in front of a door on the side toward which it opens. This requirement can create equipment organization problems that are difficult to solve satisfactorily. On balance, the best solution seems to be to provide doors that open into auxiliary areas and corridors. Doors that open into corridors should be inset so that they do not project into lanes of traffic.

Wherever possible, doors should be located in the corners of rooms or in other places where they travel through an angle of 90 degrees before being stopped against walls or partitions. Doors that are placed in the centers of partitions and walls must swing through arcs of 180 degrees before contacting stops. They waste an inordinate amount of floor space, can be dangerous, and are inefficient to operate.

There should be one door between the main work area of a laboratory and the corridor that borders it. Two or more exits can make it more difficult for a teacher to maintain effective control of classes; and good functional design rarely, if ever, requires more than one exit. Multiple exits can, in fact, detract from the validity of a laboratory design, because equipment should not be installed within five feet of a door. The resulting loss of floor space can adversely affect equipment organization. Auxiliary areas should not be given access to corridors.

ROOFS

A flat roof neither adds greatly to nor detracts seriously from the appearance of a well-designed building. It is the most common type of school roof in current use, because it has the potential to do all that is required of it yet is relatively low in cost.

A main concern of an industrial teacher is that the roof of a laboratory be strong, weather-tight, and fire-resistant. Its performance as a ceiling, or as the support for a ceiling, is of major interest, because the ceiling contributes much to the overall safety, convenience, comfort, and appearance of a laboratory.

104 STRUCTURAL TECHNIQUES AND MATERIALS

A flat roof can be framed in several ways. Typically, wide flange steel beams, open-web steel joists (bar joists — Fig. 5.6), reinforced concrete beams, precast prestressed concrete beams, or laminated wood beams are used to support a flat deck. Combinations of types of framing members are also used. To achieve maximum space utility, it is necessary to avoid roof support columns in laboratories. Columns decrease the usefulness of a laboratory because of the detrimental effect they have on equipment organization. Beams that can span entire laboratories without support should always be used.

The most widely used type of roof deck includes ribbed steel decking, a light-weight insulating concrete slab or a structural concrete slab, and built-up roofing. The steel decking is welded to structural support members and is used to support the concrete as it hardens. Slab depth ranges from 2½ inches to 7½ inches, depending on the load. It is reinforced with welded wire fabric. The built-up roof consists of alternate layers of tar (or plastic roofing compound) and waterproof felt paper. A five-ply roof is usually sufficient to provide good service. A layer of stone embedded in the top coat of tar adds durability. The stone may be common pea rock or some other kind of stone.

Another effective type of roof deck is constructed of ½-inch gypsum formboards installed in steel subpurlins, a 2-inch gypsum concrete slab, and

Figure 5.6 *Open-web steel joist installation details.* (Steel Joist Institute)

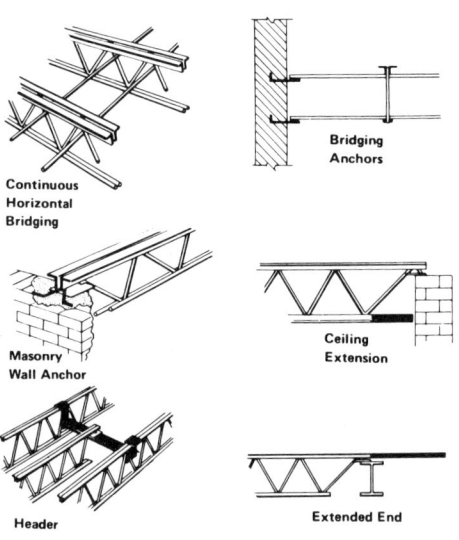

Figure 5.7 *Open-web steel joist roof framing.*

built-up roofing. The subpurlins are placed atop and perpendicular to the structural supports and welded in place. The slab, which is cast over the formboards, is reinforced with welded wire fabric.

Precast, prestressed roof decks are also in use. Precast slabs vary in thickness from four inches to twelve inches and have round or rectangular voids that run lengthwise from end to end. Joint keys between the slabs on the top surface are filled with grout and leveled to produce a flat, smooth deck. Rigid insulation is installed on the top surface to help control heat loss and heat gain, and built-up roofing makes the deck weathertight.

If a roof is framed with laminated wood beams and purlins, plank decking is used to enclose it. Plank decking is produced in both solid and laminated forms. The width of each plank is usually 6 inches, but widths up to 12 inches are available. Plank thickness ranges from 1⅞ inches to 5 inches. Each plank is single or double tongue-and-grooved on both edges. The decking is sealed with a sheet-plastic vapor barrier and faced with rigid insulation before built-up roofing is applied. If the roof has sufficient pitch, asphalt, cedar, or aluminum shingles will make it weathertight.

CEILINGS

Ceilings must be designed with the following factors in mind:

1. Appearance
2. Light reflectance

3. Sound absorption
4. Fire resistance
5. Moisture resistance
6. Resistance to sagging and cracking
7. Surface durability
8. Resistance to vermin
9. Control of heat loss and heat gain
10. Cost

Ceiling height is of critical importance to good teaching and learning. Heat, odors, and dust can become much too concentrated in rooms that have low ceilings. Noise control in such rooms is difficult, too. The concentration of noise caused by a low ceiling can make reflection and reverberation problems difficult to solve economically. Thus, it is recommended that the finished ceilings of most main work areas and auxiliary areas be at least fourteen feet above floor level. Drawing laboratory ceilings should be no less than twelve feet high.

The most commonly used types of ceilings are the open-beam ceiling and the suspended ceiling. An open-beam ceiling is formed entirely by the underside of a roof. It is economical to paint structural supports and decking — or leave them in their natural state — and allow them to serve as the ceiling of a laboratory. Plumbing pipes, ductwork, and electrical conduit can be carried in the open below and between framing members, where they are completely accessible for repair and redesign.

Accessibility of utilities systems and economy, however, are the only two significant advantages of an open-beam ceiling; and there are several serious objections to it. First of all, the appearance of an open-beam ceiling is, at best, poor. (A roof constructed of laminated wood beams and plank decking is an exception to this, but its naturally fine appearance can be marred by the presence of utilities systems.) Second, framing members and utilities systems collect dust and are difficult to clean. Third, they also break up the circulation of air along the ceiling. Fourth, the light reflectance of an open-beam ceiling is likely to be inadequate. Fifth, noise is not absorbed well and, in fact, can be reflected from a number of points. Where cost makes an open-beam ceiling a necessity, appearance and light reflectance can be improved by painting the roof decking, structural supports, and utilities systems an off-white color.

The suspended ceiling (Fig. 5.8) is a fairly recent development, but it has become the predominant type of ceiling for both renovation and new construction. In essence, a suspended ceiling consists of a metal framework, or grid, which is suspended horizontally by steel hanger wires. The wires are attached to structural support members. Ceiling panels are supported in

Figure 5.8 *Suspended ceiling*. (Armstrong Cork Company)

the grid to form a flat, level ceiling. Depending on its design, the grid can be flush with the panels, recessed, or concealed.

The various parts of a grid are fabricated of galvanized steel. Main runners, cross tees, and wall angles are available with a baked enamel finish or a wood-grain vinyl coating. Several colors of each are available.

Some grid systems are designed so that they do not deform when exposed to intense heat or fire. This design keeps the ceiling panels in place and helps to prevent a fire from spreading.

Ceiling panels are made of mineral fiber, processed wood fiber, plastic, and other materials and combinations of materials. Mineral fiber panels absorb sound well (up to 55 per cent absorption) and are the most fire-retardant. The exposed surfaces of vinyl coated panels are washable.

Common ceiling panel sizes are 24 × 24 inches and 24 × 48 inches. Panel thickness ranges from ½ inch to 1 inch. Panels are normally an off-white color and are produced in a variety of textures and patterns. The light reflectance of a ceiling panel depends on its color value and texture, but it is usually high.

Luminaires can be installed above a suspended ceiling. The regular ceiling panel is replaced by a translucent plastic panel wherever there is a luminaire. Several patterns of luminous panels are available. An entire ceiling can be constructed of this type of panel but at the expense of proper sound absorption, adequate fire protection, and effective control of heat loss and heat gain.

Luminaires that replace standard 24 × 48 inch ceiling panels are also available. This type of unit contains four 40-watt, rapid-start fluorescent lamps. It is dropped in place in the grid.

The space above a suspended ceiling is often used to house the ductwork of a mechanical ventilation system. Air diffusers mounted in the ceiling panels distribute air to all parts of the room. One type of ventilation system introduces fresh air into the entire space above the ceiling and creates enough pressure to force air through tiny perforations in the panels.

To summarize, a suspended ceiling offers the following advantages:

1. Fine appearance
2. Effective absorption of sound
3. Excellent light reflectance
4. Good fire protection
5. Complete concealment but easy accessibility of ducts, pipes, conduit, and equipment
6. Dry installation — no drying time or extensive cleanup required
7. Rapid assembly
8. Ease of maintenance, reconditioning, and replacement

FLOORS

The *structural* floors of a school usually include one floor placed at grade level (or below grade level) and one or more suspended floors. Both types of floors are virtually always constructed of concrete.

A floor that is at or below grade level consists of a flat slab that is cast in place with earth support. Normally, it is six inches thick, and it is reinforced with welded wire fabric.

A suspended floor may be constructed as a flat slab that is cast in place

FLOORS

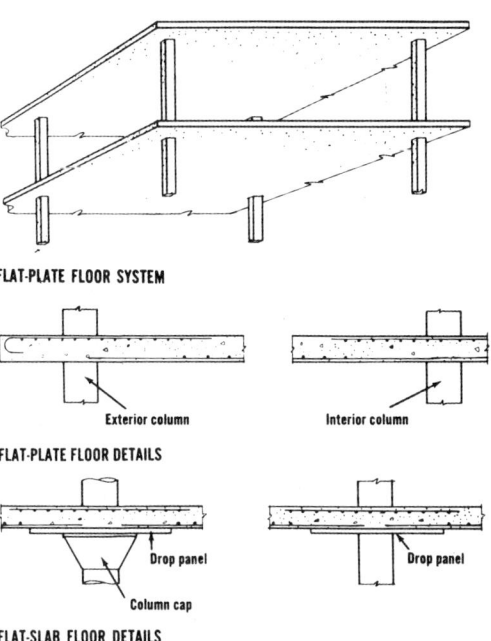

Figure 5.9 *Construction details for slab floors.* (Portland Cement Association)

(Fig. 5.9), or it may utilize any one of several other designs, such as one-way joist slab design and waffle slab design. Suspended flat slabs vary in thickness from five inches to fourteen inches.

Hollow-core slabs that are precast and prestressed are also used to fabricate suspended floors. They range in thickness from four to twelve inches, but most are either six or eight inches thick. Hollow-core slabs are often given a leveling coat of grout or concrete before the finish flooring is applied.

A structural floor serves as the base for a floor surfacing material that will provide the walking surface. Flooring materials are of substantial interest to industrial teachers because of their effects on overall laboratory design.

A floor is highly visible. Consequently it has much to do with the general appearance of a laboratory. A floor must provide strong, level support for pieces of equipment and a good surface for walking. Its light-reflecting qualities influence laboratory lighting just as the amounts of noise produced at points of impact on the floor affect laboratory acoustics.

110   STRUCTURAL TECHNIQUES AND MATERIALS

The electrical and thermal conductance, surface friction, and fire resistance of a flooring material contribute much to the comfort and safety of students. Laboratory maintenance costs depend, in part, on the flooring materials used; not all materials provide desirable protection against rust and against damage to pieces of equipment that are dropped.

Opinion concerning the effects of flooring materials on foot and leg comfort is divided. Some people believe that the type of material used makes a difference, whereas others feel that the difference is not significant. Very hard materials may make walking and standing less comfortable over long periods of time, but this characteristic does not seem important enough to affect choices of materials.

The range of available flooring materials is extensive. There are many types of materials and numerous colors, patterns, and textures within types. Among the most widely used materials are vinyl (in sheet and tile forms), vinyl asbestos tile, concrete, hardwood, brick tile, slate, ceramic tile, terrazzo, and carpet. Most of these can be eliminated from consideration for use in industrial education laboratories on the basis of cost or general suitability. Four materials — solid hardwood block, concrete, vinyl, and vinyl asbestos tile — stand out as being the most useful. Collectively they

Figure 5.10 *Nonslip materials make floors safer.*

offer a sufficiently broad range of choice so that any flooring need can be met. Each of the four is a very versatile material.

Concrete

Concrete is a hard, durable substance composed of cement, sand, gravel, and water. It is one of the oldest and most suitable flooring materials in use. Its cost is relatively low, and it has a long service life. Concrete is highly resistant to fire, chemicals, and impact damage. A concrete floor provides excellent surface friction, resistance to indentation, and strength.

The major weaknesses of concrete are its rather uninteresting natural appearance, its good electrical conductance when wet, the lack of protection it affords equipment, its tendency to soil and stain easily, and the likelihood that it will roughen, crack, craze, powder, or chip — or do all of these things — if it is not properly mixed, reinforced, finished, and cured. Nevertheless concrete is a valuable material because it can be modified to correct all but a few of its deficiencies.

Hardwood block flooring

Hardwood block flooring can be purchased in several types, sizes, and thicknesses. Laminated block may be fabricated from one species of hardwood, or it may be made of two or more hardwoods. For example, a laminated block may include a top ply of red oak and two or more additional plies of some other hardwood. Solid hardwood block — preferably maple — should be used to surface laboratory floors. The hardness and close grain structure of maple make it a truly superior flooring material. Solid block is made of strips that are tongue-and-grooved on the edges and ends and glued edge to edge with a waterproof adhesive, such as urea resin glue.

Although solid block flooring is available in prefinished form, it is probably best to finish a block floor after it has been laid so that it can be sanded level before the finish is applied. Finishes applied on site are easier to repair than factory finishes, because factory colors can be difficult to match.

Hardwood block should be applied only to suspended slabs and to slabs that are cast at grade level. As a general rule, moisture makes below-grade applications unsuccessful.

The appearance of hardwood block flooring is universally popular. It has an exceptionally long service life, offers maximum protection to tools and equipment, and provides a comfortable walking surface. For all practical purposes, hardwood is a nonconductor of electricity and heat, and it is reasonably resistant to chemical and impact damage.

The chief disadvantages of hardwood are its low surface friction (especially with sawdust on it), lack of resistance to fire, tendency to stain easily, and need for careful and regular maintenance to retain its original appearance.

Vinyl

Vinyl is a synthetic material. It is composed of vinyl resins, plasticizers, color pigments, and inert filler materials. Backed vinyl often has a backing of asbestos fiber felt bonded to it.

Vinyl is available in sheet and tile forms. Both are relatively thin, varying in thickness from 0.065 inch to 0.165 inch. The 0.165-inch (commercial) thickness should be used for all school applications.

Vinyl tile and sheet vinyl are produced in a vast assortment of colors, textures, and patterns. All are durable and resistant to chemical damage and staining. Vinyl is a nonconductor of electricity and a poor conductor of heat. Tool and equipment damage is minimized by a vinyl floor covering, although the thinner coverings do not perform as well in this respect. The only serious limitation of vinyl is its somewhat low resistance to burns.

In drawing and electricity/electronics laboratories, classrooms, libraries, design centers, teachers' offices, audiovisual rooms, and other areas where the demands on a floor surfacing material are not unusually great, vinyl can be used to good advantage. In certain of these places, the appearance of vinyl and its fine functional qualities can make it an outstanding floor covering.

Vinyl asbestos

Vinyl asbestos is a synthetic that is compounded of vinyl resins, asbestos fibers, color pigments, and inert filler materials. Since it is somewhat brittle, it is produced only in tile form. The two common tile sizes are 9×9 inches and 12×12 inches. Vinyl asbestos tile is produced in $1/16$-inch and $1/8$-inch thicknesses, and it is unbacked. The $1/8$-inch (commercial) thickness is recommended for school use.

Vinyl asbestos tile can be applied to concrete slabs that are in contact with the earth or suspended. It wears well, resists staining very well, is easy to maintain, and provides satisfactory underfoot comfort. Resistance to indentation and impact damage as well as its quietness can be considered to be fair to good. The two major advantages of vinyl asbestos tile are its low cost and its outstanding ability to resist alkalis, oil, grease, and many common solvents.

Vinyl asbestos tile can serve well in corridors, offices, classrooms, drafting laboratories, electricity/electronics laboratories, design centers, libraries, and storage rooms. Many colors and patterns are available.

Qualities that should be possessed by flooring materials are presented in Table 5.1, where each of the materials previously discussed is rated with respect to each quality. As the ratings make clear, none of the four materials is ideal. However, it is important to keep two facts in mind. First, the qualities listed in the chart are not weighted. Obviously some are more important than others. For example, a low rating concerning underfoot comfort is not as serious as a low service-life rating, because any differences in comfort are probably slight. Second, some deficiencies are more easily corrected than others. To illustrate, concrete's lack of resistance to staining is not necessarily serious because paint or a clear sealer can eliminate staining almost completely. Vulnerability to burns, on the other hand, can be impossible to correct — as it is in the case of vinyl. Therefore, information contained in the chart represents a broad comparison of the flooring materials listed and must be applied with care in the selection of a material. The best materials, of course, are those that have the fewest important and/or unalterable limitations.

In some cases, a desirable quality in flooring material can be diminished by improper installation or maintenance. The potentially excellent surface friction of concrete, for example, can be all but lost through incorrect troweling, application of a high gloss paint or sealer, or contamination by sawdust or oil.

All four of the recommended flooring materials can be slippery in day-to-day service; therefore, the danger areas of a floor or stair should be treated with a nonslip material.

Most nonslip materials include either a base material (such as paint or epoxy plastic) that is impregnated with abrasive particles or a metal or fabric base in which abrasive particles are embedded or to which they are bonded. The abrasive is usually carborundum, aluminum oxide, or a mixture of the two.

Nonslip materials can be purchased in a limited number of colors and in a variety of forms, including: abrasive mixes that are applied by troweling, brushing, or spraying; abrasive-coated fabric strips that have contact adhesive backings; and metal castings (iron, bronze, aluminum, and

STRUCTURAL TECHNIQUES AND MATERIALS

Table 5.1 COMPARISON OF SELECTED FLOORING MATERIALS

	Flooring Material			
Characteristic	*Maple block, finished*	*Concrete, natural*	*Vinyl*	*Vinyl asbestos*
Appearance	A	C	A	A
Cost	B	A	C	A
Life expectancy	A	A	B	B
Ease of maintenance	C	C	B	A
Protection of tools, equipment	A	D	A	B
Underfoot comfort	B	D	B	B
Low electrical conductance	A	D	A	A
Low thermal conductance	A	D	A	A
Optimum light reflectance	A	C	A	A
Noise at point of impact	C	C	B	B
Amount of surface friction	C	A	B	B
Maintenance of original color	C	B	B	B
Resistance to wear, abrasion	B	B	B	B
Resistance to indentation	B	A	B	B
Resistance to vermin	B	A	A	A
Resistance to decay	B	A	A	A
Resistance to staining	C	D	A	A
Resistance to burns	D	A	D	B
Resistance to soil absorption	B	C	B	B
Resistance to moisture absorption	C	D	A	A
Resistance to oil and grease	C	D	A	A
Resistance to alkali	B	B	A	A
Point rating	63	54	74	78

Rating Scale:

    A excellent (4)
    B good (3)
    C fair (2)
    D poor (1)

Table 5.2 FLOORING MATERIALS RECOMMENDED FOR USE IN INDUSTRIAL EDUCATION FACILITIES

Laboratory or Auxiliary Area	Recommended Flooring Material
General laboratory	Maple
Woods	Maple
Metals	Concrete
Crafts	Maple
Graphic arts	Maple, vinyl asbestos, vinyl, concrete
Electricity/electronics	Maple, vinyl asbestos, vinyl
Drawing	Maple, carpet, vinyl asbestos, vinyl
Automotive technology	Concrete
Class area	Maple, vinyl asbestos, vinyl, carpet
Teacher's office	Maple, carpet, vinyl asbestos, vinyl
Design center	Maple, vinyl asbestos, vinyl, carpet
Laboratory library	Maple, vinyl asbestos, vinyl, carpet
Demonstration area	Same as main work area
Locker area	Same as main work area
Project storage room	Same as main work area
Materials storage room	Same as main work area
Equipment storage room	Same as main work area
Project assembly area	Same as main work area
Toilet and lavatory	Terrazzo, ceramic tile
Wash area	Same as main work area
Finishing room	Concrete
Darkroom	Concrete, vinyl asbestos, vinyl, carpet
Materials testing center	Maple

nickel-bronze) that have abrasive particles embedded in their surfaces. Castings are bolted or cast in place on stair treads and thresholds and in other places that present slipping hazards.

It is recommended that floor areas on which students stand while operating machines have nonslip surfaces. Floors that carry substantial amounts of traffic or can become contaminated with water, oil, or some other material that reduces surface friction should also be treated with nonslip materials. Trade names of nonslip materials include Amcolun, Feralun, Alumalun, Bronzalun, Nicalun, Fera-Flow, Martex, Ferrox, Fera-Mat, and Epoxo.[2]

The two flooring materials that perform best in school laboratories are

[2]Products of American Abrasive Metals Company, Irvington, N.J.

solid maple block and concrete. More than the others, they are modifiable, and they can be economically transformed into essentially "A" materials. For the most satisfactory service, maple block should be the heavy-duty industrial type ($^{33}/_{32}$ inch thick, 9×9 inches square). It should be bonded to a concrete structural floor with flooring mastic and sealed with a clear, semigloss finish. A concrete floor should be painted, or the mix should be colored and the hardened floor coated with a clear, semigloss sealer. Specific flooring recommendations pertaining to the several laboratories and auxiliary areas are presented in Table 5.2.

It may be desirable to use more than one type of flooring material in some laboratories. Maple, for example, is the preferred material for a crafts laboratory. But in portions of the main work area where hot or molten metals are handled and where activities in ceramics are carried on, concrete is clearly preferable. Combining flooring materials means added expense, and, of course, it does tend to inhibit laboratory reorganization.

FOR FURTHER READING

American Council on Industrial Arts Teacher Education. *Planning Industrial Arts Facilities.* 8th yearbook. Bloomington, Ill.: McKnight Publishing Co., 1959.

Baas, Alan M. *System Building Techniques.* Eugene, Ore.: EROC Clearinghouse on Educational Management, 1972.

Benedict, Lowell. "When a Program Changes, They Move a Wall." *Industrial Education,* March 1975, p. 48.

Campbell, Edward A. "Flooring — a Vital Environmental Element." *Industrial Arts and Vocational Education,* March 1965, p. 48.

Castaldi, Basil. *Creative Planning of Educational Facilities.* Chicago: Rand McNally, 1969.

Davis, Edward W., and White, Lindsay. "How to Avoid Construction Headaches." *Harvard Business Review,* March-April 1973.

Griffin, C. W., Jr. *Systems — an Approach to School Construction.* New York: Educational Facilities Laboratories, 1971.

McGuinness, William J., and Stein, Benjamin. *Building Technology: Mechanical and Electrical Systems.* New York: John Wiley & Sons, 1977.

Modern School Shop Planning. 7th ed., rev. Ann Arbor, Mich.: Prakken Publications, 1976.

Ramsey, Charles G., and Sleeper, Harold R. *Architectural Graphic Standards,* 6th ed., rev. New York: John Wiley & Sons, 1970.

Sumption, Merle R., and Landes, Jack L. *Planning Functional School Buildings.* New York: Harper and Brothers, 1957.

6

The Visual Environment

INTRODUCTION

The laboratory environment in which an industrial education student works can have a significant effect on his or her emotional well-being and physical health, quantity and quality of work produced, and, consequently, rate and retention of learning. One important facet of laboratory environment is the visual environment, which includes both color and lighting. Efforts to establish a good visual environment can be expensive, but they cost much less than the decreased educational opportunities that result where seeing conditions are unfavorable.

COLOR

Human beings have always liked and needed color; now, more than ever, they prefer it in abundance. Even before people possessed an appreciable understanding of color, they undoubtedly perceived it — as we do today — as a force that could add interest to their surroundings and increase their satisfaction with life. Properly used, color can achieve results that are measurable, and it offers truly outstanding ways of improving the design of any industrial education laboratory. These include:

1. *Control of light reflection* — The light-reflecting qualities of floors, walls, partitions, ceilings, and working surfaces help determine both the level of general illumination and the uniformity of illumination in a room. Light reflection is influenced by color value.
2. *Reduction of fatigue* — Color is useful in aiding mental concentration and avoiding the eyestrain and general muscular fatigue that are concomitants of many laboratory activities.
3. *Creation of useful optical effects* — The proportions of rooms can be visually altered by the application of color. Objects and surfaces can be made to advance, recede, appear smaller, and loom larger. Optical illusions produced by color can make a laboratory safer and visually more comfortable.
4. *Creation of psychological effects* — If students are to be most productive, they must be interested in the work at hand and should possess a feeling of mental well-being (but not exuberance or complacency). Color can help to create a mental state that is conducive to learning.
5. *Achievement of desired aesthetic qualities* — Industrial education facilities should be attractive and interesting in order to encourage proper housekeeping and promote learning. Color is one of the main avenues to good appearance.
6. *Promotion of safety* — Color-coding machinery to identify parts that are likely to cause injuries can be effective in preventing accidents. Color-coding other potential danger points, such as traffic lanes, stairs, and projections of various kinds, is equally valuable.
7. *Provision of useful information* — Color coding adds to the utility of tool panels and helps to identify fire fighting equipment, first aid equipment, and materials carried in pipes.

The phenomenon that is color has its basis in light. Light waves stimulate photoreceptors, called rods and cones, in the retina of the eye, and the responses are conveyed by the optic nerve to the brain for interpretation as light and color.

The *electromagnetic wave theory* holds that light is a composition of all visible electromagnetic waves found in an extremely narrow, near-center portion of the electromagnetic spectrum. Essentially the spectrum is an organization of electromagnetic wave lengths, from shortest to longest, on

COLOR 119

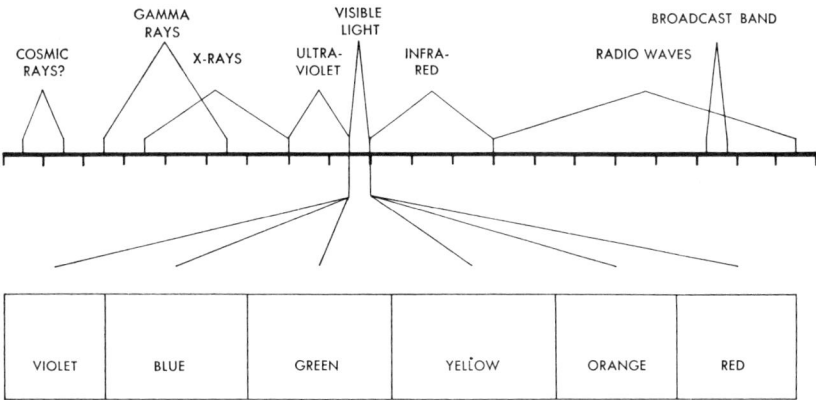

Figure 6.1 *The electromagnetic spectrum.* (PPG Industries, Incorporated)

COLOR	WAVE LENGTH
limit of visible violet	16 millionths of 1 inch
heart of violet	17 millionths of 1 inch
heart of indigo	18 millionths of 1 inch
heart of blue	19 millionths of 1 inch
heart of green	20 millionths of 1 inch
heart of yellow	22 millionths of 1 inch
heart of orange	26 millionths of 1 inch
heart of red	30 millionths of 1 inch
limit of visible red	32 millionths of 1 inch

Figure 6.2 *Lengths of visible electromagnetic waves.*

a continuum (Fig. 6.1). Included are waves of all known lengths, from short, invisible cosmic rays to long, invisible power transmission waves. All possess radiant energy.[1] Visible waves range in length from the limit of visible violet (16 millionths of an inch) to the limit of visible red (32 millionths of an inch). Ultraviolet is invisible, as is infrared.

The *quantum theory* of light states that light is radiant energy emitted by luminous bodies, such as the sun. These bodies emit energy particles, called photons, that stimulate the rods and cones of the eye.

An electromagnetic wave is produced by the oscillation of an electrical current. Waves vary in length, amplitude (height), and frequency. Since all

[1]PPG Industries, Inc., *Pittsburgh Color Dynamics: Scientific Utilization of the Energy in Color to Promote Efficiency in Industry* (Pittsburgh: PPG Industries), p. 4.

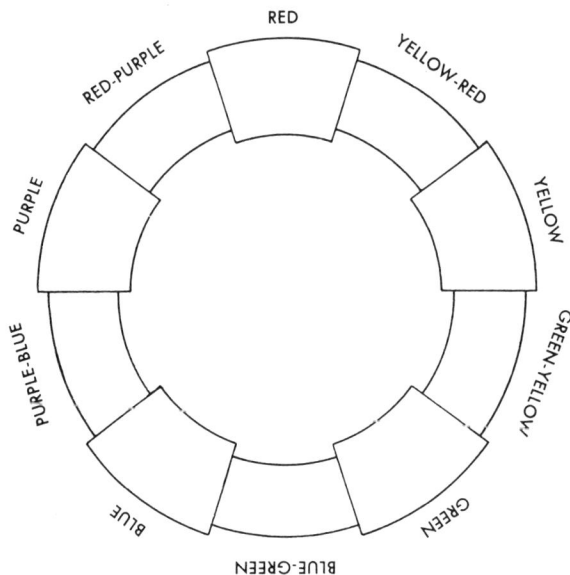

Figure 6.3 *The Munsell hue wheel.* (PPG Industries, Incorporated)

radiant energy travels at a speed of approximately 186,000 miles per second, shorter waves have less amplitude and greater frequency; that is, they oscillate more often during a given time interval. Different wavelengths create different color sensations.

White light, such as ordinary daylight, is composed of visible waves of every color. Reflecting surfaces, however, differ with respect to contour, composition, texture, and pigments contained. Pigments are light-absorbing substances that absorb certain wavelengths and reflect others. The color of a surface is determined by the specific wavelengths that it reflects (Fig. 6.2). For example, if a surface absorbs most medium and short visible waves and reflects a majority of long waves, the brain "sees" the color red.[2]

The properties of color can be described through the use of three terms — hue, value, and chroma. *Hue* (a term not in popular use) is synonymous with the term color. The hue wheel developed by A. H. Munsell includes five primary hues (purple, red, yellow, green, and blue) and five secondary hues (red-purple, yellow-red, green-yellow, blue-green, and purple-blue) arranged in the order of the electromagnetic spectrum

[2]Ibid.

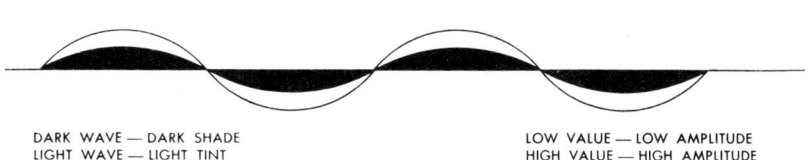

DARK WAVE — DARK SHADE
LIGHT WAVE — LIGHT TINT

LOW VALUE — LOW AMPLITUDE
HIGH VALUE — HIGH AMPLITUDE

Figure 6.4 *Electromagnetic wave amplitude.*

(Fig. 6.3).[3] Complementary hues lie opposite each other on the hue wheel. Equal amounts of two complementary hues produce white or gray.

Munsell's hue wheel is an arbitrary organization: hues exist on a continuum and there are no sharp lines of demarcation between them. Moreover, they are pure only in a theoretical sense and within infinitely narrow bands on the electromagnetic spectrum. Nevertheless, the hue wheel is useful because it permits us to deal with individual hues.

Value refers to the relative lightness or darkness of a color. A dark blue is a color of dark value, whereas a light green is a color of light value. Color values are determined by the amplitudes of light waves (Fig. 6.4). Light colors are visible waves of high amplitude. Dark values and low amplitudes are similarly related. Tint and shade are terms used to specify color values. A tint is a color of lighter value produced by adding white to a base hue. A shade is a color of darker value that results from combining a base hue with a specific amount of black.

Color value is the major factor governing the amount of light a surface reflects. Generally speaking, the lighter the value of the color of a surface, the more light it reflects, although hue, chroma, surface texture, and surface configuration determine reflection in varying and lesser degrees.

Chroma describes the relative intensity of a color, that is, its strength or weakness. A dull red is low in chroma, while a brilliant yellow is a color of high chroma. Chroma is directly related to the percentage of light waves of the same general length that a surface reflects: the higher the percentage, the higher the chroma.

All of the effects that color can be used to achieve result from variations in and combinations of hue, value, and chroma; and the possibilities are virtually limitless.

The psychologically warm colors — red, orange, and yellow — have relatively long wavelengths. They can produce feelings of warmth, and they are known to be stimulating. Cool colors — blue, green, and violet — have short wavelengths. They tend to subdue and even depress emotions and create impressions of coolness.

[3]Produced by the Allcolor Company, Inc., New York, N.Y.

Warm colors seem closer, cool colors farther away. Chroma and value also affect such impressions. Colors of light value and/or low chroma appear more distant than those of dark value and/or high chroma.

The apparent size of an object can be increased by painting it a warm hue that is light in value and high in chroma. The opposite approach will reduce apparent size. Yellow is the *largest* hue. It is followed, in order of decreasing size, by white, red, green, blue, and black.[4]

The quality called psychological weight is also a variable that depends in part on color.[5] Warm colors of high chroma and dark value appear heavier than cool colors that are low in chroma and light in value.

It is not accidental that a leading manufacturer of road-building equipment paints its products a vibrant yellow. The image of power, vitality, size, and weight called up by this color is unmistakable.

Visibility and light reflectance are physical phenomena that can be modified through the use of color. Both are important in the design of industrial education laboratories. Certain aspects of laboratory safety are dependent on visibility; and eyestrain, general muscular fatigue, and inferior performance can result from light reflectances that are too great, too little, or too strongly contrasted.

The visibility of a color seems most dependent on its value and chroma, although hue has some effect. Generally speaking, warm colors are more visible than cool colors. Yellow is the color of highest visibility, but red and red-orange are outstanding with respect to attention-attracting qualities. Strong contrasts in value and/or chroma are very effective in achieving visibility. In addition, certain combinations of hues can be used to advantage in signs, posters, color codes, and objects that must be especially noticeable. Black on yellow is excellent for making a surface conspicuous. Other good combinations are red on white, green on white, blue on white, and black on white. In all combinations, visibility is greatest if the background is a color of very light value, because the background occupies the largest area. A color of darker value should be used as the image color. The fact that the eye focuses more sharply on red, orange, and yellow than on blue and green is important in the selection of image colors.[6]

A hue's ability to reflect light is mainly dependent on three factors: its value and the form and texture of the surface to which it is applied. Light

---

[4]E. I. du Pont de Nemours and Company, Inc., *Color Conditioning Report No. 9: Size, Dimension and Weight in Color* (Wilmington, Del.: E. I. du Pont de Nemours and Co.), p. 1.

[5]PPG Industries, Inc., *Pittsburgh Color Dynamics: Scientific Utilization of the Energy in Color to Promote Efficiency in Industry* (Pittsburgh: PPG Industries), p. 4.

[6]E. I. du Pont de Nemours and Company, Inc., *Color Conditioning Report No. 8: Color and Visibility* (Wilmington, Del.: E. I. du Pont de Nemours and Company), p. 1.

values reflect much more light than dark values, while gloss surfaces reflect more light than matte surfaces. Chroma is of minor importance to light reflectance, and hue is least important.

Color systems should be planned to achieve a balance of reflected light so that excessive contrasts in reflectance (high brightness ratios) are not created. Brightness ratio is defined as the ratio of the light reflectances of two surfaces. If one surface reflects 10 per cent of the light that strikes it and another reflects 90 per cent, their brightness ratio is 1:9.

Since steady and prolonged viewing of a surface is fatiguing, it is desirable that direction of sight be frequently changed. However, if the eye is repeatedly forced to adjust from a surface of low reflectance to one of high reflectance (or the reverse), eyestrain and loss of working efficiency can result. Eyestrain is not usually recognizable as eye muscle fatigue. Instead it is often communicated to other parts of the body where it manifests itself as a feeling of general tiredness.[7] Du Pont color specialists believe that where brightness ratios do not exceed 1:5, the human eye can function for long periods of time without excessive fatigue.[8] Therefore, it is recommended that the minimum light reflectance of any surface in an industrial education laboratory be approximately 20 per cent and the greatest light reflectance be 90 per cent.

If a surface is viewed intently for even a short period of time, the retina of the eye becomes overstimulated by the color of the surface and reacts — when the view is shifted — by *seeing* an afterimage. The afterimage is a transparent silhouette of the first surface. It appears in the complementary color and is superimposed on a second surface. For example, if a red triangle is examined closely for fifteen seconds and the gaze is then transferred to a wall, a transparent green triangle appears on the wall.

In a production situation, it is desirable that the direction of a worker's view be shifted now and then in order to minimize eyestrain. But if afterimage accompanies each shift, momentary confusion may result and, in time, the worker can become fatigued. To counteract afterimage, surfaces adjacent to the principal surface can be painted the complementary color, if this is practical. If not, a change in the hue of the principal surface or a reduction in its chroma or value or the employment of all three procedures can solve the problem.

Planning the color scheme for an industrial education laboratory involves the selection of appropriate hues, values, chromas, and surface

[7]PPG Industries, Inc., *Pittsburgh Color Dynamics: Scientific Utilization of the Energy in Color to Promote Efficiency in Industry* (Pittsburgh: PPG Industries), p. 5.

[8]E. I. du Pont de Nemours and Company, Inc., *Color Conditioning Report No. 1: Brightness Engineering* (Wilmington, Del.: E. I. du Pont de Nemours and Company), p. 1.

textures for floors, walls, partitions, ceilings, and equipment. Every color scheme must be coordinated to produce the desired total impact, and the individual colors should be carefully chosen.

Several fundamental qualities of a valid color scheme can be set forth. It should utilize a base hue, tints and/or shades of the base hue, and a limited number of other colors. Six separate colors, not including those used in color codes, should be considered the maximum number that can be employed without producing a needlessly gaudy and unattractive appearance. Fewer colors should be used if it can be done without affecting the quality of the system. Only the base hue should be used extensively. Additional colors, especially those of high chroma or unusually light value, should be used sparingly and only to achieve specific results. A small area of vibrant color is much more effective than the unrestrained use of such a color. If color is to be helpful in improving concentration and increasing learning, no part of the color system should call an undue amount of attention to itself. On the other hand, drabness and monotony are undesirable and a six-color system can prevent both.

Known color preferences can and should be taken into consideration when a color scheme is planned. Blue, red, and green are the best-liked colors. Violet, orange, and yellow are less popular. Green is not, as is sometimes supposed, less likely to contribute to eyestrain. Visual comfort depends largely on reflectance and brightness ratio, not hue. But because green is the dominant color in nature, it is liked by most people.[9] Tints and shades are more pleasing to women than to men, and both sexes like tints better than shades. Pure hues are preferred to grayed ones.[10]

It is well to remember, however, that color preferences can and do change and that people are educable with respect to color. Some of the less popular colors have been successfully promoted in automobiles, house paint, table furnishings, clothing, and other products. But these colors have been used in moderation and mainly to produce accents of various kinds. A few violet automobiles might be interesting; a city full of them would be absurd.

If industrial education laboratories are adequately heated, cooled, and ventilated and if they are provided with optimum amounts of glare-free natural and artificial light, it is less important that color be used to promote feelings of coolness or warmth. It is possible (and certainly desirable) to create laboratories in which the efficiency of the learning environment is not dependent on the sun, but there are many existing

---

[9]E. I. du Pont de Nemours and Company, Inc., *Color Conditioning Report No. 3: Emotional Reaction to Color* (Wilmington, Del.: E. I. du Pont de Nemours and Company), p. 1.

[10]E. I. du Pont de Nemours and Company, Inc., *Color Conditioning Report No. 2: Color Preferences* (Wilmington, Del.: E. I. du Pont de Nemours and Company), p. 1.

facilities, including some very new ones, in which color should be used to provide increased or decreased psychological warmth.

A room that receives a relatively small amount of natural light and has a predominantly northern exposure should have light walls if its general illumination depends upon natural light to any significant degree. A tint of a warm color can make a north-facing room seem less bleak and raise the level of general illumination. A room having a west or south exposure, which makes it uncomfortably warm and light in the afternoon, should be painted a cool color of darker value.

Warm colors can be used in air-conditioned rooms to counteract psychological chilliness. Cool colors can have the opposite effect in rooms actually made uncomfortable by heat-producing activities, such as welding or foundry work.

A wall or partition that an instructor faces while teaching should have a light reflectance of approximately 30 per cent. A darker value of either the base hue or a hue that contrasts with that of the other walls can provide the proper reflectance as well as increased interest.

If a room receives a preponderance of natural light from one side, good brightness ratios and a more satisfactory level of general illumination can be obtained by painting the wall that receives the light a hue of comparatively dark value, the end walls a lighter value, and the wall from which the light comes the lightest value.[11]

Apparent room proportions can be altered by the application of color. Light values of colors make rooms appear larger, and dark values make them look smaller. Cool colors and light values cause ceilings to recede, while warm colors and dark values bring them down. A square room can be made to appear rectangular if one wall is painted either a noticeably lighter or darker value of the base hue or a contrasting hue of different value. Long, narrow rooms can be made to seem wider if the end walls are painted a color of darker value and the side walls a lighter value or contrasting color.[12] The same technique can be used to focus attention. A wall or partition — say, one containing a chalkboard — that is painted differently tends to attract the eye.

Tints of warm colors are mildly stimulating; and tints of cool colors can suppress emotions, especially if they are applied to large wall and partition surfaces.

If the surfaces of walls and partitions are to contribute to a room's

[11]PPG Industries, Inc., *Pittsburgh Color Dynamics for Grade Schools, High Schools and Colleges* (Pittsburgh: PPG Industries), p. 5.

[12]E. I. du Pont de Nemours and Company, Inc., *Color Conditioning Report No. 9: Size, Dimension and Weight in Color* (Wilmington, Del.: E. I. du Pont de Nemours and Company), p. 1.

general illumination, they should reflect from 50 per cent to 65 per cent of the light that falls on them. Chalkboards should have a reflectance of 15–20 per cent. Better brightness ratios can be obtained by finishing the lowest third of a wall or partition with a color of darker value that reflects roughly 50 per cent of the light. The upper two-thirds should be painted the same color but in a slightly lighter value that produces a reflectance of 60–65 per cent. This scheme, of course, increases the cost of decorating, but because darker values appear heavier, it has the additional advantages of contributing to good proportion and promoting a feeling of stability.

Gloss paints should be avoided because they produce glare. Flat paints can be difficult to keep clean and should be used, if at all, only on upper wall and partition surfaces and on ceilings. Semigloss paint is by far the best choice. All paints used should be fast drying, odorless, self-leveling, lead-free, durable, color-fast, easy to clean, and free of objectionable glare. Many of the latex paints provide very good general service, as well as surfaces that reflect light efficiently and without glare.

A ceiling should reflect at least 75 per cent of the light that falls on it, and a reflectance of 85 per cent or more is considered entirely appropriate. If artificial lighting is semi-indirect or indirect, it is especially necessary that ceiling reflectance be high. Very light values of colors — white, off-white, ivory, cream, and light tints of wall colors — should be applied to ceilings to achieve proper reflectance.

It is desirable that floors have a light reflectance of approximately 30 per cent.[13] The semigloss natural finish that should be applied to maple block floors can produce a light reflectance greater than 30 per cent, but it will not often be objectionably high, and the natural appearance of hardwood is well worth preserving. Concrete floors should be painted or the concrete mix should be colored and the cured floor sealed with a clear, semigloss sealer. Both methods provide adequate light reflectance. Warm colors and colors of high chroma should not be applied to concrete floors because of the large, highly visible areas to be covered. Medium gray and medium green are effective floor colors.

All pieces of equipment in an industrial education laboratory should be painted the same base color. The color value chosen must provide a light reflectance of approximately 40 per cent. The base hue should recede. It may be different from the hues of walls, partitions, and floors; or it may contrast only to the extent of having a moderately lighter or darker value. Variations in chroma can also be useful in establishing contrasts.

Critical parts of equipment — electrical switches, levers, handwheels,

---

[13]E. I. du Pont de Nemours and Company, Inc., *Color Conditioning Report No. 1: Brightness Engineering* (Wilmington, Del.: E. I. du Pont de Nemours and Company), p. 1.

tool rests, and others — should be painted in colors that advance. Colors used to focus attention may differ in value from the base hue, but the brightness ratios should not exceed 1:5. Work surfaces, such as bench tops and machine tables, should reflect 35–40 per cent of the light that strikes them.

As a general rule, nonmoving parts of a piece of equipment should be painted and moving parts should not. For example, the bed but not the chuck of a metal lathe should be painted. However, there are many exceptions to this rule. Machine tables, other work surfaces, and parts against which other parts slide (such as drill press columns) are never painted, even though they are stationary.

The use of color codes to increase the efficiency of tool storage and inventory control systems is discussed in Chapter 11. Coding can also be used to make laboratories safer, to identify materials carried in pipes, and to indicate the location of shopkeeping equipment and temporary storage facilities. Relatively small areas of a color chosen for its attention-commanding power, if they are properly placed, can be highly effective in calling attention to:

1. Collision hazards
2. Stumbling and falling hazards
3. Places of unusual danger, such as areas around machines
4. Traffic lanes
5. Waste receptacles
6. Pieces of equipment that are out of order
7. First aid supplies
8. Fire fighting equipment
9. Pipes carrying water, steam, gas, compressed air, and other materials

The color systems developed by PPG Industries, Inc., and E. I. du Pont de Nemours and Company, Inc., are outstanding examples of color in action. The names given to the two systems are Color Dynamics (PPG Industries) and Color Conditioning (du Pont). Both are attractive, versatile, and valid both psychologically and physiologically. Despite many fundamental similarities, they represent two distinct approaches to the problem of developing attractive and workable color schemes. In both systems, color is used to achieve a visual separation of critical parts of equipment from noncritical parts. Critical parts are made to stand out, without excessive contrasts in light reflectance, while noncritical parts recede. Thus an operator's attention is focused on points of importance and eyestrain is minimized. Each system includes specifications for floor, wall, partition, and ceiling colors that provide good appearance and adequate light reflectance. Each is flexible enough to meet individual color preferences and fit unique conditions of temperature, exposure, room configuration, and building construction.

In outline form, with specific reference to industrial education laboratories and with certain explanatory notes added, the two color systems are as follows:

COLOR DYNAMICS
- A. *Machines, stands, bases, other equipment*
  1. Main body — Vista Green
  2. Electrical switches — Focal Orange
  3. Focal areas (e.g., the table insert on a circular saw)
     a. Woodworking machines — Focal Orange
     b. Metalworking machines — Focal Ivory
  4. Handwheels (except for rims) — Focal Beige
  5. Levers (except for handles) — Focal Beige
  6. Dangerous projections (e.g., a flywheel) — Focal Yellow striped with Focal Black
- B. *Walls, partitions, columns, trim* — light-to-medium green hues
- C. *Doors* — natural wood finish or Vista Green
- D. *Ceilings* — white, off-white, cream, ivory, very light tint of green
- E. *Floors* — natural wood finish or medium gray
- F. *Color coding for safety*
  1. Watch out — Focal Yellow striped with Focal Black. Warns against falling, stumbling, and projecting hazards. Four-inch Focal Yellow stripes on floors mark traffic lanes and danger areas around machines
  2. On guard — Focal Orange. Warns against dangerous parts and areas of equipment. Included are electrical switchboxes, machine guards, the insides of fuse box and circuit breaker box doors, and the areas around crushing and cutting edges
  3. Fire protection — red. Marks the location of fire fighting equipment and identifies individual pieces, such as fire extinguishers.
  4. Out-of-service — blue. Blue disks are hung on pieces of equipment that are not to be used. "Out of order" is lettered in white on the blue background
  5. First aid — green. Marks the location of first aid supplies. A white cross on a green background further identifies a first

aid cabinet. Entrances to first aid stations are identified by white crosses bordered with green
6. Housekeeping facilities — white. Painted areas of floors indicate locations of waste receptacles. Temporary floor storage spaces are outlined by four-inch white stripes
7. Pipe line identification
   a. Fire protection materials (e.g., sprinkler systems) — red
   b. Dangerous materials (e.g., acids, gases, steam at a temperature higher than 212°F.) — yellow or orange
   c. Safe materials (e.g., drinking water, compressed air, steam at a temperature of 212°F.) — green, light gray, white, dark gray, black
   d. Protective materials (e.g., gases or liquids used as antidotes to dangerous materials) — blue
   e. Extra-valuable materials (e.g., materials that are usually safe but of high value) — purple

NOTE: When a pipe is coded, it should not be painted the code color along its entire length. Instead:
   1. Paint the pipe the color of the surface to which it is adjacent
   2. At intervals, paint valves, flanges, or couplings the code color *or*
   3. Band the pipe with the code color where it enters and leaves each room *or*
   4. At intervals, band the pipe with the code color *or*
   5. In each room, tag the pipe with a disk painted the code color. (A band or disk may have the identity of the material stenciled in black on it)

COLOR CONDITIONING
A. *Machines, stands, bases, other equipment*
   1. Main body — Horizon Gray
   2. Electrical switchboxes — blue
   3. Focal areas (e.g., levers, centers of handwheels, machinery guards, areas around points of operation) — Spotlight Buff
   4. Dangerous projections (e.g., a flywheel) — yellow striped with black
   5. Alert area (e.g., areas around parts that can cut or crush and the insides of machinery part covers) — orange
B. *Walls, partitions, columns*
   1. Lower third — medium gray or medium green
   2. Upper two-thirds — light green

- C. *Doors, trim* — natural wood finish, medium gray, or medium green
- D. *Ceilings* — white or ivory
- E. *Floors* — natural wood finish or medium gray
- F. *Color coding for safety*
  The Color Dynamics and Color Conditioning safety codes are the same with the exception of the colors specified for electrical switchboxes. The Color Dynamics code specifies Focal Orange, and the Color Conditioning code specifies blue

Both color systems can be employed in an industrial education facility that includes several laboratories. Monotony can result if exactly the same color scheme is applied throughout an entire department. Together, Color Dynamics and Color Conditioning offer enough variety to avoid any suggestion of sameness. It is recommended that the two systems not be mixed within a laboratory.

LIGHTING

Light and color are inseparable as areas of knowledge and investigation. A hue is composed of a limited number of visible electromagnetic waves of similar length, while white light is a blend of *all* visible electromagnetic waves. As planning topics, however, light and color are treated separately. They represent distinct though closely related aspects of building design. Colors are used to assist in the control of light but also to achieve certain functional, aesthetic, and psychological goals that are not directly related to lighting. Color properties can be used to control the reflection and absorption of light, but colors do not contribute to the emission of light. Lighting, on the other hand, is concerned mainly with the quantity and quality of light emitted by natural and artificial sources and with the control of light in order to produce good visual environments.

If industrial arts or vocational-technical students are to learn well, they must be able to see everything of importance going on during class periods. Therefore an essential part of laboratory planning is designing lighting systems that make seeing effective, comfortable, and free of distraction. For most students, a satisfactory visual environment leads to greater total learning, the development of more efficient work habits, better self-discipline, minimal eyestrain and general muscular fatigue, fewer accidents, improved craftsmanship, and the acquisition of better housekeeping habits. These advantages accrue to all students, and significantly, they represent some of the most important objectives of industrial education. Viewed in this context, the importance of lighting is obvious.

Most laboratory activities are primarily visual in nature, and they can make strenuous demands on the eyesight of students. Tasks range from large to minute, simple to complex, and mechanical to judgmental. In order to fulfill an industrial education program's broad obligation to maintain or improve, rather than impair, the mental and physical capabilities of students, the laboratories in which instruction takes place must provide unusually good seeing conditions. If this is done, most students' sight will be dramatically improved. For example, the results will be better and expenditure of time and effort will be less when automobile parts are examined for defects, drawing line work is evaluated, wood surfaces are prepared for finishing, and a wide variety of other visual tasks are undertaken.[14]

The level of general illumination provided in a laboratory is determined by both need and practicality. In recent years, these two considerations have become much less mutually exclusive. The intensity of natural illumination in a shaded outdoor area on a sunny day ranges from 400 to 1200 footcandles. Most people find intensity in this range excellent for a majority of visual tasks. It permits the normal eye to see comfortably and well. Ideally, this level of general illumination should be provided in industrial education laboratories. But equipment, installation, and operating costs still combine to keep current recommended illumination intensities well below what is manifestly desirable. Even so, enough progress has been made so that relatively high levels of general illumination are feasible. Local lighting of machines and other pieces of equipment must furnish the requisite supplementary illumination.

All aspects of school construction are expensive. Most building costs have greatly increased in recent years. But in a relative sense, lighting costs have declined. The result is that the purchase and operation of a system that provides good artificial light requires an expenditure that is less than 2 per cent of the total cost of education in most communities.[15]

The cost of adequate lighting consumes a smaller percentage of the education dollar than it did in 1940, although levels of general illumination have risen a great deal. This is not to say that the costs of luminaires, distribution systems, and control devices have actually decreased. They have not. It simply means that lighting equipment costs have increased less rapidly than many other building costs, the cost of electricity has risen

[14]General Electric, *Footcandles in Modern Lighting*, Report TP-128 (prepared by the Large Lamp Department) (Cleveland, Ohio: General Electric, October 1964), p. 5.

[15]General Electric, *School Lighting*, Report TP-102 (prepared by the Large Lamp Department) (Cleveland, Ohio: General Electric), p. 2.

132 THE VISUAL ENVIRONMENT

only moderately, and the efficiency of all lamps has been vastly improved. Before 1938, for example, the incandescent lamp was universally used to provide artificial light. Since then, there has been a nationwide swing to the fluorescent lamp, which costs significantly less to operate.

Proper lighting is, in fact, well within the reach of any school district that can afford to build a school at all, and there is little excuse for a classroom in the United States to be poorly lighted. Parenthetically, seeing conditions in all classrooms can be improved through the use of instructional materials printed in ten point or larger type, simple type styles,

Figure 6.5 *Local lighting supplements a general illumination system.* (Rockwell International, Power Tool Division)

matte paper, clean chalkboards, white chalk, and good-quality duplicated materials. Chalkboard technique is also important. Writing and diagrams should be large, distinct, and legible.

In addition to its effect on laboratory function, artificial lighting helps to determine the quality of a laboratory's aesthetic design insofar as color rendition, overhead appearance, and certain accents contribute to good design. The quality of light emitted by lamps should be such that colors appear natural and laboratories are attractive. Luminaires should be unobtrusive but well designed, so that they represent points of at least moderate interest. Sufficient progress has been made in luminaire design to ensure good appearance if discriminating choices are made. Local lighting can be used to create accents that relieve the monotony that is often a by-product of the uniformity produced by a general lighting system.

The terminology that has been developed to permit accurate descriptions of the production and utilization of light is extensive, as it is in any highly specialized field of knowledge. Part of this vocabulary should be understood by anyone who must make recommendations concerning lighting systems to be installed in schools and who must judge the effectiveness of these systems. An understanding of each of the following terms is basic to effective knowledge of the fundamentals of lighting:[16]

1. *Light* — Radiant energy that includes all visible electromagnetic waves varying in length from 16 millionths of an inch to 32 millionths of an inch.
2. *Lamp* — Any artificial light source.
3. *General lighting* — Lighting that produces a reasonably uniform level of illumination throughout an area.
4. *Supplementary lighting* — Local lighting used to provide a high intensity of illumination on a surface if general lighting cannot be economically used for this purpose.
5. *Incandescent filament lamp* — An artificial light source that produces light through the action of an electric current that passes through a filament and heats it to incandescence (usually white heat).
6. *Fluorescent lamp* — An electric discharge lamp in which a phosphor coating transforms into light some of the ultraviolet energy produced by the discharge.
7. *Luminaire* — A complete light-emitting unit that includes an

---

[16]See Illuminating Engineering Society, *American Standard Guide for School Lighting* (New York: Illuminating Engineering Society, 1962), p. 36.

artificial light source or sources, and all essential parts, such as globes, reflectors, louvers, and housings.

8. *Luminous ceiling* — A general lighting system in which an entire ceiling is constructed of a light diffusing material (or device) with incident light sources positioned above it.

9. *International candle* — The international unit of luminous intensity. Theoretically, it is the intensity of light produced by five square millimeters of platinum at the temperature of solidification (3191°F.).

10. *Candela* — One international candle.

11. *Candlepower* — The luminous intensity of a light source expressed as a certain number of international candles.

12. *Footcandle* — The intensity of illumination on a surface that is at all points one foot distant from a uniform point source equal to one international candle.

13. *Illumination* — The intensity of illumination that falls on a surface (usually expressed as a certain number of footcandles).

14. *Regular transmission* — A condition in which light is passed through a medium with little diffusion and absorption. (The direction of the transmitted light is geometrically related to the angle at which the light strikes the receiving surface.)

15. *Diffuse transmission* — The uniform emission of light in all directions from a surface other than the one on which the light first falls.

16. *Transmission factor* — The percentage of light transmitted by a medium.

17. *Specular reflection* — Regular reflection. (The angle of reflection is equal to the angle at which light strikes a reflecting surface.)

18. *Diffuse reflection* — The uniform reflection of light in all directions from a reflecting surface.

19. *Reflectance* — The percentage of light reflected by a surface.

20. *Brightness* — The luminous intensity of a surface. Brightness is the product of the intensity of light falling on a surface and the reflectance of the surface.

21. *Brightness ratio* — The ratio of the percentages of light reflected by two surfaces.

22. *Lumen* — The unit used to express quantity of light. It is the light emitted in a unit solid angle by a uniform point source of one international candle. By definition, one lumen of light falls on each square foot of a sphere's surface — regardless of the shape of the area — if one international candle is placed one foot from all points on the surface.

23. *Footlambert* — A unit of brightness equal to the uniform brightness of a perfectly diffusing surface that reflects light at the rate of one lumen per square foot. (The average brightness of a surface, expressed in footlamberts, is the product of the intensity of illumination on the surface, expressed in footcandles, and the reflectance of the surface.)
24. *Direct glare* — The visual effect of a surface of high brightness (or an insufficiently shielded light source) in the field of vision.
25. *Reflected glare* — The visual effect of a surface of high brightness (or an insufficiently shielded light source) that is reflected by a polished surface in the field of vision.
26. *Louver* — An opaque or translucent part that is used to shield a light source from direct view or to absorb superfluous light.

Three types of light are utilized in industrial education laboratories: natural light, incandescent light, and fluorescent light. Natural light can be used in a limited way to improve laboratory appearance and to prevent the feeling of claustrophobia that can trouble some people in windowless rooms. Unfortunately natural light is anything but dependable. It must always be supplemented by enough artificial lighting capacity to provide the recommended level of general illumination for a laboratory that is used by an evening class. During daylight hours, there are few times when laboratory lights can be turned off and adequate illumination obtained solely from natural light. Normal weather and the daily cycle of daylight and dark with its buildup and decline of intensity of illumination make this impossible. Therefore no reduction in artificial lighting costs can be achieved through the extensive introduction of natural light. Anyone who designs a laboratory should regard natural light as nothing more than a pleasant adjunct to an effective artificial lighting system.

Daylight can be brought into laboratories by means of windows, clerestories, and skylights. Windows and clerestories do not distribute light as evenly as skylights, but they permit vision as well as the entrance of light. A sawtooth roof can provide satisfactory skylighting, as can a series of Plexiglas domes. Plexiglas domes can be used as incident light sources that are, in effect, similar to luminaires. The utility of any type of skylight, however, is often reduced by water leakage, its limited dependability as an incident light source, heat loss, glare, its tendency to create a hot spot on the floor, and the difficulty of keeping it clean.

Natural light must be diffused to control shadows, glare, and heat. Glass in the form of matte panels, clear panels with prismatic surfaces (available with pebbled, vertical prism, diamond prism, horizontally ribbed, fluted, and other patterns), clear tinted panels, and block can be used to diffuse light. Matte and tinted panels have lower transmission

136 THE VISUAL ENVIRONMENT

factors that reduce glare. Glass block and prismatic surfaces diffuse light by refracting it.

Louvers, venetian blinds, and drapes can also be employed to minimize glare, but their use can cause self-defeating reductions in vision and in the quantity of daylight admitted. An exterior device such as the overhang of a roof or a vertical concrete screen can be an effective means of diffusing light and eliminating sky brightness and the direct rays of the sun from the field of vision (Fig. 6.6).

High-level windows offer an exceptionally good way of obtaining the benefits of natural light while avoiding most of the disadvantages of conventional windows and skylights. A well designed high-level window section often runs the entire length of a wall and extends vertically from a point nine feet above floor level to the ceiling. A transmitting material that diffuses light, an exterior concrete screen, or the overhang of the roof should be used to eliminate glare. In some cases, it is necessary to use a combination of light control methods to achieve window brightness that approximates the brightness of wall and partition surfaces.

In addition to their light-transmitting function, high-level windows provide two advantages that are important to industrial teachers. By consuming upper wall space that would not otherwise be used, they preserve valuable lower wall space for chalkboards, bulletin boards, tool

Figure 6.6 *Contemporary concrete screens control sunlight and enhance building appearance.*

cabinets, and other pieces of laboratory equipment. Finally, the position of a high-level window eliminates one source of discipline problems by preventing students from being distracted by events taking place outside the classroom.

The incandescent filament lamp was invented in 1879. Its chief advantages are low cost, simplicity of operation and control, good color rendition, good performance at low ambient temperatures, the ease with which the light output of a given luminaire can be varied, usefulness in providing local lighting that requires a point source of light, and ease of dimming over a wide light output range. The important limitations of an incandescent lamp are high heat output, glare and shadow problems, and comparatively low efficiency. Its overall operating cost is much greater than that of a fluorescent lamp. Consequently it is usually prohibitively expensive to use incandescent lamps to establish a high level of general illumination in a laboratory.

The usual general-service incandescent lamp has a rated life of 750 to 1000 hours.[17] Light output diminishes, often seriously, in the latter third of its life.

Standard incandescent lamps emit light containing a relatively large amount of red and small amount of blue. They assist in the creation of visual environments that are psychologically warm. Incandescent lamps that provide other kinds of color rendition are available, but the range of rendition offered is fairly limited.

One recently developed type of incandescent lamp that appears promising for general illumination and local lighting is the tungsten halogen lamp. The tungsten filament in this kind of lamp operates in an atmosphere containing a halogen gas, such as iodine or bromine. A tungsten halogen lamp offers long filament life, excellent color rendition, compactness, and high efficiency throughout its service life. It is available in several forms. Lamps designed for general illumination range in size from 200 watts to 2000 watts. The cost of tungsten halogen lamps is high. These lamps are vulnerable to shock, especially when hot, and the quartz bulbs must be kept completely free of contamination.

Fluorescent light became commercially available in the United States in 1938. A fluorescent lamp has two small tungsten filaments — one at each end of a sealed glass tube. The tube contains argon gas or argon and neon gas and a small quantity of mercury. It is coated on the inside with a phosphor. Electricity heats the filaments, vaporizes the mercury, and arcs across the tube from one filament to the other. Ultraviolet rays are

---

[17]Westinghouse Electric Corporation, *Light Bulbs and Fluorescent Tubes*, a bulletin prepared by the Westinghouse Lamp Division (Bloomfield, N. J.: Westinghouse Electric Corporation), p. 11.

produced when electrons from the arc strike the atoms of mercury. The ultraviolet rays are changed to visible light by the phosphor coating. Different colors of light can be obtained by coating the tube with chemically different phosphors.

A fluorescent lamp is capable of delivering up to four times more light per watt of electricity than an incandescent lamp, and far less heat is generated in the process. Rated fluorescent lamp life ranges up to 20,000 hours, depending on the type and size of lamp, but it is reduced by frequent switching on and off.

The light output of a fluorescent luminaire cannot be increased or decreased by substituting lamps of different wattages. Each luminaire is designed for a specific lamp length, and the lengths of lamps are different for different wattages. Consequently, if a luminaire is designed for a twenty-watt lamp, no other size will fit. Rapid start fluorescent lamps can be dimmed almost as well as incandescent lamps, but special dimming equipment is required.

The advantages of the fluorescent lamp are its long life, great light output, low heat generation, low operating cost, and excellent color rendition. It is without peer where a line of light is needed. Disadvantages include high lamp replacement cost, a complex control system, vulnerability to frequent on-off switching, and poor performance at low ambient temperatures. There is little question, however, that fluorescent luminaires are much better than incandescent luminaires for the general lighting of industrial education laboratories.

One of the best fluorescent lamps is the rapid start type that lights almost instantly without the use of a starter. It should be the choice whenever a general lighting system is designed. Incandescent lamps are more useful for solving local lighting problems.

Light switches should be mounted on walls and partitions just inside entrances to rooms on the latch sides of doors. Forty-two inches above floor level is a comfortable switch height. Silent mercury switches are recommended for general use. Finishing rooms and other enclosed areas in which flammable concentrations of waste materials can develop should be equipped with arc-proof switches and vapor-proof luminaires. Incandescent and fluorescent vapor-proof luminaires are available.

Each row of luminaires in a main work area should have its own electrical circuit so that circuit failure cannot darken the entire room and so that it will be possible to light only parts of the room when this is desirable. Every auxiliary room should have one or more light circuits of its own. Eventual redesign will be easier if several unused circuit breakers are provided at the lighting control panel. The provision of one spare circuit breaker for every four in use should enable a school to maintain the effectiveness of its laboratory lighting for a considerable period of time without extensive reconstruction.

When a lighting system is planned, the *quality* and *quantity* of light it must provide are the two major considerations. Good light quality is characterized by absence of shadows, elimination of glare, proper brightness ratios, and excellent color rendition. An annoying and possibly dangerous situation exists where the shadow of a student or the shadow of the piece of equipment being used obscures the point of operation. Shadows result when light is emitted by bright, widely separated light sources. Therefore, it is desirable to place luminaires close together and to use lamps having large light-emitting surfaces that are low in brightness.

Generalizing the source of light rather than concentrating it can eliminate most shadows. A luminous ceiling diffuses light evenly and is virtually shadowfree. So is indirect lighting in which 90 to 100 per cent of the light is directed up and reflected to all parts of a room by the ceiling and upper wall and partition surfaces. A semi-indirect lighting system that directs 60 to 90 per cent of the light upward and 10 to 40 per cent down is somewhat less shadowfree. Other methods of directing light (direct-indirect, semi-direct, and direct) are much more likely to cause shadows, unless the light sources are large in surface area, close together, low in brightness, and equipped with efficient diffusion systems.[18]

Glare may be direct or reflected. Both kinds can be distracting, fatigue-inducing, and dangerous if they cause any reduction of vision. Direct glare can be eliminated by shielding a light source or by placing it out of the normal field of vision — for example, more than 45 degrees above the horizontal line of sight of a person standing erect. It can be minimized by controlling the brightness of the light source and by establishing a low brightness ratio between the light source and the area surrounding it.

The greatest amount of reflected glare is produced by a bright light source located above and in front of a student and directed on a polished surface, especially a dark one. Semi-direct and direct lighting can be serious offenders in this respect. Ideally light should fall on a working surface at approximately the same angle as a student's line of sight. But because an industrial education laboratory is used at any given time by many students who change positions frequently, it is rarely possible to place luminaires so that the light parallels lines of sight. The best means of avoiding reflected glare are those that effectively combat shadow formation — matte surfaces, larger and less bright light-emitting surfaces, luminaires placed close together, proper lamp shielding, and the use of

[18]Illuminating Engineering Society, *American Standard Guide for School Lighting* (New York: Illuminating Engineering Society, 1962), p. 18.

diffusing or refracting materials. Luminous ceilings, indirect lighting, and semi-indirect lighting can reduce reflected glare to a minimum.

Some lighting specialists believe that the height of suspended fluorescent luminaires designed for semi-indirect or direct-indirect lighting is important to proper illumination. Optimum luminaire height promotes adequate and uniform ceiling brightness, high reflectance, and good diffusion of light and thus materially aids in the reduction of glare and shadows.

Luminaires, of course, must be high enough to avoid dominating a room and creating the illusion of insufficient head room. As room size and the number of luminaires increase, such an illusion tends to become more pronounced. If the height of a ceiling is 14 feet and room width is 35 feet or more, as recommended, suspension of luminaires at 12 feet above floor level strikes a satisfactory balance between functional and aesthetic needs. When 15-foot ceilings are used, luminaires should be placed 12½ feet above floor level, and with 16-foot ceilings, luminaire suspension should be at 13 feet.[19]

Simple arrangements of luminaires are preferable. Continuous-row luminaires that are uniformly spaced and run parallel to walls and partitions can be excellent, both functionally and aesthetically. This arrangement also permits economical installation. Rows of luminaires that run laterally in a room make the room appear wider; longitudinal rows make it look longer. Diagonal rows of luminaires may be useful in minimizing shadows cast by instruments in drawing laboratories, but there is little evidence to support this conjecture. Tilting drawing surfaces so that they are vertical or near vertical is probably a more productive technique. Luminaires should be kept at least twelve inches away from walls and partitions to avoid the appearance of crowding. Placement more than thirty inches away, on the other hand, may make it difficult to provide the proper intensity of illumination around the edges of a room.

Brightness ratios, discussed earlier in this chapter, have much to do with the quality of light in a laboratory. The ratios between a working surface and the background and between a working surface and surrounding surfaces should be small so that drastic eye adjustments will not be necessary.

The most beneficial color schemes cause colors to appear natural. This effect can be achieved only by light sources that render colors well. Seven varieties of white fluorescent lamps are commonly available: standard cool white, deluxe cool white, standard warm white, deluxe warm white, white,

---

[19]Westinghouse Electric Corporation, *Lighting Application Aids*, a bulletin prepared by the Westinghouse Lamp Division (Bloomfield, N. J.: Westinghouse Electric Corporation), p. 4.

natural, and daylight. Each produces its own type of color rendition, and its use results in a distinct visual environment. Standard cool white and deluxe cool white lamps are best for use in industrial education laboratories. Both approach the color of daylight, are psychologically cool, and render colors accurately. Deluxe cool white fluorescent light is the better of the two with respect to color rendition. Cool white has a graying effect on reds and gives slight emphasis to blue, blue-green, yellow-green, and yellow.

Cool white lamps are superior to deluxe cool white lamps with respect to lighting efficiency. A cool white lamp emits approximately 25 per cent more light than a deluxe cool white lamp of the same wattage.[20] Consequently the type of lamp that will be used must be specified when a lighting system is planned so that the system can be designed to provide the required level of general illumination. If a system is designed for cool white fluorescent lamps and deluxe cool white lamps are substituted, the level of general illumination that the system provides may be inadequate.

To summarize, a lighting system for an industrial education laboratory should utilize fluorescent luminaires equipped with cool white or deluxe cool white lamps for general illumination. Incandescent luminaires should be used to provide local lighting where necessary. Good light quality is achieved through:

1. Light-emitting surfaces that are relatively large in area and low in brightness
2. Efficient shielding of light sources
3. Good light diffusion
4. Luminaires placed close to each other
5. Luminaires placed at correct heights and in effective patterns
6. Matte surfaces used wherever possible
7. Proper reflectances and brightness ratios

The levels of general illumination required in industrial education laboratories are necessarily higher than those provided in many other educational facilities. Values presented in Table 6.1 are achievable and practical in terms of cost and teacher-student needs. Initial light intensities should probably be somewhat higher than the ones listed in order to compensate for reduced levels of illumination due to soiling of walls, partitions, ceilings, equipment, and luminaires and to decreased lamp output that results from service. Regular maintenance can reduce the

[20]Westinghouse Electric Corporation, *Light Bulbs and Fluorescent Tubes*, a bulletin prepared by the Westinghouse Lamp Division (Bloomfield, N. J.: Westinghouse Electric Corporation), p. 8.

Table 6.1 RECOMMENDED MINIMUM LEVELS OF GENERAL ILLUMINATION

Type of Facility	Footcandles at the Working Surface[a]
Laboratories	
drawing	200
metals	150
woods	150
crafts	200
automotive technology	150
graphic arts	150
electricity/electronics	200
general laboratory	150
Auxiliary Areas	
design center	200
class area	150
teacher's office	150
demonstration area	150
laboratory library	150
student locker area	30
project storage room	50
materials storage room	30
equipment storage room	50
project assembly area	150
toilet and lavatory room	30
wash area	30
finishing room	150
darkroom	50
materials or equipment testing room	150

[a]Considered to be thirty inches above floor level.

need for higher initial intensities, but this is not always provided. Soiled luminaires and lamps that have been in service too long can decrease light intensities by as much as 50 per cent. Periodic cleaning and lamp replacement prior to burnout result in maintenance of recommended levels of illumination, better laboratory appearance, and greater learning.

Certain tasks — such as the precision welding of very small parts, intricate assembly procedures, and highly accurate machining operations — require as much as 5000 footcandles of illumination for proper performance. Local lighting will provide the needed intensities at reasonable cost. It should be considered an integral part of a total lighting system and included in every laboratory.

Although light variation is probably less important in industrial education laboratories than in stores, places of public entertainment, and homes, general illumination that is uniform enough to be monotonous should be avoided. The local lighting of chalkboards, bulletin boards, display facilities, pieces of equipment, and certain parts of rooms can add welcome accents of brightness.

FOR FURTHER READING

E. I. du Pont de Nemours and Company, Inc. *Du Pont Color Conditioning*. Wilmington, Del.: E. I. du Pont de Nemours and Co.

E. I. du Pont de Nemours and Company, Inc. *Du Pont Color Conditioning Report Series*. Wilmington, Del.: E. I. du Pont de Nemours and Co. Titles in the series are: *Brightness Engineering; Color Preferences; Emotional Reaction to Color; "Warmth" and "Coolness" in Color; Featuring Color Through Complementation; Color and Climate; Color and Visibility; Size, Dimension and Weight in Color; Attention Through Brightness;* and *Color and Illumination*.

E. I. du Pont de Nemours and Company, Inc. *Du Pont Safety Color Code*. Wilmington, Del.: E. I. du Pont de Nemours and Co.

Illuminating Engineering Society. *IES Lighting Handbook*. 5th ed. New York: Illuminating Engineering Society.

Large Lamp Department, General Electric. *Footcandles in Modern Lighting*. TP-128. Cleveland, Ohio: General Electric.

Large Lamp Department, General Electric. *Industrial Lighting*. TP-108. Cleveland, Ohio: General Electric.

Large Lamp Department, General Electric. *School Lighting*. TP-102. Cleveland, Ohio: General Electric.

Lighting Division, Westinghouse Electric Corporation. *Lighting Application Aids*. Cleveland, Ohio: Westinghouse Electric Corp.

McGuinness, William J., and Stein, Benjamin. *Building Technology: Mechanical and Electrical Systems*. New York: John Wiley & Sons, 1977.

PPG Industries, Inc. *Color Dynamics*. Pittsburgh: PPG Industries.

PPG Industries, Inc. *Color Dynamics for Grade Schools, High Schools and Colleges*. Pittsburgh: PPG Industries.

Ramsey, Charles G., and Sleeper, Harold R. *Architectural Graphic Standards*. 6th ed. Rev. New York: John Wiley & Sons, 1970.

Stein, Richard G. "Saving Energy in Vocational Schools." *School Shop*, April 1976, p. 51.

Westinghouse Lamp Division, Westinghouse Electric Corporation. *Footcandle Levels and Interior Lighting Design*. Bloomfield, N. J.: Westinghouse Electric Corp.

Westinghouse Lamp Division, Westinghouse Electric Corporation. *Light Bulbs and Fluorescent Tubes*. Bloomfield, N. J.: Westinghouse Electric Corp.

7

The Auditory Environment

INTRODUCTION

The impact of teaching diminishes if students are unable to hear well. Effective hearing relates directly to students' physical condition and to the quality of the auditory environment in which they work. Schools recognize the importance of good physical condition and for many years have sought to identify students having hearing difficulties. Special seating arrangements, special classes, individualized instruction, and professional treatment have been employed to help solve hearing problems.

Less attention has been paid to environmental conditions that can rob even individuals with normal hearing of their ability to distinguish sounds accurately. Lack of knowledge about the effects of sound and methods of sound control undoubtedly has slowed progress in this important area, but school districts' unwillingness to spend enough money to create good auditory environments and their at least tacit willingness for students to endure levels of sound that are far too high have been even more detrimental. Clearly the services of acoustical engineering firms are essential during the design and construction of new schools and the renovation of older ones so that the full potential of educational facilities can be realized.

THE NATURE OF SOUND

Sound is a wave motion of energy in the atmosphere. It is generated by a vibrating body that causes successive increases and decreases in air pressure. Sound waves travel through air at the rate of 1130 feet per second. The frequency of a sound is the number of complete vibrations (cycles) per second of the vibrating body. Frequency is expressed in Hertz (Hz); 1 Hertz is equal to one cycle per second. The brain interprets frequency as pitch — the higher the frequency, the higher the pitch. Normal hearing functions within a frequency range that is approximately 20 Hz to 22,000 Hz. A given sound may be a compound of many frequencies and intensities.

Sound may be entirely airborne, or it may be partially structure-borne, as is the case when the vibrations of a machine are transmitted by the floor to another part of the building where they become recognizable as sound. Structure-borne sound is called "impact sound." In either case, airborne sound waves ultimately stimulate portions of the ear, and the resulting impulses are conveyed to the brain for interpretation.

A great many sounds are pleasing and important, if not essential, to our general well-being. Other sounds, while not necessarily pleasing, make it possible to perform useful tasks. For example, an automotive technician can learn much about an engine by listening to it and interpreting the sounds that it makes. Sonar equipment uses sound echoes to calculate distances and directions from a base point to underwater objects.

Much of the sound created by human beings and by nature is unwanted and is, by definition, noise. As societies have developed, noises have invariably increased in variety, intensity, and duration. New products have brought noise problems as well as increases in living standards. A naturally ventilated home is usually warmer and more humid than one cooled by refrigeration, but it may well be less noisy.

General noise levels have also risen a great deal. The result is that people now live in a world that is noisier than it has ever been, and they are finding it necessary to preserve emotional and physical health by eliminating and controlling the noise they have been instrumental in creating.

The relative loudness (intensity) of sounds is measured in decibels (db.). A decibel is a unit that is approximately equal to the smallest difference in intensity detectable by a normal human ear. Average speech has an intensity of about 60 decibels. The range of intensity within which human hearing can function extends from the threshold of audibility (0–20 db.) to approximately 130 decibels.

Sound can cause physical damage to human beings. Prolonged exposure to a sound intensity greater than 85 decibels — a condition easily reached in an industrial education laboratory — may temporarily or permanently impair hearing. Short periods of exposure to sound intensities that exceed 105 decibels involve serious risk that impairment will occur. Damage can be almost immediate in cases of exposure to sound intensities greater than 130 decibels.[1]

The common responses to noise are emotional ones. They include irritation, inability to concentrate, tension, depression, and loss of interest. One result of physical damage to hearing is that a student may not be able to learn easily or rapidly. Emotional responses to excessive noise make it likely that the teaching-learning process will not be efficient.

CONTROL OF NOISE GENERATION

Architectural acoustics is an immensely complex field of knowledge. Even so, much has been learned about the nature, generation, effects, and control of sound. A good base of theory exists, and valid acoustical designs can be created in most cases. But a skillful design performance can be nullified by a window that fits loosely or a machine that has not been properly maintained. Therefore the need remains to attack problems of noise control on an operational as well as theoretical level and to proceed quite often in an eclectic and experimental manner.

In broad form, the two available approaches to effective noise control are: to prevent, by any practical means, the generation of noise and to minimize, by absorption, insulation, isolation, and masking, the harmful effects of noise that cannot be prevented. Noise is a concomitant of many laboratory activities. However, noise levels can be much lower than we have thus far accepted.

Proper location is an important means of noise prevention. Industrial education laboratories should be built away from playgrounds, busy streets, railroad rights-of-way, and the approach or take-off paths of airports. If any one of these locations is unavoidable, elaborate and expensive noise control measures may be necessary. At least one school

---

[1]Armand Lerner, "Stop That Noise!!!" *Reproduction Methods for Business and Industry,* March 1962, p. 44.

district has built an entire school underground to escape the noise of a jet airport.

A laboratory must also be isolated from noise produced in other parts of the school. It is unwise to locate laboratories near band, orchestra, and choral practice rooms; gymnasiums; other noisier laboratories; and certain physical plant facilities, such as furnace rooms and repair shops. Noise that can be kept out of a laboratory is noise that does not have to be controlled within the laboratory.

Fortunately, procedures that minimize noise problems are often helpful for other reasons. For example, single-story building design is preferable for several reasons in addition to its effectiveness in preventing transmission of noise from a laboratory to others above and below it. If this type of design is not possible in a given situation, the next best solution is to locate the noisiest laboratories at ground level and employ every available means of preventing vertical noise transmission.

Industrial education laboratories should be as large as possible, and ceilings should be fourteen feet or more above floor level in order to minimize concentrations of noise. In general, the larger the room, the less noticeable the noise produced in it, but ceiling height is a key factor. Even a spacious laboratory is likely to be noisy if it has a low ceiling.

A curved ceiling is not a good design, because the concavity tends to reflect noise to one or more parts of a room and concentrate it there. A correct curvature and/or the application of sound-absorbing materials to a curved ceiling can counteract reflection, but at best, it is an involved problem. Usually it is far better to avoid it, since the aesthetic and structural advantages of a curved ceiling in an industrial education laboratory are slight, if they exist at all.

Rooms should be as nearly square as is consistent with architectural validity and good equipment organization. Long, narrow rooms lead to reverberation — an uncomfortable situation in which incident noise is followed by a series of multiple echoes of decreasing intensity as the sound reflects back and forth between side walls that are too close together.[2]

Only full-height partitions should be used. Partial-height partitions allow noise to pass over them from one room to another. Extending a partition from floor level to the underside of a suspended ceiling or dropping a suspended ceiling below the top of a partial-height partition can be equally ineffective because it is rarely possible to achieve airtightness where the partition joins the ceiling. Cracks furnish excellent passage-

---

[2]Paul E. Sabine, *Theory and Use of Acoustical Materials*, 2nd ed. (New York: Acoustical Materials Association, 1950), p. 9.

ways for noise, and the space above a suspended ceiling can serve as a plenum for transmitting noise from one room to another.

Gloss finishing and surfacing materials — for example, gloss wall paint and gloss-glazed brick — reflect sound in much the same way that a mirror reflects light. Their use in industrial education laboratories leads to echo and reverberation.

In laboratories that must be relatively quiet, even a noise of low intensity, such as the hum produced by some fluorescent luminaires, can be distracting to students. Proper lighting system maintenance will eliminate hum, and the use of mercury light switches excludes another source of noise. Background music can be used to mask low-intensity noise that cannot be economically prevented if the intensity of the music is slightly greater than that of the noise.

Exhaust systems can be prolific noise producers unless they are carefully designed, manufactured, and installed. Even so, noise created by a good exhaust system, while it might not be especially noticeable, is steady and is a potential source of fatigue and tension. But exhaust systems are necessary in several types of laboratories, so the noise cannot be eliminated. The best procedure is to transfer as much of it as possible to the atmosphere by installing collectors and storage hoppers outdoors. They should not be placed in front of windows or rigidly connected to buildings. Noise- and vibration-absorbing pads that insulate exhaust system mounts from buildings can be helpful. Additional noise reduction can be achieved through the use of:

1. Slow-speed electric motors
2. Large, slow-turning fans that move air at the lowest effective velocity
3. Large ducts having smooth inside surfaces and gradual bends
4. Flexible connectors placed between ducts and dust collectors
5. Firm but nonrigid duct mounts used on overhead duct systems
6. Carefully designed hoods and grilles that promote smooth, whistle-free air flow
7. Collector motors wired through the starter switches of machines serviced (ensures that exhaust systems will operate only when machines are running)

The use of sound-absorbing surfacing materials on ceilings and upper walls and partitions (above the forty-two-inch level) can result in materially reduced noise reflection and transmission. Sound-absorbing batts suspended from a ceiling by nonrigid connectors can be used to quiet portions of laboratories in which concentrations of noise exist. The effectiveness of an absorbent material depends largely on its porosity. Air inside the pores is set in motion by sound waves. The movement results in friction between the air and the walls of the pores, thereby generating heat and changing a portion of the energy of each sound wave to heat energy that is dissipated in the atmosphere.

Equipment selection offers many opportunities to prevent noise in industrial education laboratories. In general, the better the quality of the equipment, the less noise it produces. A piece of equipment that is heavy, rigid, manufactured to close tolerances, strongly constructed, tightly assembled, balanced and counterbalanced, acoustically treated by its manufacturer, and provided with an effective system of lubrication will be as inherently quiet in operation as a unit of its type can be. Even in pieces of hand-operated equipment, noise reduction is important and can be accomplished. As an example, one manufacturer of woodworkers' vises installs thick rubber washers near the ends of the metal handle of each vise to minimize the noise created when the handle falls from one position to another — a minor point, perhaps, but one that is indicative of the manufacturer's awareness of noise problems.

Machines equipped with cast iron stands, bases, and housings tend to produce less noise than those constructed of sheet metal. If cost or some other factor makes it necessary to purchase a machine built of sheet metal, it will operate more quietly if the insides of all sheet metal enclosures are coated with a sound-absorbing material that is troweled, sprayed, or cemented in place. The coatings applied to interior sheet metal surfaces of automobile doors and the blankets of insulation attached to the undersides of automobile hoods are examples of this method of noise control.

It is well to purchase machines that are no larger than they must be to function effectively in industrial education programs. Usually, large machines make more noise than smaller ones of the same quality, although many exceptions exist. However, essential machine capacity should never be sacrificed for a small decrease in noise level.

If its performance is good, a machine that operates at moderate speeds is preferable to one that must run at high rates of speed. Machine speed and noise generation are positively related.

In general, electric motors should be mounted with flexible mounts. One common nonrigid mount that governs drive belt tension by using the belt to support the weight of the motor should be avoided, however, because of the excessive noise produced. A motorhead drive is exceptionally quiet. Its spindle is an extension of the motor shaft; consequently, noises produced by the movement of belts, pulleys, gears, and chains are absent.

If a motorhead drive is too costly or undesirable for some other reason, a slow-speed motor should be employed and the speed varied through the use of a V-belt and step-cone or split pulley drive that is as short as possible. Optimum belt tension, exact pulley alignment, and good belt and pulley condition are essential to minimize noise.

Machines that "freewheel" (coast to a stop over a relatively long period of time after being switched off) should not be purchased if the additional noise they produce will be detrimental. For the most part, they employ motorhead drives and are fundamentally more quiet than other types, but they may generate higher total amounts of noise by virtue of the fact that they do not stop quickly. Brakes are always desirable features on such machines.

If it is impossible to purchase a new piece of equipment that is relatively quiet or if reconditioning cannot reduce the noise generated by a used machine to an acceptable level, isolation is a final resort. The noise of an air compressor, for example, is often incompatible with class operation. Enclosures of various kinds can be used to isolate an air compressor from other parts of a laboratory. Heat buildup is nearly always a problem, but it can be solved by a power vent system that discharges some of the heat to the atmosphere. Installation outdoors in a vented, weatherproof enclosure is a possible solution, as is placement in an area of the school where the noise will not be heard.

How equipment is installed can affect noise generation and transmission in the laboratory. The following precautions will minimize the amount of noise caused by equipment operation: fastening benches to floors to prevent sliding and minimize impact sound; placing vibration-absorbing pads under machinery, benches, and surfaces used for hammering; installing rubber tips on the legs of stools and chairs; spacing machinery as widely as possible to avoid concentrations of noise; and keeping pieces of equipment from touching walls, partitions, and columns.

Air-Loc,[3] a material fabricated of cork, sisal fiber, and vinyl resin, is useful for insulating equipment from floors. Wedgemounts[4] are partly constructed of Air-Loc and are used to insulate and level equipment and to bolt it to the floor (Fig. 7.1). According to its manufacturer, Air-Loc is 85 per cent effective in eliminating transmission of vibration, shock, and noise and is impervious to oil, water, acid, and alkali.

Regular, painstaking maintenance of equipment offers an excellent way to reduce noise levels. A piece of equipment that is not in its best

---

[3]Produced by the Air-Loc Division of Clark-Cutler-McDermott Company, Franklin, Massachusetts.
[4]Ibid.

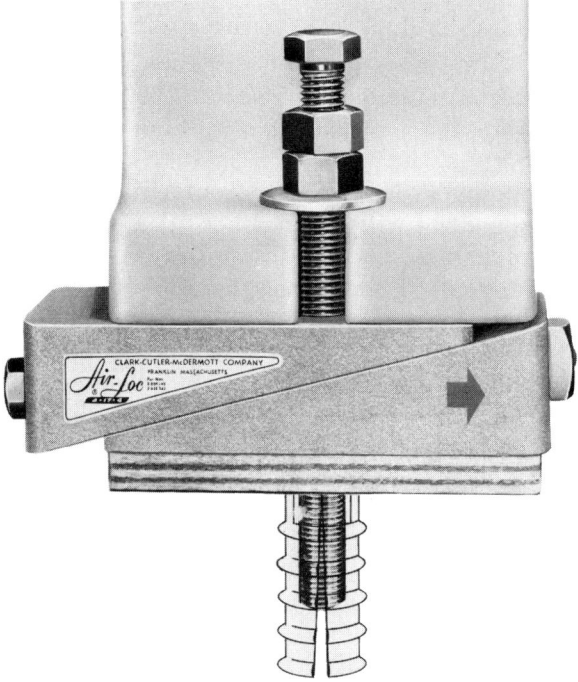

Figure 7.1 *Wedgmounts permit leveling and assist in vibration control.* (Air-Loc Products)

working condition can generate much more noise than necessary. The following precautions will effectively prevent noise that can result from poor equipment condition:

1. Proper maintenance of cutting edges (a dull jointer knife makes more noise than a sharp one because there is excessive contact and friction between the knife and the stock; in addition, the stock cannot be fed as fast and the noise lasts longer)
2. Periodic lubrication, which eliminates sheet metal squeaks, gear growls, bearing howls, thread squeals, and other operating noises
3. Careful mechanical adjustment to prevent noises made by moving parts that are too loose, too tight, or out of alignment
4. Prompt replacement of worn and damaged parts
5. Installation of mufflers on all internal combustion engines operated indoors or in outdoor compounds.

CONTROL OF NOISE GENERATION

Students should always follow the best work procedures. Not surprisingly, good procedures are usually less noisy than inefficient or careless ones. Noise that results from the normal use of laboratory equipment can be sharply decreased by:

1. Operating machines at the slowest safe speeds that permit accurate work
2. Avoiding excessively heavy cuts and too-rapid feeds (equipment should not be forced to operate beyond its designed capacity)
3. Switching machines off when they are not being used
4. Regulating machines properly (a table-saw blade that is too high creates more noise than one at the proper height)
5. Using the best tool for each job (a table-saw crosscut blade does not cut along the grain of wood as quietly as a rip blade)
6. Working skillfully so as to reduce the contact between tools and between tools and work (three times as much noise is produced when six hammer blows are struck where two accurate ones should suffice)
7. Using pieces of equipment that produce large amounts of noise as sparingly as possible (a planer should not be used to reduce a board from one inch to three-eighths inch in thickness; resawing the board before planing it is a less noisy procedure)
8. Running dust collection systems only when machines are being used (at times, a dust collection system must run continuously, but needless continuous operation is poor practice; intermittent use can be ensured, as suggested before, by wiring a dust collection system motor through the starter switch of each machine served by the system)
9. Using the lowest possible volume when testing electronic and audio devices
10. Seeing that students avoid: slamming doors, drawers, and covers; dropping lumber, sheet metal, and other items on the floor; and dragging materials and equipment across the floors

Effective class discipline also helps to establish a good auditory environment. Unnecessary conversation and singing, whistling, and shouting contribute to the general noise level of a laboratory. In the vast majority of class situations, these problems do not exist. However, they should be discouraged wherever they exist.

If everything that can be done to prevent and control noise *has* been done and the intensities of specific noises are still bothersome or dangerous, ear plugs or ear muffs can provide relief. They are often necessary in woods and metals laboratories.

NOISE TRANSMISSION

Proper location is also a productive way to minimize the transmission of noise from an industrial education laboratory to other areas of a school. A separate building virtually eliminates noise transmission problems but is much less desirable, from several standpoints, than an attached wing. Moreover, a buffer zone of quiet areas — such as drawing laboratories and classrooms — can, and should, be placed between noisy laboratories and the point where a wing is attached to the central portion of a school building. Creating a buffer zone serves the same purpose as constructing a separate building but does not isolate the industrial education program. Laboratories in which relatively great amounts of noise are produced should be located as far away as possible from a buffer zone.

Storage rooms, offices, libraries, and other auxiliary rooms should be used to create buffer zones between laboratories. The noisiest machines and activities should be placed farthest from such zones. If this is done on both sides of a partition that separates two laboratories and if the doors to buffer zone rooms are kept closed during class periods, sound transmission in both directions should be negligible. In fact, this should be a standard design practice wherever it can be employed without violating other important planning principles. (Fig. 11.4, a woods laboratory for senior high school, shows the creation of a buffer zone between laboratories.)

Corridors are efficient passageways for airborne noise, but noise transmission can be greatly reduced by using door-vestibule-door entries to a wing and to each laboratory in the wing. For maximum effectiveness, doors should be airtight along the four edges. If a door must be glazed, two panels of quarter-inch plate glass separated by one-half inch of dead air space will provide transparence as well as good noise control. A glass panel unit should be set in plastic or rubber gaskets on all four sides so that there is no rigid connection between the panel and the door. Thick, solid-core flush doors and steel-clad insulating doors are much more effective than hollow-core doors or standard panel doors in preventing noise transmission. Sliding (pocket) doors are inappropriate because they control noise poorly.

Doors along a corridor should be staggered in order to prevent noise from flowing directly from one laboratory into another. It is essential to keep the doors closed whenever classes are in session. An open door can nullify all efforts to reduce the transmission of noise.

Walls and partitions must be relatively thick because thickness, rather than density, is a major factor in preventing noise transmission. If a masonry wall, such as a cavity wall, is utilized in the construction of a laboratory, it should be a minimum of ten inches in thickness. Masonry partitions should be at least eight inches thick. Brick, concrete block, and lightweight block walls must be carefully pointed to prevent airborne noise from passing through cracks in mortar joints. Cracks that develop once construction is complete should be promptly repaired.

Lightweight block and concrete block walls and partitions must be sealed on one side and preferably on both sides to effectively prevent noise transmission. If they are not airtight, sound waves can pass through the pores from one side to the other. The porosity that absorbs sound on one side can leak it on the other side. A concrete block partition constructed as two four-inch partitions separated by a two-inch dead air space and sealed on both outside surfaces can be superior in sound-absorbing qualities to a solid block partition of the same weight.

Two types of partitions that are effective in reducing noise transmission are the double 2 × 4–inch wood stud partition and the 3⅝-inch steel stud partition. A double wood stud partition consists of two partitions installed side by side with a 1-inch dead air space between them (see Fig. 7.2). The studs are placed 16 inches on center (O.C.). Separate single soles and double plates provide the necessary rigidity. Both sections are packed with 3½-inch fiberglass batt insulation and surfaced on the outside with ½-inch gypsum board. Fiberglass caulk seals each sole to the subfloor and

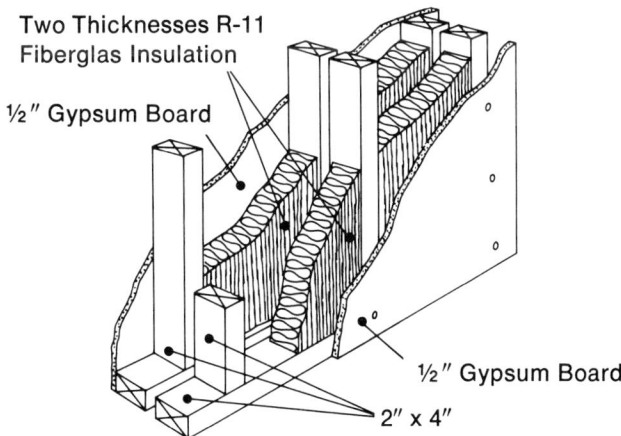

Figure 7.2 *Double wood stud sound control partitions.* (Owens-Corning Fiberglas)

156 THE AUDITORY ENVIRONMENT

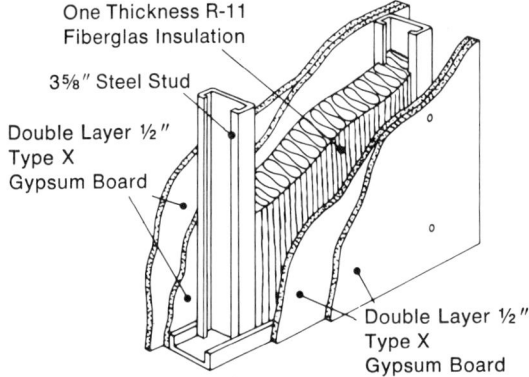

Figure 7.3 *Steel stud sound control partitions.* (Owens-Corning Fiberglas)

each plate to the ceiling joists. The double studs and fiberglass caulk break up the path of noise, while the gypsum board and fiberglass insulation both absorb noise.

A steel stud partition has steel floor and ceiling tracks, and the studs are usually set 24 inches O.C. A double layer of ½-inch gypsum board applied to each side of the partition helps control noise transmission. Spaces between studs are filled with 3½-inch fiberglass batt insulation. Fiberglass caulk seals the joints between the tracks and the subfloor and ceiling joists.

Windows (especially ones that can be opened) can transmit large amounts of noise from one laboratory to another and from an industrial education wing to other parts of the school. Walls that face sources of high-intensity noise should be windowless or equipped with relatively small windows. Fixed, high-level windows can ensure satisfactory transmission loss (TL — decrease in the intensity of sound due to passage through a structure) if they are airtight. Glass block, double glazing (with a removable storm panel), insulating glass, and ¼-inch plate glass all provide much greater TL than standard window glass.

Suspended floors that absorb sound well are essential in multistory facilities. A 10-inch reinforced concrete slab faced with $^{33}/_{32}$-inch maple block flooring is excellent in this respect, especially if a suspended ceiling having porous, sound-absorbing panels and nonrigid supports is installed below it. Nine inches of fiberglass batt insulation placed above the ceiling will further reduce the transmission of impact sound.

Ducts, pipes, and electrical conduit can increase noise transmission between rooms. In order to reduce the passage of airborne noise, a sealer or resilient packing should be used to seal openings where these sections pass through walls, partitions, ceilings, and floors.

Baffles similar to those in automobile mufflers can be used to reduce the noise transmitted by ducts if the ducts do not carry solid wastes. Sound-absorbing materials also can be sprayed on or cemented to the inside and/or outside surfaces of some ducts. Any material used for this purpose should be moistureproof, fireproof, and extremely low in thermal and electrical conductivity. Rigid, sound-absorbing materials such as fiberglass panels can be used to replace short sections of ducts or even to construct entire ducts. Cloth, neoprene, rubber, and asbestos connectors are available for joining duct sections as a means of reducing noise transmission.

Ordinarily ducts should not be rigidly mounted on structural parts of a building. Pieces of laboratory equipment and certain parts of air-handling systems produce vibrations that must be absorbed by pads and flexible mounts.

Mechanical equipment for ventilating, heating, air-conditioning, plumbing, and electrical systems should be the best obtainable, and it should be suitably isolated and correctly installed. It is difficult to overemphasize the importance to a good auditory environment of even small items, such as adequately large water pipes and quiet ballasts for fluorescent lamps.

Unit-heating, ventilating, and air-conditioning systems are often advantageous in an industrial education complex. The attendant duct systems, because they are not connected to a central system, will not transmit noise beyond the complex.

Finally, class activities carried on outdoors should be carefully supervised so that noises do not disturb nearby classes.

Most of the procedures discussed are likely to prove impracticable in certain circumstances and eminently usable in others. The decision as to whether a specific procedure will be helpful must be based on answers to the following questions:

1. What are the potential benefits?
2. Will it make possible more effective teaching and learning?
3. Will it be worth the cost?

FOR FURTHER READING

Acoustical Materials Association. *The Use of Architectural Acoustical Materials: Theory and Practice.* New York: Acoustical Materials Association.

American Council on Industrial Arts Teacher Education. *Planning Industrial Arts Facilities*. 8th yearbook. Bloomington, Ill.: McKnight Publishing Co., 1959.

Dusenbury, George. "The Noiseproof House and Apartment." *American Builder*, May 1965, p. 69.

Gilliland, John W. "Sound: Its Effect on Teaching and Learning." *Modern School Shop Planning*. 4th ed. Ann Arbor, Mich.: Prakken Publications, 1965.

Johns-Manville. *Sound Control Ceilings*. Denver, Colo.: Johns-Manville, 1973.

Lerner, Armand. "Stop That Noise!!!" *Reproduction Methods for Business and Industry*, March 1962, p. 44.

Owens-Corning Fiberglas Corporation. *Noise Control in Residential Construction*. Toledo, Ohio: Owens-Corning Fiberglas Corp., 1973.

Owens-Corning Fiberglas Corporation. *Solutions to Noise Control Problems*. Toledo, Ohio: Owens-Corning Fiberglas Corp.

Ramsey, Charles G., and Sleeper, Harold R. *Architectural Graphic Standards*. 6th ed. rev. New York: John Wiley & Sons, 1970.

Sumption, Merle R., and Landes, Jack L. *Planning Functional School Buildings*. New York: Harper and Brothers Publishers, 1957.

8

The Air Environment

INTRODUCTION

During an academic year, secondary school students are in class approximately 1100 hours. In addition, they spend considerable time in other school facilities pursuing out-of-class interests. Throughout their high school careers, students spend nearly one-fifth of *all* active hours in an air environment provided by the school district. Students who attend other types of schools, such as area vocational schools and community colleges, also occupy classrooms, laboratories, and supplementary facilities many hours per year.

It seems reasonable to assume that the amount of time students devote to school activities will increase in the future. If it is also reasonable to believe that a school district's major concern is the quality of education provided by the schools it controls, it follows that the district should be vitally interested in the air environment that exists in each school. The relationship between air environment and learning is no longer in doubt.

Both students and teachers find it more enjoyable to work in a good air environment. They tend to be happier, more interested in their work, and more productive. Student attendance is better, and there are fewer discipline problems. Teachers devote more time to the preparation of teaching materials and the organization of their courses. It appears indisputable that construction money saved by accepting a poor-quality air environment is saved at the expense of decreased educational opportunities for many students.

A good air environment is important also to the physical condition of laboratory equipment and materials. Rust and corrosion are time-consuming to remove, and they can result in the need for early replacement of equipment. The detrimental effects of very high or very low humidity and poor air circulation on lumber are well known. Light-sensitive papers, films, and numerous other materials that are stocked in quantity in industrial education laboratories can be equally sensitive to extreme air conditions. Some processes, such as wood finishing, work with fiberglass, and photographic film processing, are difficult to control unless the air environment can be regulated with at least moderate precision.

The goal of an air control system is to provide an air environment that is odorless, has no harmful impurities, is at the proper temperature, and contains sufficient moisture. To achieve this goal, classroom air must be blended with outdoor air, filtered, heated or cooled, humidified or dehumidified, and kept gently in motion. Nature does all of these things well — except where production of waste materials or other conditions prevent it — but not consistently. Therefore it is necessary to employ mechanical systems to maintain a satisfactory air environment. The tools are at hand: mechanical ventilation and exhaust systems, heating and air conditioning equipment, and humidifying and dehumidifying devices. They are effective, as well as relatively inexpensive to install and operate. All that remains is to put them to use wherever possible.

Ventilation, heating, air conditioning, and exhaust systems are closely related. Each system can and does perform several of the functions that contribute to effective air control. For convenience, they will be discussed separately.

MECHANICAL VENTILATION

Industrial education laboratories require dependable ventilation. Production of heat, odors, and harmful gaseous waste materials can be high in metals, crafts, automotive, and general laboratories and moderately high in woods and graphics laboratories. Drawing rooms and electricity/electronics laboratories require the same amount of ventilation as standard classrooms.

MECHANICAL VENTILATION

Ventilation requires movement of air. Air movement can be caused by the action of natural forces or it can be mechanically produced. Nature moves air without consuming energy but in a manner that is neither dependable nor uniform. Windows, doors, and other openings in buildings let in air that is variable in quantity and quality. Odors, dust, heat, humidity, and noise enter in uncontrollable amounts.

A good mechanical ventilation system includes a motor, drive mechanism, fan, duct system, and filtering equipment. If rooms are tight enough to permit efficient heating and air conditioning, operation of a mechanical ventilation system will build up a slightly positive air pressure, which retards the seepage of outside dust through cracks around windows and doors.

One significant advantage of mechanical ventilation is that it permits the installation of much smaller window sections. It is debatable whether or not smaller windows represent an aesthetic loss. What is not debatable is the fact that they reduce construction costs and the costs of operating heating and air conditioning systems. They also result in classrooms that are more functional and allow better control of natural light.

Central, zone, and classroom mechanical ventilation systems are in use. Central and zone systems are less noisy, and they do not include classroom ventilating units that consume floor space. They also permit using a central air-cleaning system (such as charcoal filtering, water washing, or electronic cleaning) that is easier to maintain than filters in classroom units and provides better performance.

During spring and fall seasons when the weather is moderate, a mechanical ventilation system alone can provide a satisfactory classroom air environment. When climatic conditions are more severe, however, the air in a building must be modified by the introduction of fresh air, heating or cooling, and humidification or dehumidification.

A human being requires approximately thirty-six pounds of air during every twenty-four-hour period. In comparison, one person will consume less than four pounds of food and slightly more than four pounds of water during the same period.[1] All three must be pure within fairly narrow limits in order to maintain good health.

Air movement of four cubic feet per minute per student is sufficient to introduce enough outside air to maintain a good oxygen supply in a classroom and to dissipate the carbon dioxide that is produced. Odor removal requires an airflow of from twenty to forty cubic feet per minute

---

[1] York Corporation, *Applied Air Conditioning* (York, Pa.: Borg-Warner Corporation, 1961), p. 3.

per student, depending on the odor and on the size of the room. A large room allows a smaller airflow because it contains more air. A laboratory encompassing 3000 square feet of floor space and having 14-foot ceilings will receive slightly less than one and one-half complete changes of air per sixty-minute class period, if an air movement of forty cubic feet per minute per student and a class size of twenty-four are assumed. This quantity is usually sufficient to restore oxygen, adequately dilute the carbon dioxide content, remove odors, permit effective air conditioning, and maintain a draft-free air environment. However, the specific amount of air needed must be determined for each given situation.

Proper air movement is essential if the true benefits of controlling temperature and relative humidity are to be realized and if stratification of air between floors and breathing zones is to be prevented. Mechanical ventilation offers the best means of achieving good air movement, and no industrial education laboratory should be without it.

HEATING

Heat is thermal energy. It can be changed to other forms of energy, but it cannot be destroyed. It is at once a faithful servant and a force that can be exceedingly difficult to utilize efficiently. Cold is not a measurable quality; it is simply the absence of heat.

Thermal energy is quantitatively measured in British thermal units (Btu.). One Btu. is defined as the quantity of heat needed to raise the temperature of one pound of water, at its maximum density, one degree Fahrenheit. The heat obtained by burning one large wood match is equal to approximately one Btu.

An interesting characteristic of thermal energy is that it always attempts to move from an area of higher temperature to areas of lower temperature. This transfer of energy is termed "heat loss" or, conversely, "heat gain." *Rate* of heat loss or heat gain is expressed in British thermal units transferred per hour (Btuh.).

The ways in which heat transfer takes place in the atmosphere are termed "conduction" (a material conducts heat from one place to another), "radiation" (heat passes directly through air from a warmer object to a colder one), and "convection" (a current of warm air rises, raises the temperature of cooler air by direct contact, and forces cooler air to settle to lower levels).

An industrial education laboratory constantly gains heat from several sources. Heat received from the sun is substantial even during winter months. Heat is also generated by students and the teacher. When the human body is engaged in more or less sedentary activity, it radiates heat at the rate of 400 to 450 Btuh. Heavy exertion can raise the rate to nearly 5000 Btuh. Physical activity in laboratory classes is quite varied, of course, but it is reasonable to assume a heat gain of between 12,000 and 25,000 Btuh. whenever a class of normal size is in session. Important amounts of heat are given off by luminaires (especially incandescent luminaires), pieces of laboratory equipment, and certain technical processes. In laboratories where welding, metal casting, ceramic firing, or testing internal combustion engines is carried on, the heat gain can be enormous.

The temperature within a laboratory represents a balance between heat lost to the atmosphere through the roof, walls, doors, windows, and ventilating and exhaust systems and heat gained from incident sources. The difference between this temperature and an acceptable one must be made up by a ventilating, heating, or air conditioning system. When the outdoor temperature is greater than 60°F., as it is much of the year even in colder geographic areas, heat gains from sources other than a school's heating plant make cooling, rather than heating, a necessity. Unfortunately, this fact does not seem to be generally recognized, and many American schools are overheated much of the time.

Human beings feel most comfortable when the temperature in a room is between 68°F. and 75°F. and the relative humidity — that is, the ratio of the quantity of water vapor present in air to the quantity it *could* contain at the given temperature — is between 40 and 60 per cent. Uniformity of temperature is a critical factor. Two degrees Fahrenheit should be considered the maximum permissible variation between floor level and the six-foot level. The difference in temperature at the floor and ceiling levels should not exceed 4°F. Because of the nature of laboratory work, it is recommended that temperatures in all laboratories except drawing and electricity/electronics be set at the low end of the comfort range.

A heating plant must be able to maintain room temperatures of at least 68°F. in the coldest weather that can be expected. Much of the time the task is not very demanding, but it is complicated by exhaust systems that can make it necessary to replace heat diverted to the atmosphere. If a laboratory is tight enough to afford good control of noise transmission and to minimize heat loss, not enough makeup air can be drawn in through cracks around windows and doors to replace exhausted air. The effort, however, may cause dirt to seep in and doors to resist opening. For example, the exhaust system in a finishing room may create an air pressure drop (partial vacuum) that is sufficient to draw contaminated air from an adjacent room. In any event, good temperature and humidity control can be difficult to maintain unless a makeup air system provides clean air at the desired temperature with the proper relative humidity.

At times during cold winter months, moisture should be added to a school's air environment. Although there is no consensus concerning the effects of low humidity on the human body, it does sometimes cause the skin and nasal passages to dry out. Greater comfort and other minor but useful benefits, such as a reduction in static electricity, make humidification worthwhile. On the other hand, there is little question about the value of dehumidification during spring, summer, and fall months when outdoor temperatures rise above 75°F. It is essential in maintaining a comfortable and efficient learning environment.

The two basic types of heating systems are central heating and unit heating. A central heating system consists of a main heating plant, a distribution system that conducts heat from the plant to all rooms in a building (or to all rooms in all buildings in a group), and heat radiating and/or diffusion devices in each room. With a unit heating system, one or more direct-fired heaters located in each room provide heat for that room alone. In practice, unit heating is often combined with central heating in order to provide masses of heat in small areas where it is needed and to obtain certain heating economies.

Unit heaters may be recessed in walls or ceilings or suspended from ceilings. They make it possible to heat parts of school buildings during evenings, weekends, and holiday periods. Usually, unit heaters are effective and reasonably economical to install, although they do not provide such uniform heating as most central heating systems and they can be noisy. Piping, wiring, and maintenance requirements of unit heaters are not great, however, and thermostatic control can be moderately precise.

A central heating system may employ forced air, hot water, or steam to transport heat to the areas it serves. Once heat has arrived at a room from a central heating plant, it is diffused by steam or hot water radiators, radiant coils, duct grilles that direct a flow of warm air to all parts of the room, or electric radiating units. Temperatures should be governed by thermostats installed in all rooms served by the plant. Heat-radiating surfaces must be relatively large so that surface temperatures will not cause burns and so that they will distribute heat evenly. One effective diffusion technique (called "perimeter heating") is to install radiating devices (or heat diffusers) under all windows in order to blanket the windows with warm air. This arrangement results in better heat distribution and eliminates low surface temperatures and window drafts.

Heat diffusers should be attractive and they should be recessed in walls and partitions so that they do not occupy valuable floor space. Heat transportation systems, radiators, and diffusers must operate quietly.

A metal coil laid in a concrete floor to carry hot water at a relatively low temperature represents an interesting heat transportation and diffusion system. The theory on which radiant coil heating is based is not new, but its use in the United States is comparatively recent. This type of heating has some distinct advantages, including silent operation, an invisible diffusion system, odorless performance, and low temperature radiation over an exceptionally large surface. Radiant coil heating is complex and expensive and may give rise to poor patterns of heat diffusion, although the diffusion is potentially satisfactory. Such a system is slow to warm a cold room and, if the room becomes overheated, just as slow in allowing it to cool. Therefore, under certain conditions, radiant heat is difficult to regulate. Heat loss can be severe with radiant heating unless a system is carefully designed and the building is well insulated. For these reasons, radiant coil heating has never become as popular as other systems.

Electric heating is not central heating in the usual sense of the term because it does not include a centrally located heating plant. However, it *is* central heating in that a network of wires serves to conduct potential thermal energy from a central point to all rooms in a building. Radiating units in each room transform electrical energy to thermal energy at points where heat is needed. Thus a single system serves an entire building.

Electric heating seems destined to become very important. The initial cost of an electric heating system is no higher than that of a conventional system, although the better building insulation necessary to electric heating economy is more expensive. Over a period of time, of course, added insulation will pay for itself through reduced heating and air conditioning costs.

Operating costs of electric heating have been high but are gradually being reduced as use increases and energy-efficient building designs are created. System maintenance costs are low, and future additions to a building need not mandate increasing the heating capacity. In addition, the availability for other purposes of much of the floor space occupied by a conventional heating plant is a significant advantage. Electric heat is clean, odorless, silent, and capable of quick and precise regulation in every room. It is wise to request bids on electric heating as well as on the more common systems when the time comes to choose a school heating system.

Commonly used sources of heat include coal, fuel oil, gas, and electricity. The first three can be burned by central heating plants and the last two are used to operate unit heaters. Fuel oil and gas are the predominant fuels, but the spread of electric heating has been fairly rapid. Each fuel is more economical than others in some regions, even though differences in costs have been narrowing in recent years. In a given locality, the total cost (including equipment, installation, operation, and maintenance) of heating with any of these fuels is likely to be competitive enough so that no fuel must be ruled out on the basis of cost alone. Properly utilized, all provide satisfactory heating. It is conceivable that nuclear fuel will become the most important source of thermal energy in the future. Other possible sources include solar energy, wind power, tidal power, and geothermal energy.

AIR CONDITIONING

The American Society of Heating, Air Conditioning, and Refrigeration Engineers defines air conditioning as the treating of air to control temperature, relative humidity, cleanliness, and distribution within specified limits. By this definition, air conditioning is a generic term implying the addition and subtraction of heat and moisture and the exchange of air, as necessary, to achieve certain desired air environmental conditions. Undoubtedly this is the view that should and will prevail as people begin to better understand that air is a natural resource of limitless value (but not necessarily limitless quantity) that must be modified if its full potential is to be realized. In this respect, it is like any other natural resource.

Physical and emotional reactions — headache, nervous tension, lack of interest, lack of ability to concentrate, dizziness, nausea, and fatigue — attributable to rooms that are poorly ventilated, too warm, and too humid stem from the inability of the human body to lose heat rapidly enough. Understandably such conditions seriously interfere with the teaching-learning process. They can occur when the outdoor temperature rises above 60°F. and are likely to occur when it exceeds 80°F., unless classrooms are cooled by refrigeration.

Maximum return on money spent for education will accrue only if high learning efficiency and full utilization of facilities can be achieved. Air conditioning makes both goals easier to reach. In many areas of the United States, new schools should not be built without air conditioning, and it should be added to existing schools wherever it is economically practicable to do so. In some areas, a full-year educational program is not feasible unless schools are air conditioned.

Air conditioning systems are not designed to provide cold rooms during hot weather. A room at 60°F. is not, after all, more livable at one time of the year than at another. Room temperatures falling within the range of 70–80°F. are comfortable and conducive to learning. Lower temperatures are costly to maintain and disadvantageous from the standpoints of comfort and, possibly, health. They do not improve learning efficiency.

Many physiologists believe that a twenty-degree differential between indoor and outdoor temperatures is the maximum that is desirable. Even this large a gradient may be detrimental if indoor temperatures are maintained as low as 72°F. Neuralgia and stiffness and soreness of muscles and joints have been traced to excessive temperature differentials.

Coolness may be transported from a central refrigeration system by chilled water pumped through pipes (at approximately 50°F.) or by chilled air forced through ducts. Chilled water systems use unit ventilators as room terminals. The ventilators introduce fresh air, provide fan action, and permit thermostatic control. Room heat is transferred to the water, and the water is returned to the refrigeration system so that the heat can be dispersed in the atmosphere.

Chilled air systems have low noise levels because all machinery is installed in a central location. They can do a superior job of filtering air and removing odors if the proper rate of airflow is maintained. Air conditioning requires a greater air velocity than mechanical ventilation, but it should not exceed fifty cubic feet per minute per student if drafts are to be avoided.

The cost of purchasing and installing a central air conditioning system is substantial. So are direct operating costs. It costs approximately as much to cool a school building on a hot day as it does to heat it on a cold day.

Industrial education laboratories can be difficult and expensive to air-condition. Exhaust systems transfer cool air to the atmosphere, and some laboratory activities generate a great deal of heat. Increased air-conditioning capacity, together with a control system that permits turning the air conditioning off in certain areas when heat-producing activities are in progress, seems to be a good solution. In addition, it will probably become increasingly desirable to route air that passes through exhaust systems back into laboratories.

The *differences* between the construction and operating costs of air conditioned buildings and those of buildings that are not air conditioned need not be significant if architects take advantage of economies made possible by air conditioning. Air conditioned schools can be much more compact. They need not employ finger plan and campus plan designs in order to minimize the effects of the sun and take advantage of prevailing winds.

A compact building requires less land, and it consumes a smaller weight of structural steel. Its roof area is smaller. Water, storm, sanitary, and electrical distribution systems can be more compact and less costly. The need for fewer lineal feet of wall in itself results in a significant saving. The opportunity to reduce the size of window sections and eliminate sash ventilators is also of great importance. Windows — particularly sash ventilators — are the most expensive elements in wall construction. A wall that contains a large area of glass can cost as much as 20 per cent more than a windowless wall.

A compact school needs less heating plant capacity because its smaller roof, wall, and window areas minimize heat loss. It is true that an air conditioned building must be tighter and better insulated, but higher insulation costs are eventually more than offset by lower fuel consumption.

An air conditioned school tends to remain cleaner and to require less custodial service and less frequent redecorating. Exterior maintenance costs less because there is not as much to keep in good repair.

Parenthetically, it is well to note that compact designs present several potentially serious problems. For example, compactness can result in increased noise transmission and in corridor systems too limited to prevent congestion. Unless problems like these are solved, the economies offered by a compact building will have no real meaning.

In many cases, central air conditioning adds less than two dollars per square foot to the cost of constructing a school building. Under severe climatic conditions, additional operating costs should total no more than ten cents per day per student. Moreover, the added construction and operating costs can be largely offset by construction and operating economies. It is readily apparent, however, that these savings must be achieved by constructing buildings that are more compact and have smaller window areas. If a school district decides to build an air conditioned finger plan or campus plan school with large expanses of glass, air conditioning costs will be much higher.

In the final analysis, however, it is not worthwhile to try to defend the inclusion of air conditioning on the basis of cost alone. If, as seems entirely reasonable, air conditioning improves learning efficiency by as little as 10 per cent, it is well worth having. Learning is, after all, the purpose of a school. The important questions faced by a school district are these:

1. Is air conditioning instrumental in maintaining the health and comfort of students and teachers?
2. Is air conditioning a significant aid to learning?

The answer to both questions is *yes*.

EXHAUST SYSTEMS

Waste materials produced in laboratory classes can present problems to teachers and students and even to entire schools. Odors, fumes, smoke, and dust that seep into other areas of a school from an industrial education laboratory can hamper classes and make sanitation standards more difficult to maintain. Industrial teachers and students find concentrations of waste materials to be irritating and possibly detrimental to health. Teachers are more affected because they spend much more time in laboratories than do students. Respiratory and eye irritations and aggravation of such conditions as asthma and sinusitis are more common in laboratory air environments contaminated by dust and other waste products than in clean air environments. Possible links between inhalation of waste particles and serious illnesses such as lung cancer and emphysema must be kept in mind, too. School districts, therefore, should recognize the critical nature of the problem and adopt the general policy that *all* air contamination must be eliminated through the use of exhaust systems.

Exhaust systems serve other important purposes besides cleaning the air. Nuisance waste removal is essential to good housekeeping and machine maintenance. Woods laboratories without dust collection systems can be kept clean, but the task is time-consuming and, consequently, easily put off. Usually these facilities become less and less clean as time passes, and their appearance and physical condition deteriorate. Premature wear of bearings, threads, belts, pulleys, gears, shafts, guides, and other operating parts may take place.

Exhaust systems can be instrumental in preventing accidents or making them less serious. Removal of waste materials eliminates one source of explosions and fires. It also reduces the number of slipping and stumbling accidents, as well as accidents resulting from decreased visibility in a contaminated air environment.

Certain common processes, such as wood finishing, require reasonably clean air for best results.

The broad purposes of exhaust systems, then, include:

1. Preservation of health
2. Removal of laboratory waste products
3. Prevention of accidents
4. Improvement of technical processes

Equipment to accomplish this is readily available to every school district. Exhaust systems range from single ducts that carry ammonia fumes away from print machines in drawing laboratories to complete dust collection systems for removing waste materials from woods laboratories. Every laboratory needs some type of exhaust system.

Gaseous wastes can be exhausted to the atmosphere, provided care is taken to make sure that they will not be drawn into the school's ventilating and/or air conditioning system or become a nuisance to surrounding areas

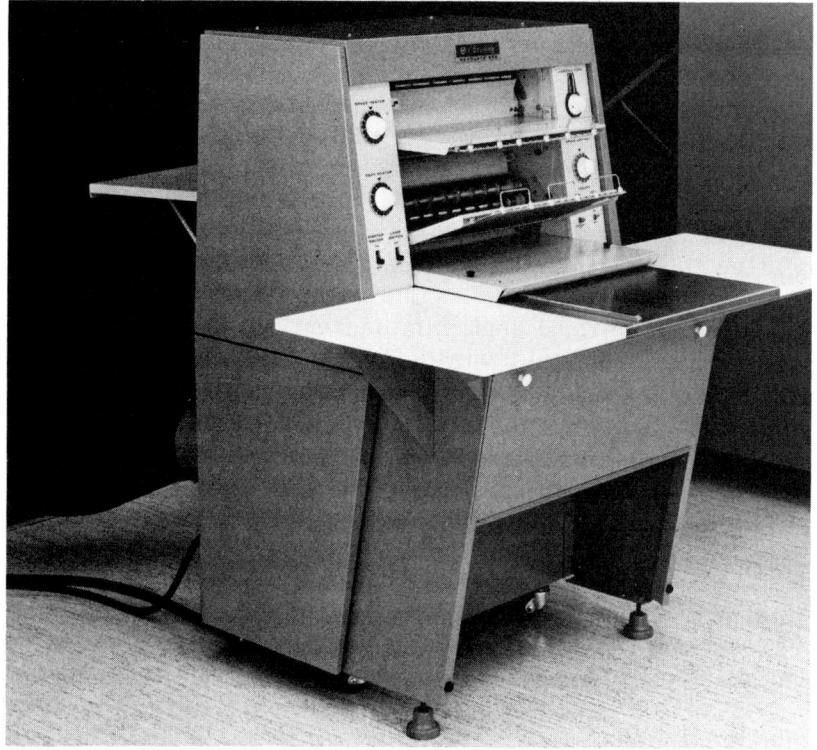

Figure 8.1 *Simple exhaust system for removing gaseous wastes.* (Bruning Division, Addressograph Multigraph)

of the community. The volume of gaseous wastes produced in a laboratory is usually insignificant except in geographic areas that have general air pollution problems. In those areas additional pollutants are unwelcome. Where statutes prohibit the release of untreated gaseous wastes to the atmosphere — and such laws are becoming common — cleaning devices must be used.

Wastes that contain substantial quantities of solid materials are the most difficult to handle, though not necessarily the most harmful, and they require comprehensive exhaust systems. For example, waste materials produced in a woods laboratory range from the fumes of finishing materials and extremely fine sanding dust to coarse sawdust and chips. Three separate exhaust systems are necessary for their removal: an exhaust fan to remove odors and fumes from the general finishing room; a water-air exhaust system to remove fumes and solid airborne materials that result from spray finishing; and a dust collection system to remove solid wastes produced by machine and hand tool operations.

A woods laboratory dust collection system consists of a number of

Figure 8.2 *Overhead duct system*. (Torit Division, Donaldson Company, Incorporated)

exhaust hoods (one or more at each machine serviced) that help to confine waste materials at their sources, a duct system to convey wastes away from the hoods, a collector (motor, fan, and housing) that reduces the air pressure at the mouth of each exhaust hood and separates waste materials from the air stream, and a storage hopper in which waste materials are deposited.

Ducts may be installed overhead or beneath the floor. Overhead installation (see Fig. 8.2) is recommended in most cases, even though it presents an aesthetic problem and may interfere with light reflectance, sound absorption, and the visibility and working space around certain machines. An overhead duct system is much easier to adjust and maintain, and it can be readily redesigned if it becomes desirable to add machines to the system or to modify the floor plan of a laboratory.

A duct system placed underfloor minimizes the amount of visible ductwork and does not usually interfere with machine performance or restrict visibility around machines. Ducts are shorter, and less noise is created by the movement of air. The disadvantages of having a duct system under the floor are that it is more expensive to install and modify — even minor changes are difficult to make — and blockages can be time-consuming to clear. An underfloor duct system can ultimately become only a partial dust collection system, if cost prohibits adding new machinery to it as it is purchased. It is likely also to freeze a floor plan in the form of its original design, since underfloor ducts must be installed before a concrete floor is poured.

Collectors and storage hoppers should be located outdoors so as to isolate motor, fan, and drive system noises and noises created by waste materials as they strike interior surfaces. There is seldom, if ever, a compelling reason for installing anything but exhaust hoods and ducts within a laboratory. Space provided around collectors and storage hoppers should be adequate to permit necessary maintenance activities.

Figure 8.3 *Underfloor duct system.*

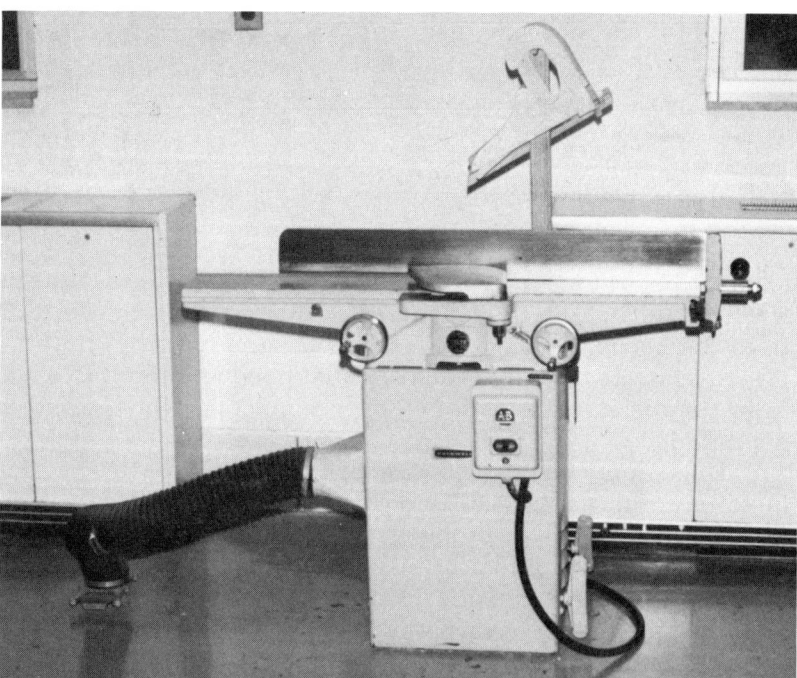

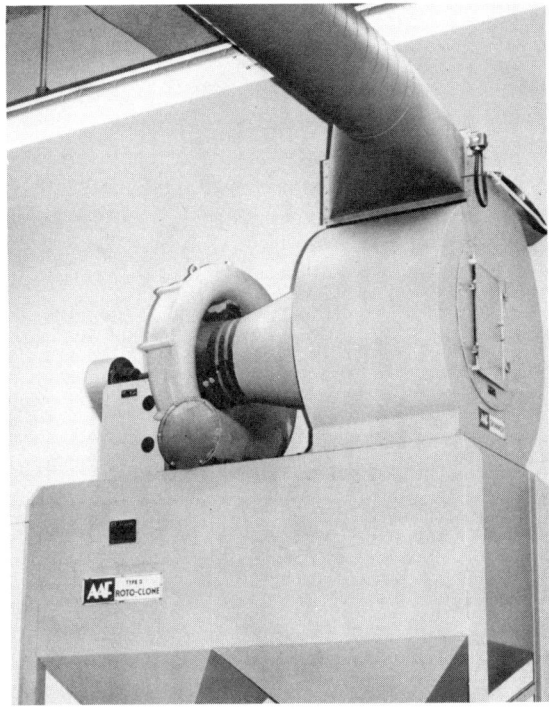

Figure 8.4 *Dust collector and storage hopper.*

To conserve fuel and electric power, air leaving a collector can be passed through a fabric filter and returned to the laboratory instead of being dispersed in the atmosphere. However, this approach is likely to increase the noise level of the dust collection system well above the desired eighty-decibel limit. The duct between the collector and the filter should be lined with a sound-absorbing material; if noise is still a problem, a silencer can also be installed between the collector and filter.

Two types of collectors useful in woods laboratories are the dry-type dynamic precipitator and the high efficiency cyclone. Both are effective and relatively inexpensive. Each provides a moderate pressure drop. In addition, they can be used to collect waste that accumulates from grinding metals, machining and sanding plastics, and many polishing operations. Neither is capable of handling extremely large exhaust volumes (as would be produced in an industrial plant), large pieces of scrap, or sticky, fibrous materials.

Dynamic precipitator operation is based on centrifugal force, which causes dust striking the fan blades to move along the blades to the periphery of the fan and forces it into the surrounding dust circuit, which

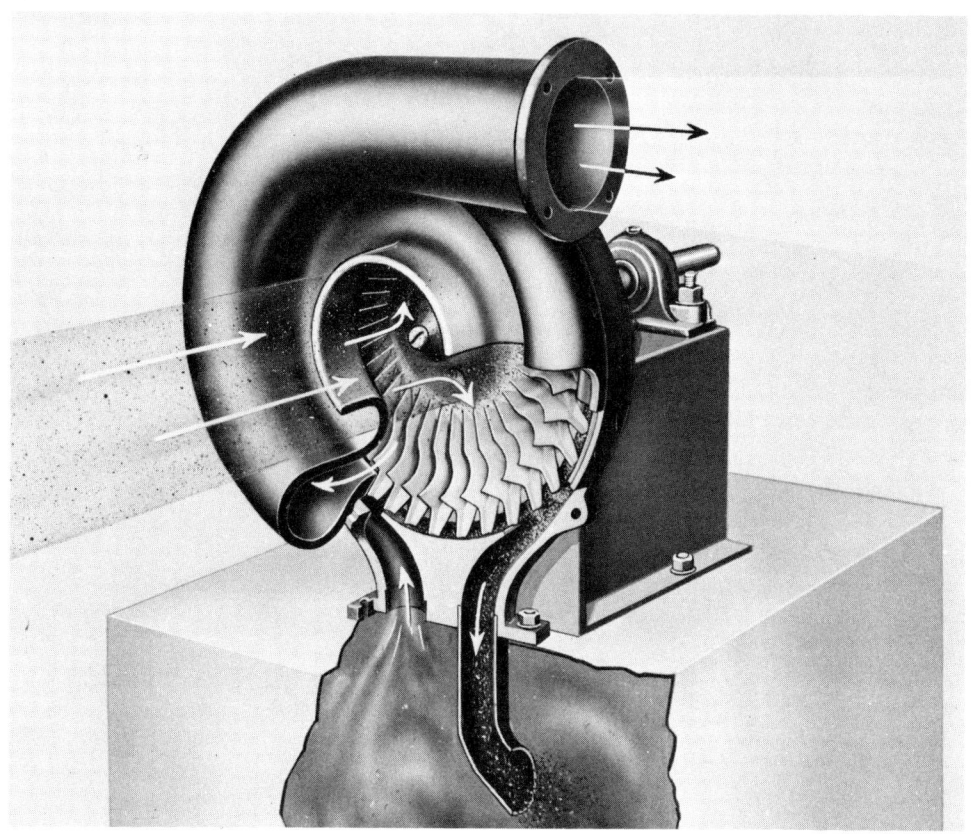

Figure 8.5 *Dry-type dynamic precipitator.* (AAF Company, Incorporated)

connects to a storage hopper.[2] It is common practice to use a precleaner to remove coarse particles from dust-laden air before it is drawn into a dynamic precipitator.

A cyclone (Fig. 8.6) uses spiral baffles to create a whirlwind air motion. Centrifugal force precipitates dust, chips, and shavings, spins them against the conical section of the collector, and forces them into a storage hopper. Fan action draws the cleaned air out of the cyclone.[3]

Whatever type of collector is used, completion of the dust collection process entails periodically emptying the storage hopper and making sure

[2]John M. Kane, "Operation, Application and Effectiveness of Dust Collection Equipment," *Air Conditioning, Heating and Ventilating. Reference Section,* August 1952; reprinted for American Air Filter Co., Inc., Louisville, Ky.

[3]Ibid.

Figure 8.6 *High-efficiency cyclone.* (Torit Division, Donaldson Company, Incorporated)

that materials removed from the hopper are not allowed to blow around the area.

A fabric-type dust collector (Fig. 8.7) avoids problems of heat loss, loss of cool air, and the need for makeup air created by standard dust collection systems. Air passed through a fabric collector is usually returned to a laboratory for reuse unless the air drawn into exhaust hoods contains toxic gases. A fabric collector is more expensive than a dynamic precipitator or cyclone. Its higher price may or may not be justified by potential reductions in a school's consumption of fuel and electric power.

Dust-laden air drawn into a fabric collector is forced to make a sharp change of direction so that centrifugal force will cause the larger particles to be precipitated into a storage hopper. The air then passes through a highly efficient fabric filter element consisting of closely spaced envelopes

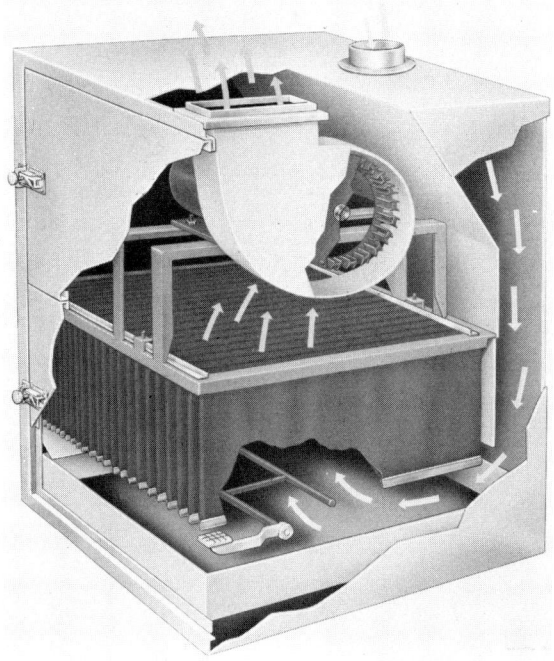

Figure 8.7 *Fabric-type dust collector.* (Torit Division, Donaldson Company, Incorporated)

of woven fiberglass or some other material. The filter element removes almost 100 per cent of the remaining dust. Most fabric collectors include a manual or motor-driven vibrator to agitate the element when the system is not in use. The dust loosened by this process falls into the storage hopper.

Through-the-wall exhaust systems with exterior fans work well where air velocity requirements are relatively modest and where waste materials are gaseous and not highly concentrated. General wood finishing rooms, photographic darkrooms, and sink areas where acid etching and other chemical processes are carried on are examples of this kind of activity. Exhaust fan motors must be spark-free, and they must operate at low temperatures so that exhaust gases can pass around them without danger of ignition. They must also be corrosionproof.

Highly concentrated and potentially lethal gaseous wastes such as fumes from internal combustion engines, welding, and foundry activities, must be removed by a more comprehensive system. The basic parts of such a system are one or more exhaust hoods, a duct system, and a collector. A squirrel cage fan with a suitable housing often acts as the collector. The collector should not be located inside the laboratory.

A company whose operation is strictly local should *not* ordinarily be employed to design and install a dust collection system or, indeed, any comprehensive exhaust system. Too often, the results are disappointing. National firms offer the best systems and service. The chosen firm will need the following information as the basis for its design work:

1. A simple floor plan of the industrial education facility, including adjacent interior and exterior areas
2. A dimensioned laboratory floor plan that shows the placement of all pieces of equipment
3. A description of the laboratory's construction — kinds of walls and partitions, luminaire placement, ceiling height, types and locations of windows, and other details that will affect the design and installation of an exhaust system
4. A list of all pieces of equipment to be serviced and their working capacities
5. A list of basic exhaust system specifications

There are many hallmarks of a good dust collection system. Design qualities that it must possess include satisfactory appearance, unobtrusiveness, silent operation, efficiency, durability, and ease of maintenance. The appearance of an overhead duct system is determined by quality of workmanship and the color and texture of paint used. It is possible to paint horizontal ducts so that they blend fairly well with a ceiling, but vertical ducts are difficult to conceal. Silent operation, efficiency, durability, and ease of maintenance result from good basic design, proper location of the collector and storage hopper, and expert workmanship during construction, installation, and testing.

The efficiency of a dust collection system depends on its ability to move enough air to pick up all waste materials at each exhaust hood. Table 8.1[4] lists branch duct diameters and branch duct air transport velocities needed to pick up and remove waste materials produced by woodworking machines. The total air transport velocity that a dust collection system must provide is found by adding branch duct velocities, since any system must be capable of servicing all machines at the same time.

The woods laboratory shown in Fig. 11.4 requires an air transport velocity of 6650 cubic feet per minute. This capacity will handle all machines except the drill presses, mortiser, grinder, and buffer. In woods laboratory operation, grinders and buffers do not produce enough waste material to require dust collection service. Drill presses and mortisers are

[4]James R. Kayse, "Dust Control for School Woodworking Shops," *Air Conditioning, Heating and Ventilating*, reprinted for American Air Filter Co., Inc., Louisville, Ky.

Table 8.1 EXHAUST SYSTEM SPECIFICATIONS FOR WOODWORKING MACHINES

Machine	Number of Branch Ducts Required	Branch Duct Diameter, Inches	Branch Duct Air Transport Velocity (cubic feet per minute)
Table saw			
up to 12" diameter	1	4	350
over 12" diameter	1	5	550
Radial arm saw			
up to 20" diameter	1	4	350
Disc sander			
up to 12" diameter	1	4	350
12" to 18" diameter	1	4½	450
Jointer			
up to 6" knives	1	4	350
6" to 12" knives	1	5	550
Planer			
up to 20" max. working width	1	6	775
20" to 26" max. working width	1	7	1050
26" to 32" max. working width	1	8	1450
32" to 38" max. working width	1	9	1800
Vertical belt sander (rear belt and both pulleys enclosed)			
up to 6" wide	1	4½ on bottom	450
6" to 9" wide	1	5 on bottom	550
Lathe	1	4½	450
Scroll saw	1	4	350
Band saw			
up to 2" wide			
bottom	1	4	350
top	1	4	350
Horizontal belt sander			
up to 6" wide			
drive pulley	1	4½	450
idler pulley	1	4	350

6" to 9" wide			
drive pulley	1	5	550
idler pulley	1	4	350
9" to 14" wide			
drive pulley	1	6	775
idler pulley	1	4	350
Shaper (average)	1	5	550
Floor sweeps			

Use 6" branch duct for fine dust and 8" branch duct for coarse material. Mouth size at floor: 4 × 10" to 5 × 12".

---

difficult to service without interfering with machine function. Fortunately, due to relatively limited use, they are not prolific producers of waste materials.

Floor sweeps need not be considered in air transport velocity calculations because they are seldom used while equipment is in operation. Moreover, because it is unlikely that all machines will ever be in simultaneous operation, there is sufficient overcapacity in a well-designed system to permit the use of the floor sweeps at any time. A minimum of two floor sweeps should be provided in every woods laboratory. One should be placed adjacent to the machine area and the other should be located near the bench area. Floor sweep mouths should measure four inches high by twelve inches wide. Each should be equipped with a coarse, hinged grille to prevent large pieces of wood from being drawn into the duct.

Additional specifications for a dust collection system are as follows:[5]

1. Exhaust hoods should be designed to utilize the natural trajectories of waste materials.
2. Each exhaust hood must be placed very close to the source of dust production. Efficiency diminishes rapidly as distance increases.
3. No exhaust hood or duct should be constructed or placed so that it interferes with machine set-up, operation, or maintenance.
4. Cross drafts at sources of dust production must be avoided.
5. Overhead ducts, except floor sweeps, should be twelve inches or more away from walls, partitions, and ceilings and six inches or more away from floors.

[5]Dust Control Division, American Air Filter Co., Inc., *Design of Roto-clone Dust Control Systems* (Louisville, Ky.: American Air Filter Co.), p. 7.

180 THE AIR ENVIRONMENT

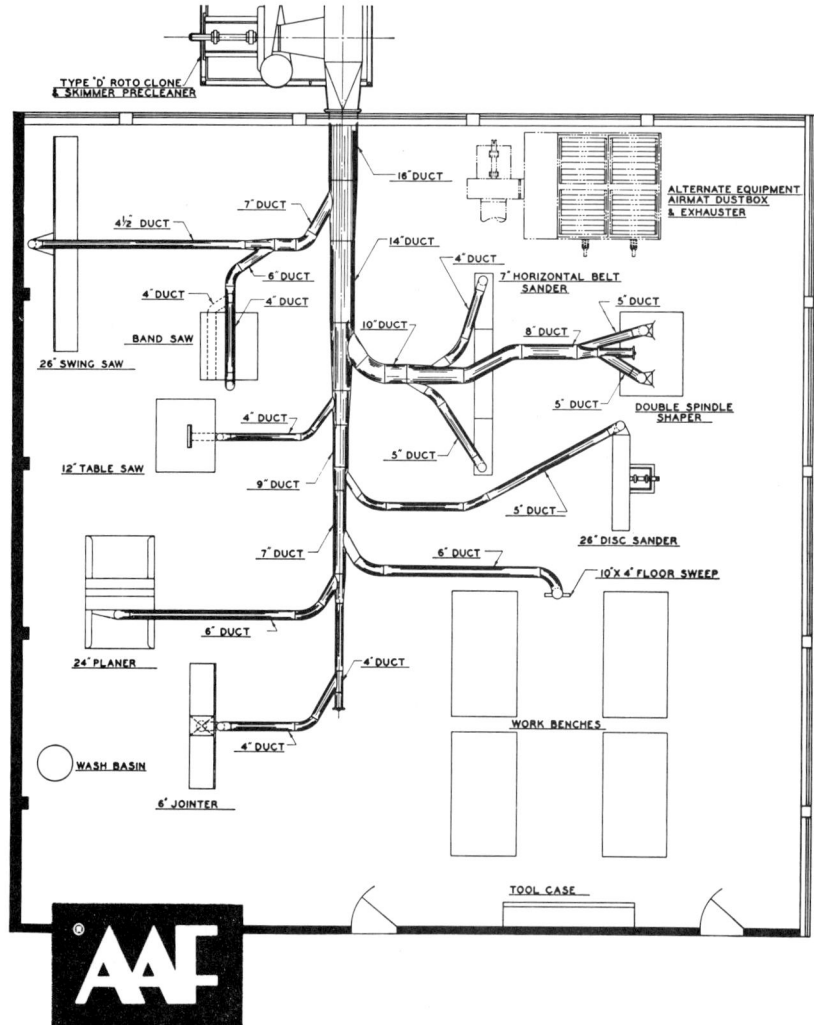

Figure 8.8 *Sample duct system layout for dust collection system.* (AAF Company, Incorporated)

6. Branch ducts must enter the main duct only on the top and sides, and they must not connect directly opposite each other.
7. Branch ducts should enter the main duct and other branch ducts at angles of forty-five degrees or less. Thirty-degree angles are preferred.

EXHAUST SYSTEMS

8. Ducts up to eight inches in diameter should be constructed of twenty-two-gauge galvanized steel. Ducts having diameters of eight inches to eighteen inches are to be constructed of twenty-gauge galvanized steel.
9. Round ducts should be used throughout. If lack of clearance makes it necessary to use a rectangular duct, it should be as nearly square as possible and equal in area to the corresponding round duct.
10. Longitudinal joints should overlap one inch, and they should be secured by double-lock seams that are riveted or spot welded on three-inch or closer centers.
11. Girth joints should overlap one inch in the direction of air flow, and they should be riveted or spot welded on three-inch or closer centers.
12. All joints should be soldered or sealed with duct tape so that they are airtight, and all other parts of the system must be airtight.
13. Elbows and angles should have inside radii equal to or greater than one duct diameter.
14. Reducers used in main and branch ducts should be designed so that the taper represents a ratio of five inches in length to every one-inch change in diameter.
15. The main duct should connect to the collector inlet with a split sleeve draw band having a length equal to the duct diameter.
16. Horizontal overhead ducts that are eight inches or less in diameter should be supported at intervals no greater than twelve feet. Larger ducts should be supported at intervals no greater than twenty feet. Supports must be able to carry the weight of the duct system, even if it is solidly filled with waste materials, without placing a load on equipment connected to the system.
17. The interior of the entire system must be free of dents, burrs, sharp edges, and other obstructions.
18. Ducts must not contain fixed screens.
19. Cleanout traps should be provided on ten-foot centers and near each elbow and junction in horizontal overhead duct sections.
20. A blast gate should be installed in every branch duct near the point where it connects to the main duct. Blast gates are used to adjust the flow of air in the system. They should be locked in position after the adjustment has been made.

21. A cut-off gate should be installed in each branch duct near the machine it serves. A cut-off gate is used to halt the flow of air from a machine while it is being set up or maintained.
22. The collector motor should be wired through the starter switch of each machine motor so that no machine can be run without the system being in operation.
23. The entire system must be electrically grounded.
24. Units installed outdoors must be constructed of corrosionproof materials and properly finished.
25. Collectors, storage hoppers, drive systems, electric motors, and electric wiring installed outdoors must be watertight.
26. Fire dampers and explosion vents must be installed as required by law. Equipment, materials, and workmanship must conform to standards of the National Fire Protection Association.

Regular maintenance is essential in preserving the efficiency of a dust collection system. Every system should receive the same kind of periodic maintenance that a production machine receives. Specifically, accumulations of waste must be removed, exhaust hoods checked for proper condition and alignment, belt drives correctly tensioned, motors and moving parts lubricated, and all parts of the system kept airtight.

Where few machines are to be serviced, portable dust collectors may be used, although they are less efficient, even in moderate use, than a central dust collection system. Because of limited storage capacity, portable collectors require more maintenance. They consume valuable floor space and are often noisy. Portable collectors do not offer a really good solution to the problem of dust removal, but they can provide adequate temporary service until a central system can be obtained.

Substantial amounts of dust will be removed by the dust bags supplied with some portable electric sanders. No sander should be purchased without such a bag.

A portable vacuum is a worthwhile addition to the equipment of any laboratory. Cleaning jobs that must be done especially well often require vacuuming.

FOR FURTHER READING

AAF, Inc. *Manual of Exhaust Hood Design*. Louisville, Ky.: AAF.
American Council on Industrial Arts Teacher Education. *Planning Industrial Arts Facilities*. 8th yearbook. Bloomington, Ill.: McKnight Publishing Co., 1959.

Dust Control Division, AAF, Inc. *Design of Roto-clone Dust Control Systems.* Louisville, Ky.: Dust Control Division, AAF, Inc.

Kayse, James R. "Dust Control for Vocational Arts." *Illinois School Board Journal*, September-October, 1957.

McGuinness, William J., and Stein, Benjamin. *Building Technology: Mechanical and Electrical Systems.* New York: John Wiley & Sons, 1977.

Ramsey, Charles G., and Sleeper, Harold R. *Architectural Graphic Standards.* 6th ed. rev. New York: John Wiley & Sons, 1970.

Rutgers, Norman L. "Heat: Its Effect on Teaching and Learning." *Modern School Shop Planning.* 4th ed. Ann Arbor, Mich.: Prakken Publications, Inc., 1965.

Stein, Richard G. "Saving Energy in Vocational Schools." *School Shop*, April 1976, p. 51.

Sumption, Merle R., and Landes, Jack L. *Planning Functional School Buildings.* New York: Harper and Brothers Publishers, 1957.

University of Iowa. *Thermal Environment and Learning.* Report prepared by the Iowa Center for Research in School Administration. Iowa City, Iowa: University of Iowa, 1962.

University of Minnesota. *School Thermal Environment.* Minneapolis, Minn.: University of Minesota, 1961.

Wiars, Dale M. "Heat Recovery System Saves Power." *School Shop*, April 1976, p. 77.

Winslow, C. E. A., and Herrington, L. P. *Temperature and Human Life.* Princeton, N. J.: Princeton University Press, 1949.

9
Utility Service Systems

INTRODUCTION

Industrial education programs make use of four utility services. They are electricity, water, gas, and compressed air. Electricity is the most important of the four. No laboratory could operate well without it. Water also is essential in most laboratories. Gas is useful chiefly where metals are to be forged, cast, welded, brazed, soldered, or heat-treated and where clay is to be fired and glazed. However, lack of gas does not pose a critical problem because electricity is an entirely adequate substitute as far as most laboratory activities are concerned. Compressed air is useful in certain cleaning processes and is a key ingredient in such operations as spray finishing, hard soldering, tire inflation, and airbrush work. Failure to include compressed air will preclude a number of activities that enrich industrial education courses.

Table 9.1 summarizes utility service needs of the several industrial education laboratories. In specific situations, activities included in courses of study may require utility services that would not normally be provided.

Utility service systems should be considered integral parts of the

Table 9.1 UTILITY SERVICES NEEDED IN INDUSTRIAL EDUCATION LABORATORIES

Laboratory	Utility Service			
	Electricity	Water	Gas	Compressed Air
Woods	√	√		√
Building construction	√	√		√
Metals	√	√	√	√
Drafting	√	√		√
Graphics	√	√		√
Electricity/electronics	√	√		√
Automotive technology	√	√	√	√
Refrigeration	√	√	√	√
Crafts	√	√	√	√
General	√	√	√	√

design of a laboratory, not appendages that will be modified at leisure as the needs of the program become known.

Utility service system designs are based on lists of laboratory activities, lists of equipment to be provided, and detailed, dimensioned floor plans of laboratories. The lists make it possible to calculate needed capacities of utility service systems, and floor plans indicate the locations of outlets of various kinds.

In the planning of utility service systems, the future is as important as the present. Systems must be designed so that additional pieces of equipment can be added and pieces initially installed can be replaced by others having greater capacity—if the change becomes desirable—without undertaking major reconstruction. There is no disadvantage in providing overcapacity and more outlets than are immediately required, since the cost of doing so is insignificant when compared to the cost of future alterations. On the other hand, inadequate systems can be both a severe handicap and dangerous. Overloaded electrical circuits, for example, often result in the interruption of class activities and can cause fires if the problem is attacked by the use of oversize fuses or circuit breakers.

Although the quantity of each utility consumed in a year's time by an industrial education department is substantial, an individual laboratory will not use a great amount of any utility at any given time. Large melting furnaces and ceramic kilns might be exceptions to the rule, but even so, more or less normal rates of consumption can be assumed.

Consequently wiring, circuit breakers, pipes, valves, faucets, pressure indicator/regulators, and other components can be purchased in standard sizes. The best obtainable quality is often the least expensive and the most satisfactory over a period of time. All accessories or options that make systems safer, more durable, or easier to operate should be installed. Good industrial education programs depend on effective utility service systems.

ELECTRICITY

Power tools and machines are driven by electric motors that vary widely with respect to horsepower rating. Thus, all laboratories should have 115-volt, single-phase and 230-volt, three-phase electric service, as well as other voltage/phase combinations needed by individual pieces of equipment. Motors rated in excess of one-half horsepower should be run on 230-volt, three-phase current for maximum operating economy. Heat-producing equipment, such as ceramic kilns, should also be operated on 230-volt current.

All electric motors, heat-producing equipment, and parts of the electrical distribution system in a laboratory should be approved by Underwriters' Laboratories, Inc., and installed in accordance with the National Electrical Code (Section 70 of the National Fire Codes), the state electrical code, and the local code. (Copies of the National Electrical Code can be obtained from the National Fire Protection Association, 470 Atlantic Avenue, Boston, Massachusetts 02210.)

An all-wire distribution system should be constructed of insulated No. 12 or heavier wire. It should be designed as a single-phase, three-wire and three-phase, four-wire system, which will provide a low-resistance path to ground for each consuming device equipped with a grounding-type power cord and plug. All connections must be made in junction boxes. Switches and convenience outlets also must be installed in boxes. Wires should be run in conduit or raceways to prevent damage to insulation.

Each circuit must be protected against overloading. In general, a circuit breaker that can be reset manually offers the best and most convenient protection. The manual reset should be easy to operate, and it should be equipped with a device that indicates whether the circuit is open or closed.

Machine and convenience outlet circuits should be separate from each other, and both must be separate from light circuits. If an all-wire distribution system is used, every machine and heat-producing device should have its own circuit. No more than three convenience outlets should be on the same circuit.

A convenience outlet circuit must be constructed so that it will not be overloaded if all outlets are used at the same time by the pieces of equipment that draw the greatest amount of amperage. The technique of installing convenience outlets that are on the same circuit in locations *not* adjacent to each other is another safeguard against overloading. Ordinarily, not all outlets on a circuit will be in simultaneous use by the largest consumers of power; but the possibility cannot be ignored.

Economical expansion of an electrical distribution system can be ensured by providing space on a laboratory switchpanel for one additional circuit breaker for every four power circuits and convenience outlet circuits in use.

An industrial education laboratory should have wall-mounted duplex convenience outlets on all sides of every room in which power equipment is operated. Except in drawing laboratories, 115-volt, single-phase outlets and 230-volt, three-phase outlets should be installed on ten-foot centers that are three feet above floor level in order to clear benches and counters. Drawing laboratories should have the same pattern of 115-volt outlets, but 230-volt outlets should be placed only where needed to serve large print machines. Additional convenience outlets should be provided wherever specific needs exist. If an under-floor distribution system is employed, 115-volt single phase outlets installed flush with the finished floor at two opposite corners of each workbench will provide service for portable power equipment. Floor outlets should include dustproof and moistureproof covers. Outlets should be suspended over benches if an overhead distribution system is used.

An industrial education facility should be equipped with a switchboard that breaks the incoming electrical current into as many large circuits as there are separate laboratories in the group. A switchboard is composed of one or more electric panels, each containing meters, circuit breakers, and a master switch. A red pilot light is often used to show that the master switch is "on." Switchboards should be centrally located in places that are secure from tampering.

Every laboratory should have a switchpanel equipped with one circuit breaker for each branch circuit and a master switch that controls the current in all branch circuits. Switchpanels should be installed in locking cabinets having charts on which outlet and circuit breaker numbers can be recorded. (The number of each circuit breaker should also be marked on each outlet it controls.) Switchpanel locations near bench areas, machine areas, main entrances, or teachers' offices are convenient. A red pilot light indicating that the master switch is "on" should be installed in

Figure 9.1 *Laboratory switchpanel equipped with circuit breakers.*

a highly visible place on or near a switch panel. One or more additional master switches located in other easily reached places will permit a teacher to break all circuits quickly in case of emergency. Because tampering is a possibility, these switches should be equipped with red pilot lights to signify that they are "on."

Each machine should have its own switchbox that contains "off" and "on" push-button switches and a mechanical switch that can be used to physically break the machine motor circuit. The "off" button should be red in color, and it should be considerably larger than the "on" button. A mechanical disconnect switch is an important safety device that enables a machine operator to halt electrical service to the machine while making setups or adjustments. Lack of such a switch necessitates trips to the switchpanel—something an operator will not always remember or take the trouble to do.

Of the various electrical distribution systems that have been developed, six can be used to advantage in industrial education laboratories. They are rigid conduit, flexible conduit, surface raceways, underfloor raceways, busways (also called bus ducts), and wireways. Essentially, all are means of enclosing electrical conductors and leading them to various outlet points. Each is an all-metal system that must be assembled in continuous form so that it provides a low-resistance path from every part of the system to the switchpanel, which is grounded. Flexible conduit and surface raceways are seldom used to construct entire distribution systems. Instead, they are usually used in conjunction with other types of systems.

It is often desirable to utilize one kind of system for major service and one or more of the other systems for supplementary service. For example, if a busway is employed to distribute current to machines, flexible conduit can be used to carry the wires that connect each machine to the busway. Rigid conduit can be used in the same system for constructing convenience outlet and light circuits and for distributing current in finishing rooms and other areas where wires and connections must be shielded from moisture and/or from flammable, explosive, or corrosive concentrations of materials.

Two types of rigid conduit are available: standard aluminum or

Figure 9.2 *Flexible conduit keeps vibration from reaching the electrical distribution system.*

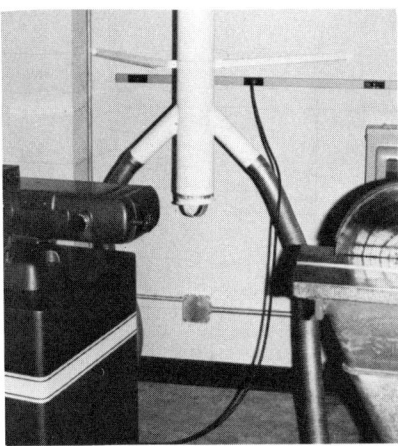

Figure 9.3 *A surface raceway can offer convenient access to electrical service.*

coated steel pipe with threaded connections and thin-wall aluminum or coated steel pipe with compression fittings. Both types may be carried in the open on walls, partitions, and ceilings or buried in masonry. Joints must be moistureproof if the conduit is used outdoors or in masonry. Boxes should be used to shield connections and for the installation of switches and convenience outlets. Rigid conduit provides good protection for insulated wires because it can withstand heavy impact. Unless rigid conduit is buried in masonry, its mediocre appearance is a handicap that can be only partially overcome by the application of paint.

Flexible conduit (trade name: Greenfield) is constructed of light-gauge, coated steel. Its chief advantages are that it can be used to connect an electrical distribution system to machinery that vibrates and it is useful in places where the number or kind of required bends makes it difficult to use rigid conduit (Fig. 9.2). Flexible conduit is easily installed. If moisturetightness is necessary, flexible conduit coated with plastic (called Sealtight) should be used. Uncoated flexible conduit should not be buried in masonry or installed outdoors, especially in unprotected places. Flexible conduit is moderately resistant to damage. Its appearance is fair, but it can be improved somewhat by paint.

A surface raceway is a stamped rectangular sheet-metal form, usually steel, that is used to enclose insulated wires. It can be mounted on walls, partitions, and ceilings in any dry location where impact damage is not likely to occur. It is not moisturetight and should not be used outdoors or buried in masonry. Surface raceway systems include junction boxes, switchboxes, and sections that have built-in convenience outlets. Prewired sections are also available. Raceway parts are sold prefinished

192 UTILITY SERVICE SYSTEMS

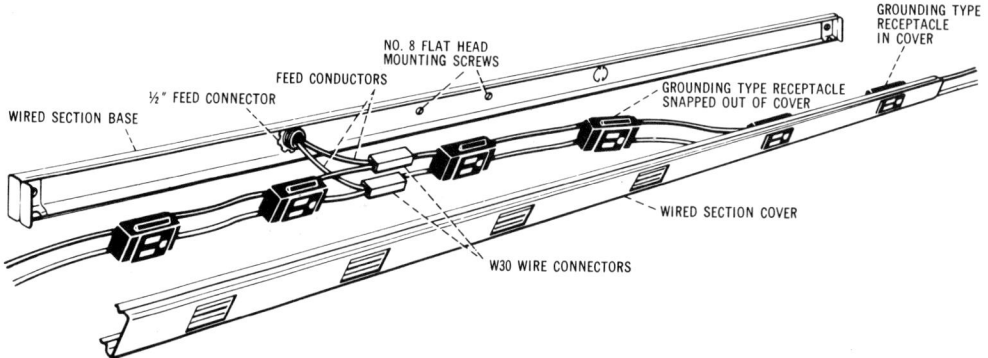

Figure 9.4 *Surface raceway construction.*

Figure 9.5 *Underfloor raceway (Q-floor tap-route system).* (H.H. Robertson Company)

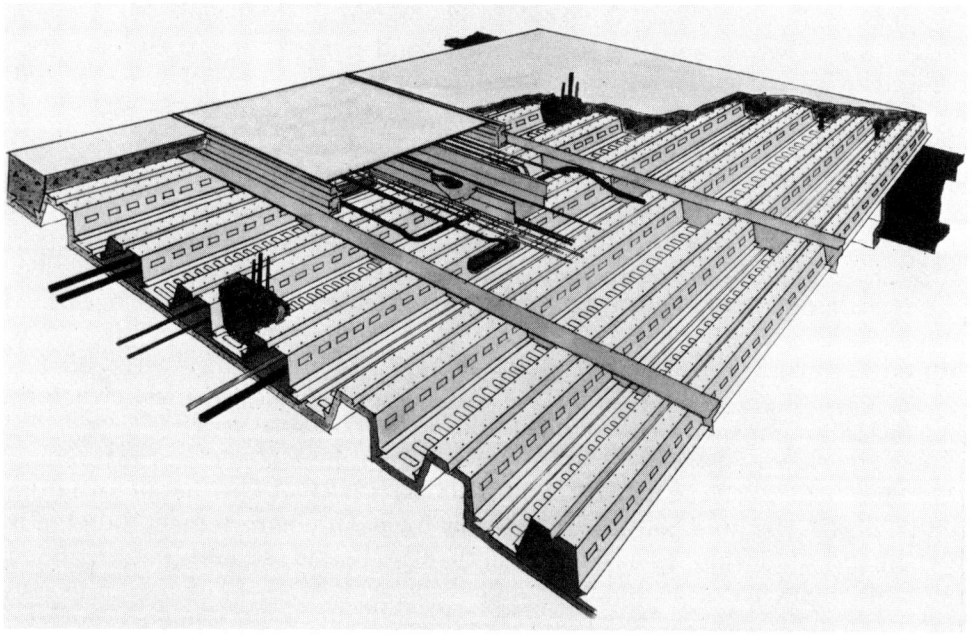

but can be easily repainted to match the surfaces on which they are mounted. The appearance of a surface raceway system is reasonably pleasing, and it is much less obtrusive than rigid or flexible conduit. A surface raceway system is useful for reconstruction jobs where it would be impracticable to bury rigid conduit in masonry or where the appearance of rigid conduit carried in the open would be a disadvantage.

An under-floor raceway is a rather complex electrical distribution system (see Fig. 9.5). The raceway is composed of a steel or fiber duct, junction boxes, couplings, elbows, offsets, and other parts that are cast in a concrete floor to carry insulated wires to outlets. Floor openings are provided wherever necessary. Each opening is equipped with a cover installed flush with the surface of the finished floor. An under-floor raceway system has the advantages of providing short, little-noticed connections that do not hamper machine operations and of virtually eliminating the use of extension cords. It is a compact, effective system that is expensive to install and even more expensive to redesign. Of course, it can be so extensive that it permits almost any reorganization of equipment, but the cost is prohibitive and the many access covers that must be provided detract from the appearance of a floor.

A busway is a large rectangular sheet-metal housing that encloses insulated or uninsulated rectangular metal bus bars supported approximately every ten feet. Supporting hangers are constructed of an insulating material, such as porcelain. A busway can be mounted on a wall, partition, or ceiling. More commonly it is suspended overhead. Bus bars are constructed of aluminum or copper, and they are usually silver-plated to eliminate corrosion. They carry the various voltage/phase combinations required by laboratory equipment and make them available at numerous points along the busway. Plug-in openings are provided on twelve-inch or twenty-four-inch centers on both sides of a busway. Cover plates seal openings that are not in use.

The advantages of a busway are its standardized construction, flexibility, low installation cost, small power loss, low operating temperature, safety, and limited space requirement. It permits extensive laboratory rearrangement without electrical distribution system redesign. Except for an uninteresting appearance, a busway has no limitations worth mentioning.

Busways are especially useful where installations of machinery and other equipment allow long, straight runs. They are prefabricated in standard ten-foot lengths that can be easily assembled in I, T, H, L, and other patterns. Busway components include straight lengths, elbows, offsets, and fittings. Usually, busways are installed in horizontal positions. In vertical installations where runs are longer than a few feet, the bus bars are supported to restrict vertical movement.

It is possible to make a variety of electrical connections to a busway. Machine motors and other consuming devices can be connected by heavy-duty rubber-covered power cords or by insulated wires run in flexible conduit. Rigid conduit is not recommended because it can transmit vibration to a building. Both permanent and plug-in connections are used. One common type of connection includes a switchbox mounted on the consuming device and a heavy-duty rubber-covered power cord that plugs into an outlet on the side of the busway.

A wireway is somewhat similar to a busway. Fundamentally it is a rectangular sheet metal housing that encloses insulated wires carrying all necessary voltage/phase combinations. It has plug-in openings equipped with cover plates on the sides and bottom so that pieces of equipment can be connected almost anywhere. Wireways are manufactured in convenient lengths that can be assembled and installed as units. The sections are equipped with flanges that bolt together. A telescoping section makes it possible to adjust the length of the final section of a system, and it permits longitudinal movement of the wireway to accom-

Figure 9.6 *Busways provide simple and effective electrical distribution systems.* (Torit Division, Donaldson Company, Incorporated)

modate expansion and contraction due to changes in ambient temperature. A wireway can be mounted on vertical and horizontal surfaces or suspended.

It is recommended that convenience outlet and equipment circuits in drawing laboratories be run in rigid conduit buried in masonry. Busways should be used to distribute current in the main work areas of other laboratories because they offer many desirable features and have few, if any, disadvantages. Rigid conduit with airtight fittings should be used in finishing rooms and in any other areas where flammable and/or explosive concentrations of materials can develop. Plug-in connections should be eliminated in such places. Standard rigid conduit is appropriate in all other auxiliary areas.

WATER

Water is used in industrial education laboratories for drinking, washing, and operating toilets and urinals. It also makes possible many processes and operations, such as compounding clay bodies, slips, and concrete; casing and moistening leather; mixing adhesives and finishing materials; diluting solvents, coolants, and acids; heat-treating and cooling metals; processing photographic films; reproducing drawings; preparing sand and plaster of Paris molds; performing certain housekeeping tasks; and combating fires. If water is to be used to best advantage, a school's plumbing system must provide a constant and adequate supply of pure water; effective control, distribution, and utilization devices; and an efficient drain system.

Both hot and cold water should be available at each wash station. Normal water pressure of approximately forty pounds per square inch (psi) and the quantity of water that can be supplied by standard one-inch pipe is satisfactory in most cases, since no laboratory consumes an unusually large quantity of water or has need of an extraordinarily high rate of flow. In fact, the amount of water consumed in an industrial education laboratory during a school day is less than that used in a typical household.

The inclusion of water softening equipment should be considered whenever a plumbing system is designed for a laboratory. There is little question that water that has been softened and filtered to remove hardness elements, sediment, and gaseous particles keeps valves, faucets, spray nozzles, drinking fountains, and fixtures in better condition. Water softening may also lead to better results in processing photographic films, compounding ceramic glazes, and carrying on other activities in which water is an important ingredient. The presence of large amounts of minerals in water can affect colors, textures, and other characteristics of materials. Fully automatic water softening equipment is the most desirable type. Good quality units are trouble-free in operation, and they avoid the marked inconvenience of manual regeneration. In many schools, the advantages of soft water can easily justify the modest costs of providing it.

Once the floor plan of a laboratory has been designed, the locations of water distribution points will be available to the plumbing contractor. Water outlets should be placed so that water utilization is safe and convenient. Locations where water spillage can make the floor around machines slippery, where a wet or damp floor can become an electrical safety hazard, and where splashed water can cause equipment to rust should be avoided.

Every school's water supply system and drain system must be well designed. Rearrangement is expensive, especially if pipes are buried in masonry. Open piping that is supported on walls, partitions, and ceilings has the advantage of being easily accessible for repair and reconstruction. The appearance is poor, but the application of paint can help it to blend fairly well with nearby surfaces. Open piping can also be carried above a suspended ceiling where it will be concealed yet accessible. Buried pipe systems must have access panels at junctions for repairs and modification.

Water system control is relatively simple. A large, hand-operated master valve should be installed in the main water line shortly beyond the point where it enters a school building. The valve should be easy to reach but safe from tampering. Submaster valves should be used to control water supplied to rooms and/or areas within the building. For example, water supplied to each industrial education laboratory complex should be controlled by a submaster valve installed within the complex in a convenient and secure location. In addition, a valve should be placed in every hot and cold water line near the point where it connects to a faucet or some other utilization device. Thus the entire system, a specific area, or an individual utilization device can be taken out of service for repair.

Water distribution systems are most often constructed of galvanized steel pipe with threaded fittings or rigid copper pipe assembled with soldered fittings. Copper pipe is the better choice because mineral deposits do not collect as rapidly on interior surfaces, copper does not corrode as easily as steel, and exterior diameters are smaller. Total costs are substantially the same. Rigid copper pipe is superior to soft copper tubing with respect to strength and appearance. Tubing assembled with compression fittings is often more useful where unusual bends must be made. In time, plastic may supplant copper as the predominant water pipe material. New types of plastics and better methods of fabrication seem likely to make the cost and reliability of plastic competitive. At present, polyvinyl chloride (PVC) is satisfactory for cold water piping; and chlorinated polyvinyl chloride (CPVC) is a good choice for hot water piping.

Water pipes in industrial education laboratories should be no less than one inch in inside diameter (I.D.), except in places where they are reduced for attachment to utilization devices.

Each rise pipe in a water distribution system should be equipped with a vertical air chamber placed at the highest point. An air chamber is a capped section of pipe (of the same diameter as the rise pipe on which it is installed) that is approximately twenty-four inches long. Because it provides a cushion of air to absorb some of the energy of the flow, an air chamber can effectively eliminate the "water hammer" that occurs when the flow of water through a pipe suddenly stops. Additional air chambers should be installed in the hot and cold water lines at each faucet and at all other distribution points.

Water utilization devices purchased for industrial education laboratories should be of the best available quality in order to minimize service interruptions and obtain the lowest overall operating costs. Weight is one evidence of quality. Generally speaking, a heavy unit is higher in quality than a light one. Construction materials provide additional indications of quality. They must be strong, highly resistant to wear and corrosion, and pleasing in appearance. Bronze (with low zinc content) valves and stainless steel or heavily chrome-plated brass faucets, aerators, spray nozzles, and bubblers provide good service.

Toilets and urinals should be made of vitreous glazed china. Bowls and sinks should be constructed of heavy-gauge stainless steel or porcelain enameled cast iron. Acid-proof sinks of precast marble or stone belong in crafts laboratories and others where etching, pickling, and similar activities that make use of corrosive chemicals take place. Single lever faucets are recommended because they offer maximum dispensing convenience and accurate temperature control.

One drinking fountain should be provided for each class of twenty-four or fewer students. Fountains that are recessed in partitions save floor space. Since drinking water temperature should be between 45°F. and 65°F., refrigerated fountains are best. Good quality refrigerators do not produce enough noise to be objectionable, and they present few service problems.

Automatic sprinkler systems give worthwhile protection against fire and can be valuable additions to industrial education laboratories, although laboratory fires have not been a serious problem. Sprinkler systems should be completely separate from regular water distribution systems. Inclusion of a sprinkler system reduces fire insurance costs.

A wet pipe system is effective. It is full of water at all times, and it discharges only through sprinklers opened by heat, thus avoiding unnecessary water damage. In foundries, welding areas, and other places where heat buildup is a natural by-product of class activities, sprinkler plugs that have higher melting points may be needed to compensate for the comparatively high room temperatures that can occur.

A dry pipe system contains compressed air. When heat melts one or more of the sprinkler plugs, loss of air pressure allows normal water pressure to open a valve so that water can flow to the open sprinklers. The valve is called a dry pipe valve.

Most sprinkler systems are automatically activated, but they must be manually deactivated. Therefore they are connected to fire alarms and to fire departments.

An exposed sprinkler system is unsightly, and the pattern of pipes further complicates overhead spaces that contain exhaust system ducts, electrical conduit, light fixtures, and other equipment. Paint can improve the appearance of sprinkler pipes, but it will not completely solve the problem. Therefore suspended ceilings that conceal everything except the sprinklers must be installed with this kind of system.

Oversize drains should be provided in all laboratories. A two-inch diameter drain is the minimum size that should be used with a sink. Every sink drain should be equipped with a water-seal trap and cleanout plug. Floor drains should be at least three inches in diameter. They are needed in hoist and wash areas of automotive laboratories, photographic darkrooms, foundries, ceramics laboratories, and toilet/lavatory rooms. Floor drains should have special sand and grease traps, as well as cleanouts.

Waste stacks, soil stacks, vent stacks, and branches are often constructed of rigid copper pipe assembled with soldered fittings. Smooth inside surfaces give copper pipe a self-scavenging quality that tends to reduce the frequency and seriousness of clogging. In this respect, it is much better than galvanized steel or cast iron pipe.

The cost of the pipe used in an all-copper drain system will far exceed the cost of pipe used in an iron or steel system, but it is less expensive to assemble copper pipe. Consequently the total cost will be moderately higher. Traps, cleanout plugs, and other visible parts of sink drains should be fabricated of chrome-plated brass or stainless steel.

Acrylonitrile-butadiene-styrene (ABS) plastic drain piping also is self-cleaning. It is light in weight, easily fabricated, and durable. In the future, ABS or some other type of plastic may become the most important drain pipe material.

Building drains and building sewers should be constructed of cast iron rather than fiber pipe, ABS pipe, or some other material. Cast iron is relatively expensive, but it lasts indefinitely.

If a water system is to work well in an industrial education laboratory, it must have all of the attributes of a good residential system. In addition, its control and utilization devices should be more heavily constructed, and pipe diameters should be larger. The system should meet requirements of state and local plumbing codes, as well as those of the National Standard Plumbing Code.

GAS

Natural gas is a mixture of hydrocarbons. It is composed primarily of methane and small amounts of ethane, propane, and butane. Traces of nonhydrocarbons such as nitrogen, hydrogen sulfide, carbon dioxide, helium, and water vapor are also present. Gas deposits are found underground with deposits of petroleum and by themselves in porous rock formations.

Natural gas is an excellent fuel that has many uses in industrial education laboratories. Its main advantages are:

1. Excellent combustion
2. Dependability (as regards thermal energy content per unit)
3. Economy (as compared with other common fuels, such as fuel oil and electricity)
4. Ease of control
5. Safety

Although fuel costs fluctuate from time to time and cost differentials between common fuels have diminished, gas remains the least costly source of heat in areas where it is readily available. It provides considerably more thermal energy per dollar than electricity and somewhat more than fuel oil. Bottled liquid propane gas is more expensive than natural gas, but furnaces, ovens, and kilns used in industrial education laboratories can be operated on bottled gas as cheaply as on electricity.

Future developments in the fuel industry, of course, may result in changes in the relative costs of fuels.

Natural gas provides economical heat for soft and hard soldering, foundry activities, heat-treating, certain types of metal finishing, ceramics firing, metal enameling, jewelry casting, light brazing, and plastics forming. Equipment manufacturers have developed a variety of torches, furnaces, ovens, and kilns that effectively utilize gas.

A gas system must be designed to ensure safety and convenience. The cost of redesigning a system can be substantial. Therefore present needs must be met and provision made for future expansion. Construction materials and utilization equipment should be the best obtainable.

Gas appliance manufacturers and gas companies can provide useful information during the design and construction of gas systems. Both types of work, however, are the responsibility of heating contractors whose efforts are governed by state and local building codes.

The floor plan of a laboratory provides the basis for planning a gas system. The designer must know the exact location of each utilization device as well as its Btuh. input requirement. Manufacturers' specifications concerning Btuh. input requirements are usually found on plates attached to their products. For example, the plate on one popular three-burner bench soldering furnace designed for heating soldering coppers and melting solder specifies an input of 39,000 Btuh. when all three burners are in operation. The *total* required gas-supplying capability of a system is the sum of the requirements of all utilization devices to be served plus a predetermined overcapacity to meet expanded future needs.

Individual and total Btuh. input values must be translated into pipe diameters that are appropriate for main lines, branch circuits, and lead lines. In the case of the bench soldering furnace mentioned, a half-inch lead line can supply enough gas to operate it at its full rated capacity. Equipment manufacturers customarily provide information concerning necessary lead pipe diameters. They range from one-quarter inch for a single-burner bench soldering furnace to one and one-half inches for large heat treating, melting, and hardening furnaces. Main lines and branch circuit pipes must be able to supply enough gas so that all utilization devices in a laboratory can be operated simultaneously at maximum temperatures.

The total cost of a gas system can be minimized by using short supply lines and as few bends and junctions as working convenience will permit. All gas-utilizing devices should be located in the same general area of a laboratory, provided this arrangement will not interfere with the effective organization of equipment. A compact system saves space, is economical to install, and is easier to maintain. Compactness, however, should not be considered more important than safety and utility. The width of traffic lanes and the spacing of pieces of equipment can affect a program, but construction economy that results from a reduction in the amount of gas pipe used does not.

Gas can be carried in black iron, copper, and aluminum pipe. Experiments with various plastics are being conducted, and it is possible that plastic piping will be the most useful carrier in the future. At present, however, many building codes do not permit using a piping material other than black iron or copper, even though it can give satisfactory service. Future amendments are likely to make those codes more realistic.

The gas supply line to a building should be equipped with a locking, hand-operated cut-off valve installed inside the building near the point where the pipe connects to the gas meter. Each branch line that serves an industrial education laboratory should have a similar valve located inside the laboratory. Gas supplied to each utilization device should be controlled by a valve in the lead line near the point of connection to the device. Such a control system ensures that gas service to the entire building, to parts of it, or to individual utilization devices can be interrupted while repairs are being made. Inconvenience is minimized in all cases except those requiring total termination of service.

The low point in a gas distribution system and the bottoms of vertical pipes should be equipped with sumps that trap moisture and help to prevent corrosion. A sump is a six-inch vertical pipe (of the same inside diameter as that used in the line) that is capped to permit periodic draining.

Furnace and kiln temperatures can be controlled within broad limits through the use of manual gas-flow regulating valves. Accurate control, however, requires an instrument that both indicates and maintains desired temperatures. Several types are available. One control unit employs a platinum-rhodium thermocouple and a rheostat, which govern blower motor speed and the flow of gas through a diaphragm valve assembly. Another effective indicating controller uses a solenoid valve to regulate the flow of gas to burners. Both units regulate temperature within narrow limits in the range of 0°F. to 3000°F. Thermostatic controls of various kinds can be used to regulate oven temperatures in the range of 100°F. to 650°F.

Four types of operating defects can occur in the temperature control systems of furnaces, kilns, and ovens. They are:

1. Pilot light or electric ignition system failure
2. Interruption of gas service

3. Electrical failure (in blower-type furnaces)
4. Air failure (in blower-type furnaces)

All four conditions can result in dangerous accumulations of unburned gas in combustion chambers. Consequently devices that utilize pilot lights, electric ignition systems, or blowers must be equipped with automatic safety solenoid valves that stop the flow of gas in case of electrical, gas, or air failure. These solenoids should be the manual-reset type.[1]

Gas leakage at valves, joints, connections, and temperature control units can cause fires and explosions. Proper room ventilation helps to prevent gas concentrations from reaching dangerous levels. Leaks can be avoided (and corrected if they occur) through the use of good construction materials and expert workmanship. Gas storage tanks must be kept outside buildings to dissipate leaked gas and to minimize damage should an explosion occur. Large tanks should be installed thirty feet or more away from buildings. Tank controls must be covered with locking shields.

Acetylene is a manufactured gas that is extremely useful as a source of thermal energy in welding, brazing, case-hardening, annealing, flame cutting, and other technical processes. When ignited and mixed with the proper amount of pure oxygen, acetylene produces a flame temperature of approximately 6300°F. Acetylene is a hydrocarbon composed of two parts of hydrogen and two parts of carbon. It is produced during the chemical reaction of calcium carbide and water. It is colorless, foul smelling, and chemically unstable if subjected to pressures greater than 15 psi. Therefore, acetylene is stored in steel cylinders containing a porous material saturated with acetone. Acetone absorbs acetylene without chemical reactions at pressures greater than 15 psi.

An oxyacetylene system should comprise the best available oxygen and acetylene cylinders, regulators, piping (if it is a stationary system), cart (if it is a portable system), hoses, torches, and torch accessories. All components should have the approval of Underwriters' Laboratories, Inc. Each component must be regularly inspected and kept in good repair. The system must be designed to yield maximum operating convenience and safety. Working space and traffic lanes should be generous, and the entire area should be isolated from other laboratory activities.

Regulators are installed on oxygen and acetylene cylinders to provide proper working pressures. Each regulator has two gauges—one to indicate cylinder pressure and the other to indicate working pressure. Single-stage and two-stage regulators are available. A two-stage reg-

---

[1]Johnson Gas Appliance Co., *Catalog No. 62* (Cedar Rapids, Iowa: Johnson Gas Appliance Company), p. 19.

ulator (Fig. 9.7) reduces from cylinder pressure to working pressure in two steps. The first step lowers oxygen pressure to approximately 200 psi and acetylene pressure to 50 psi. The second step further reduces the pressure to whatever is required for the work at hand. A single-stage regulator reduces pressure from normal cylinder pressure to working pressure in one step. As cylinder pressure decreases, a single-stage regulator requires more adjustment than a two-stage regulator. The main advantage of a single-stage regulator is that its price is much less than that of a two-stage unit.

Oxygen cylinders are tall and relatively small in diameter. They are usually painted orange (in accordance with Compressed Gas Association Standards) and labeled "oxygen." Full cylinder pressure is 2150 psi. Acetylene cylinders are painted black and labeled "acetylene." They are

Figure 9.7 *Two-stage pressure regulator.* (Victor Equipment Company)

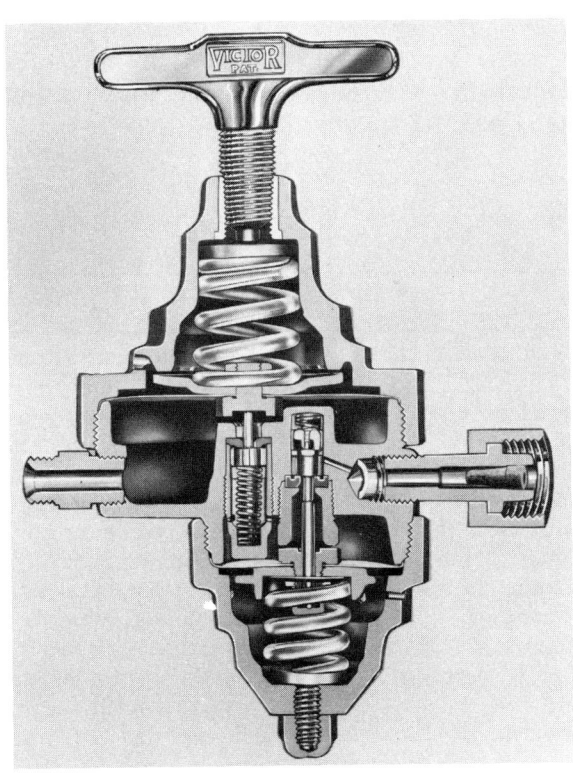

shorter and larger in diameter than comparable sizes of oxygen cylinders. A full cylinder of acetylene is under a pressure of 225 psi.

All cylinders must be protected by pressure-operated safety devices, which are incorporated in their valves. Oxygen and acetylene cylinders may be stored in the laboratory, provided they are kept in a cool (70°F. or less), well ventilated room equipped with an explosionproof door. Direct rays of the sun should not be allowed to strike the cylinders.

COMPRESSED AIR

Compressed air is an important source of energy. When the force holding it in compression is removed, compressed air expands until it exerts normal atmospheric pressure (approximately 14.7 psi at sea level). As it expands, it releases energy that can be used to perform useful work.

Air compression is expressed in pounds of pressure applied to each square inch of the inside surface of a storage tank or other containing device. Manufacturers of compressed air utilization equipment always specify the pressures at which their products should be operated, and builders of air-compressing machinery provide information concerning pressures produced by each of their units.

Table 9.2 USES OF COMPRESSED AIR IN INDUSTRIAL EDUCATION LABORATORIES

Activity	*Laboratory*
Spray finishing	Woods, metals, automotive, general
Parts washer operation	Automotive, metals, general
Abrasive cleaning	Metals, general
Hard soldering	Crafts, metals, general
Metal casting	Crafts, metals, general
Hoist operation	Automotive, general
Spark plug cleaning	Automotive, general
Spark plug testing	Automotive, general
Impact tool operation	Automotive, general
Lubrication	Automotive, general
Tire inflation	Automotive, general
Air brush illustration	Drawing, graphics, general
Spray glazing	Crafts, general
Direct cleaning	All

Compressed air volume (or rate of air flow) is expressed in cubic feet of air movement per minute (cfm). Makers of utilization equipment supply information regarding the air volume requirements of their products, while air compressing machinery manufacturers furnish output specifications for each compressor they make. Usually, pressure and air volume requirements and compressed air production data are marked on small plates attached to pieces of equipment.

Most industrial education laboratories can make good use of compressed air. Table 9.2 summarizes major activities in which compressed air is either essential or highly desirable. For reasons of safety, compressed air should not be used for machine cleanup in metals laboratories. Air-driven fragments of metal can destroy eyesight instantly. It is, in fact, doubtful that compressed air should be used for general cleanup in any laboratory. The relatively great velocity of the air results, more often than not, in a redistribution of waste materials on pieces of equipment rather than in a transfer of these materials to the floor. If air is needed for a specific cleanup task, it can be supplied—with more effort but with greatly increased safety and effectiveness—by hand-operated bellows. However, compressed air is occasionally essential for *complete* removal of dust from mechanisms, parts, and projects, so it should be available. For a compressed air system to be truly useful, it must be planned so that proper pressures and adequate amounts of clean, dry air will be on hand when (and where) needed.

A compressed air system has three major components. They are compressing machinery, a distribution system, and utilization devices. In most cases, compressing machinery includes an air compressor; an electric motor; a drive system; a storage tank; a control system; and a number of protective devices that prevent accidents, make them less serious, and lengthen the service lives of basic units. A distribution system is composed of pipes, control valves, takeoffs, hoses, fittings, pressure indicator-regulators, water legs, supplementary storage tanks, and air-cleaning devices. There are many compressed air utilization devices, and the number will increase as more and more uses for compressed air are found. At present, the most common ones are those used in carrying on activities listed in Table 9.2.

Because the compressor is the heart of any compressed air system, it is important to select a unit that will give good service. Four factors govern the choice of a compressor: minimum required pressure, total volume of air needed, compressor quality, and manufacturer's reputation.

Minimum required pressure is the highest pressure needed by any utilization device to be served by a system, and the compressor must be able to produce it. But there is no advantage in generating pressure that is very much higher than necessary. Doing so, in fact, increases the possibility that air leakage and moisture condensation will become serious problems and that compressor wear will be accelerated. In addition, it will increase power consumption. Pressure requirements in industrial education laboratories are moderate, and it is doubtful that pressures in excess of 125 psi need be provided.

Typical air pressure and volume requirements of a variety of utilization devices are presented in Table 9.3. Manufacturers' recommendations should be observed in specific cases because individual brands may vary with respect to their air needs.

The air volume requirement of a system is based on the sum of the requirements of individual utilization devices. However, estimating initial and future needs is not a very exact procedure because several variables must be taken into account. Thus it is necessary to err in the direction of overcapacity. Air volume requirements specified by manufacturers of utilization devices should be increased by 5 to 10 per cent because they are

Table 9.3 COMPRESSED AIR VOLUME AND PRESSURE REQUIREMENTS OF SELECTED UTILIZATION DEVICES

Utilization Device	*Air Volume (cfm)*
Below 80 psi	
finish spray gun	5.0–10.0
ceramic glaze spray gun	5.0–10.0
air brush	0.5–6.0
parts washer	4.0–6.0
hard soldering torch	5.0–10.0
furnace	13.0–75.0
air hose (tire inflation)	1.0–2.0
80–125 psi	
air hoist	1.0–4.0
abrasive cleaner	2.0–4.0
spark plug cleaner	4.0–6.0
spark plug tester	0.5–1.0
impact wrench	2.0–10.0
blow gun	2.5–15.5
125–200 psi	
lubrication gun	2.0–4.0

Source: *Champion Pneumatic Machinery Co., Inc., Selecting Your Air Compressor (Princeton, Ill.: Champion Pneumatic Machinery Co.), p. 4.*

Table 9.4 COMPRESSED AIR VOLUME COMPUTATION

Utilization Device	Number of Devices	Individual Air Volume Requirement (cfm)	Total Air Volume Requirement (cfm)
Finish spray gun	2	8	16
Air brush	3	3	9
Parts washer	1	5	5
Hard soldering torch	1	8	8
Melting furnace	1	35	35
Spark plug cleaner and tester	1	5	5
Abrasive cleaner	1	3	3
Blow gun	2	9	18
Total			99
+35%			35
Total			134

usually somewhat modest. Leakage and line loss due to friction can also be significant. Good basic design and expert workmanship can reduce these losses, but they cannot be entirely eliminated. Approximately 10 per cent of additional air volume supplying capacity will compensate for leakage and line loss in a good system.[2] In nearly every situation, the demand for compressed air will increase as an industrial education program develops. New utilization devices will be added, and all devices will receive more use. While it is difficult to predict growth, it seems reasonable to assume that after most compressed air systems have been in operation for several years they will be called upon to supply from 10 to 20 per cent more air volume than at first. Finally, in spite of good maintenance, compressor efficiency will slowly diminish. Thus it is evident that in order for a compressed air system to give satisfactory service, the compressor must be able to supply a volume of air that is approximately 35 per cent greater than the basic requirement when the system is built.

The volume of compressed air needed by a hypothetical industrial education department is shown in Table 9.4. Once the total volume and

[2]Champion Pneumatic Machinery Co., Inc., *Compressors, Pumps, and Hi-pressure Washers Catalog* (Princeton, Ill.: Champion Pneumatic Machinery Co.), p. 3.

208 UTILITY SERVICE SYSTEMS

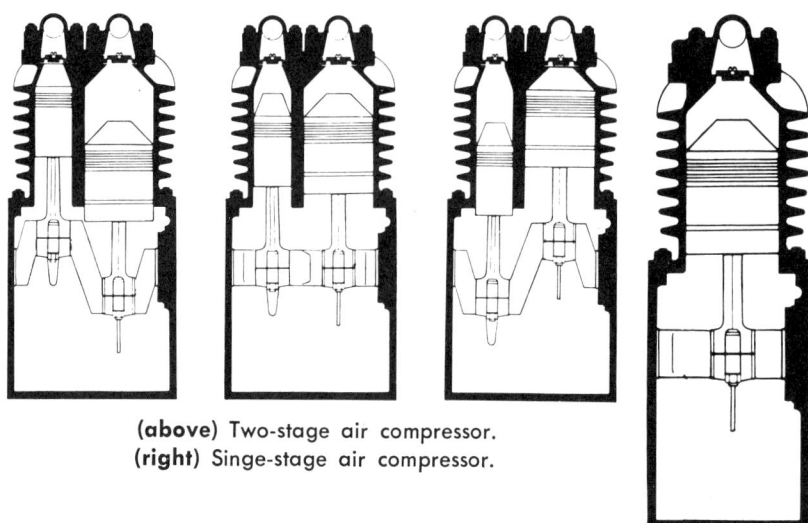

(above) Two-stage air compressor.
(right) Singe-stage air compressor.

Figure 9.8 *Reciprocating air compressor design.* (Amerad Advertising Services, Incorporated)

Figure 9.9 *Dual compressors provide good service for multiple laboratory facilities.* (Amerad Advertising Services, Incorporated)

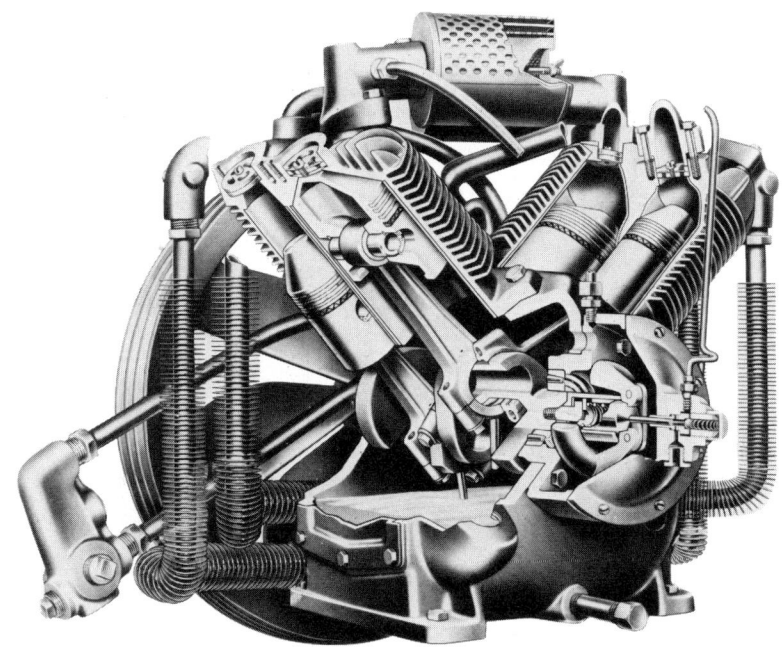

Figure 9.10 *Two-stage reciprocating air compressor.* (Amerad Advertising Services, Incorporated)

the type of service—continuous or intermittent—are known, air-compressing equipment can be selected and pipe sizes can be specified for the distribution system.

The electric motor-driven *reciprocating* air compressor is satisfactory for use in industrial education laboratories. It is comparatively inexpensive, efficient, and long-lasting. Its major weakness is that it is noisy, but this problem can be solved by isolating it from the laboratories it serves.

Reciprocating compressors are available as single-stage or two-stage units (Fig. 9.8). A single-stage compressor uses the downstroke of its piston to draw air through an inlet valve into the cylinder. The outlet valve is closed on the downstroke. On the upstroke, the inlet valve is closed and the outlet valve is open.[3] Air is compressed into the distribution system for immediate use or, more commonly, into a storage tank for subsequent use. The piston acts against line or tank pressure at all times. A single-stage compressor serves best where a medium volume of air and moderate pressures are needed. It is the less costly of the two types and it

[3]Ibid.

Figure 9.11 *Screw-type compressors are quiet and effective.* (Joy Manufacturing Company)

is easier to maintain. But it operates at relatively high cylinder temperatures, consumes more electric power, and has a shorter service life than a two-stage compressor.

In a two-stage compressor, one or more pairs of cylinders compress air in two steps. Each pair includes a larger low pressure cylinder and a smaller high pressure cylinder (see Fig. 9.10). Air is drawn into the low-pressure cylinder, compressed to approximately 45 psi, and passed through a water-cooled intercooler into the high pressure cylinder, where it is compressed to line or tank pressure. The advantage of two-stage design is that the compressor operates at a lower temperature and, as a result, is more efficient and longer-lasting.[4] A two-stage compressor is especially effective where a large volume of air and relatively high pressure are required.

Wherever possible, no reciprocating compressor should be operated at more than three-fourths of maximum speed. Lower speeds increase piston ring, cylinder wall, valve, and bearing life. It is more economical to use two compressors (with both serving the same storage tank) than to

[4]Champion Pneumatic Machinery Co., Inc., *Selecting Your Air Compressor* (Princeton, Ill.: Champion Pneumatic Machinery Co.), p. 4.

COMPRESSED AIR

operate one compressor at capacity. Moreover, two compressors driven by one electric motor and serving a single storage tank make it possible to shut one unit down for maintenance without interrupting the service. A cutoff valve in the line between each compressor and the tank makes partial shutdown possible.

The positive displacement, single-stage, *screw-type* compressor is an efficient, long-lasting machine (Fig. 9.11.) One of the leading manufacturers of air compressing equipment produces a series of screw-type compressors that range in size from 7½ to 300 horsepower (h.p.). The output of this kind of compressor is excellent. For example, a 30 h.p. unit will produce an air volume of 112 cfm and a maximum pressure of 125 psi. It discharges into a 120-gallon storage tank and is designed to operate in ambient temperatures of 50°F. to 105°F.

The basic parts of a typical screw-type compressor include a housing (stator), two screws (rotors), bearings, bearing housings, and end caps.

Figure 9.12 *The rotors are the heart of a screw-type compressor.* (Amerad Advertising Services, Inc.)

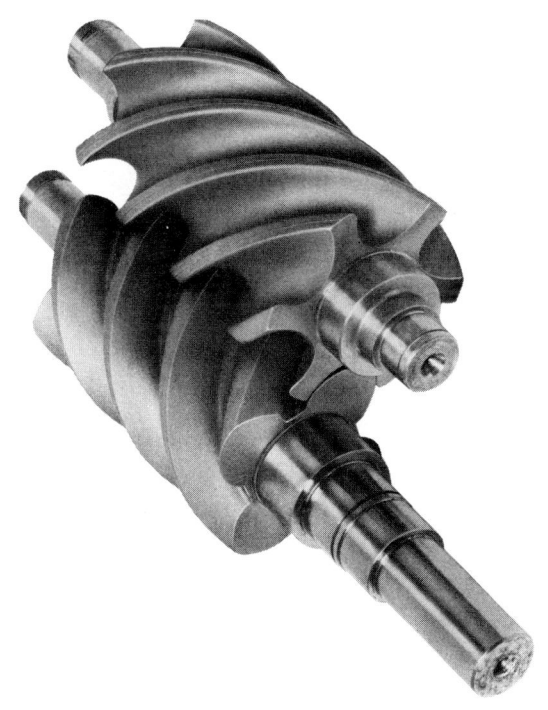

212 UTILITY SERVICE SYSTEMS

The male (driving) rotor has four lobes and turns at a specified input shaft speed. The female (driven) rotor has six lobes; therefore it turns at two-thirds of male rotor speed. Air drawn into the intake port by rotor action is trapped between the threads and compressed as it moves along the threads toward the discharge port (Fig. 9.12).

Since a screw-type compressor is a rotary machine, it operates with very little noise and vibration. This characteristic, as well as its compact size and fine output, make it suitable for use in industrial education laboratories.

Continuous operation is a condition in which the demand for compressed air exceeds 50 per cent of compressing capacity and is steady throughout the work period. Intermittent operation is a condition in which demands for air are infrequent and of short duration. Three types of compressor controls are available: start-stop, constant speed, and dual. Start-stop controls are used where the demand for air is intermittent. A constant speed control runs a compressor continuously and maintains a uniform tank pressure so that all compressed air utilization devices can be in steady operation. A constant speed control offers economies in

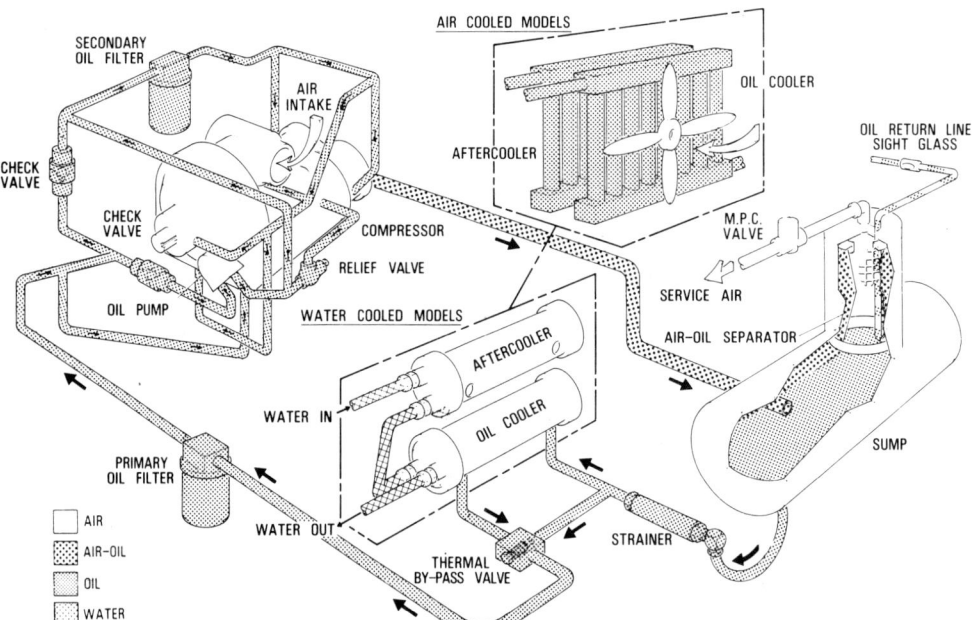

Figure 9.13 *Air/oil/water flow—screw-type compressor.* (Joy Manufacturing Company)

COMPRESSED AIR

electric current consumption and in the cost of control equipment, but maintenance costs may be somewhat higher. A dual control is a flexible unit that permits constant speed compressor operation during peak loads and start-stop operation the balance of the time.

For the most part, demands of industrial education laboratories for compressed air occur intermittently and do not involve unusually high pressures and large air volumes. Therefore, if a reciprocating air compressor is chosen, two recommendations are:

1. An individual industrial education laboratory should be equipped with a two-stage, two- or four-cylinder compressor rated at ½ to 10 h.p., depending on need. A start-stop control should be provided, and storage tank capacity should be 60–120 gallons.
2. A multiple-laboratory department should be served by dual, heavy-duty compressors that compress air into a single 120-gallon storage tank. Each compressor should be a two-stage, four-cylinder unit rated at 7½ to 10 h.p. A start-stop control should be employed. If a single-stage, screw-type compressor is chosen, it should be a 7½–40 h.p. unit equipped with a dual control and a 120-gallon storage tank.

Information presented in Tables 9.5 and 9.6 can be used to select a reciprocating compressor that will meet a specific air volume require-

Table 9.5 SELECTOR CHART — SINGLE-STAGE SYSTEM

Continuous Operation		*Intermittent Operation*	
Free Air Needed by System (cfm)	*Reciprocating Compressor Needed (h.p.)*	*Free Air Needed by System (cfm)*	*Reciprocating Compressor Needed (h.p.)*
up to 1.9	½	up to 6.6	½
2.9–3.0	¾	6.7–10.5	¾
3.1–3.9	1	10.6–13.6	1
4.0–5.8	1½	13.7–20.3	1½
5.9–7.6	2	20.4–26.6	2
7.7–10.2	3	26.7–32.5	3
10.3–18.0	5	32.6–38.0	5

Source: *Champion Pneumatic Machinery Co., Inc., Selecting Your Air Compressor (Princeton, Ill.: Champion Pneumatic Machinery Co.), p. 5.*

Table 9.6 SELECTOR CHART — TWO-STAGE SYSTEM

Continuous Operation		Intermittent Operation	
Free Air Needed by System (cfm)	*Reciprocating Compressor Needed (h.p.)*	*Free Air Needed by System (cfm)*	*Reciprocating Compressor Needed (h.p.)*
up to 4.2	1	up to 14.7	1
4.3–6.4	1½	14.8–22.4	1½
6.5–8.7	2	22.5–30.4	2
8.8–13.2	3	30.5–46.2	3
13.3–20.0	5	46.3–60.0	5
20.1–29.2	7½	60.1–73.0	7½
29.3–40.0	10	73.1–100.0	10
40.1–60.0	15	100.1–150.0	15
60.1–80.0	20	150.1–200.0	20

Source: *Champion Pneumatic Machinery Co., Inc., Selecting Your Air Compressor (Princeton, Ill.: Champion Pneumatic Machinery Co.), p. 5.*

ment. Based on these values, the compressors chosen for the hypothetical multiple-laboratory facility described earlier will be dual, two-stage, four-cylinder compressors rated at 7½ h.p. each.

In addition to the design qualities discussed, reciprocating air compressors for industrial education laboratories should possess the following features:

Figure 9.14 *Oil monitor: (left) low oil position; (right) normal operating position.* (Amerad Advertising Services, Incorporated)

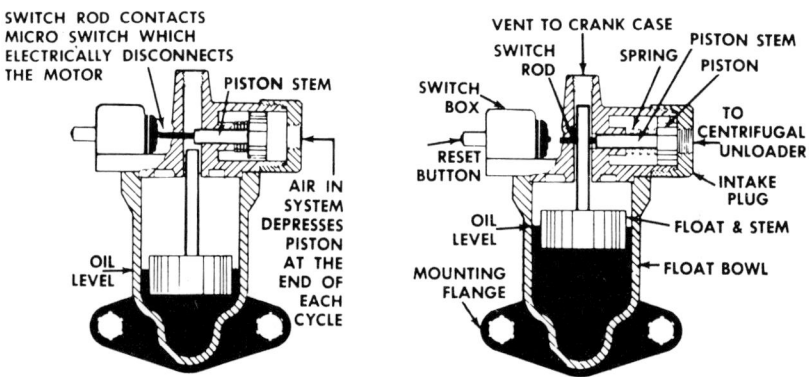

1. An unloader that ensures no-load starts by releasing the compression in the cylinders, intercooler, and aftercooler when the compressor stops
2. An oil cut-out switch (Fig. 9.14) that shuts off the motor and prevents the compressor from starting whenever the oil level in the crankcase falls below a predetermined point (the switch should have a manual reset)
3. A large oil reservoir that helps to maintain lower oil operating temperatures
4. A multiple V-belt drive
5. A rapid-acting belt-tension-adjusting device
6. A belt guard
7. An effective air cleaner to filter air drawn into the compressor
8. Replaceable piston pin bushings, connecting rod bearings, and crankshaft bearings
9. Easily removable valve assemblies
10. A fan-type flywheel
11. A water-cooled aftercooler that reduces the temperature of the air before it goes into the storage tank (reducing the temperature has the effect of increasing the capacity of the tank, since moisture condenses in the aftercooler before it reaches the tank and pipes)
12. Electrical apparatus approved by Underwriters' Laboratories, Inc.
13. 230-volt, three-phase operation
14. A vibration switch that shuts off the motor whenever compressor vibration reaches a predetermined intensity (the switch should have a manual reset)
15. A thermal overload switch that shuts off the motor whenever compressor temperature reaches a predetermined level (the switch should have a manual reset)
16. A thermal overload switch that shuts off the motor whenever motor temperature reaches a predetermined level (the switch should have a manual reset)
17. A storage tank approved by the American Society of Mechanical Engineers (ASME) National Board for 200 psi working pressure and tested to 400 psi
18. A storage tank drain—either manual or automatic
19. A storage tank safety valve set to function at 250 psi
20. A storage tank service valve that permits manual release of pressure
21. A storage tank pressure indicator that registers pressures in the 0–300 psi range at 5 lb. intervals

Compressed air can be distributed by galvanized steel pipe assembled with threaded fittings or by rigid copper pipe having soldered or compression fittings. Either type of pipe is satisfactory if assembled so that it can stand testing to 400 psi. Copper pipe offers the advantages of greater resistance to corrosion, smaller outside diameters, less weight, and easier assembly.

A compressed air distribution system must be free of leaks, since even a small leak can waste up to 4 h.p. at the compressor. There should be relatively few fittings in order to minimize the number of potential leak points and to reduce pressure losses due to pipe friction. The pressure drop between the main storage tank and the most distant utilization device should not exceed 4 psi.

Exposed pipes are often preferable. They detract from the appearance of the laboratory, but they make it easier to repair or modify a distribution system. It is essential that all pipes be adequate in diameter, since undersize diameters can greatly reduce the effectiveness of utilization devices. Fortunately the additional cost of larger pipes is nominal.

Table 9.7 PIPE SIZES FOR COMPRESSED AIR LINES

Air (cfm)	Length of Pipe Lines (ft.)							
	25	50	75	100	150	200	250	300
1	½	½	½	½	½	½	½	½
2	½	½	½	½	½	½	½	½
3	½	½	½	½	½	½	½	½
5	½	½	½	½	½	½	½	½
10	½	½	½	¾	¾	¾	¾	¾
15	½	¾	¾	¾	¾	¾	¾	¾
20	¾	¾	¾	¾	¾	¾	¾	¾
25	¾	¾	¾	¾	¾	1	1	1
30	¾	¾	¾	¾	1	1	1	1
35	¾	¾	1	1	1	1	1	1
40	¾	1	1	1	1	1	1	1
50	1	1	1	1	1	1	1	1
60	1	1	1	1	1¼	1¼	1¼	1¼
70	1	1	1	1	1¼	1¼	1¼	1¼

Source: *Champion Pneumatic Machinery Co., Inc., Selecting Your Air Compressor (Princeton, Ill.: Champion Pneumatic Machinery Co.), p. 7.*

Pipe diameter can be increased 50 per cent at an increase in installed cost of 20 per cent or less. Each main pipe in a distribution system should be at least as large in diameter as the storage tank outlet. Long runs and large air volumes require increased pipe diameters. Table 9.7 shows the relationship between air volume, pipe length, and pipe diameter.

The following minimum pipe diameters are recommended for multiple industrial education laboratory distribution systems in which the air volume is 150 cfm or less and the pressure is no more than 125 psi:

1. *Main pipe from storage tank to each laboratory*—2 inches for automotive, woods, building construction, metals, and general; 1 inch for drafting, graphics, crafts, electricity/electronics, and refrigeration
2. *Major loop runs within each laboratory*—1½ inches for automotive, woods, building construction, metals, and general; ¾ inch for drafting, graphics, crafts, electricity/electronics, and refrigeration
3. *Secondary loop runs and crossovers*—1¼ inches for automotive, woods, building construction, metals, and general; ¾ inch for drafting, graphics, crafts, electricity/electronics, and refrigeration
4. *Takeoffs*—¾ inch for all types

All pipes must be firmly supported with nonrigid supports in order to minimize the generation and transmission of noise. Pipes not correctly supported can pulsate.

Air hoses used to connect takeoffs to utilization devices must be designed to promote an efficient flow of air. Inadequate diameters, poorly designed fittings, and excessive hose lengths can sharply reduce air volume. Heavy-gauge, fabric-reinforced rubber tubing is recommended. It should be highly resistant to moisture and petroleum products. Hose reels add to working convenience and keep hoses in better condition. All hoses should be as short as possible — preferably less than twelve feet in length — since hose friction is relatively high. Diameters should rarely be smaller than three-eighths of an inch. Fittings must have smooth interior surfaces and diameters that are equal to or greater than the hoses they assemble. Numerous T-type takeoffs for hoses should be provided in all parts of a laboratory. They should be installed on the top sides of pipes to reduce the amount of moisture entering the hoses.

The effectiveness of a compressed air distribution system can be improved by installing a supplementary eighty-gallon storage tank at the point farthest away from the compressor. The supplementary tank will

218 UTILITY SERVICE SYSTEMS

help to equalize the pressure throughout the system, make it possible to handle large short-term demands that may occur in foundries and other areas, and reduce the amount of moisture in the pipes. A supplementary tank must be equipped with a drain.

Water legs should be installed at regular intervals in a distribution system. A water leg is a short vertical section of pipe (usually twelve inches or less in length) installed on the underside of a horizontal pipe. It provides a place where moisture can collect. Each water leg should be equipped with a valve so that it can be drained when necessary. The pipes

Figure 9.15 *Types of compressed air distribution systems.* (Amerad Advertising Services, Incorporated)

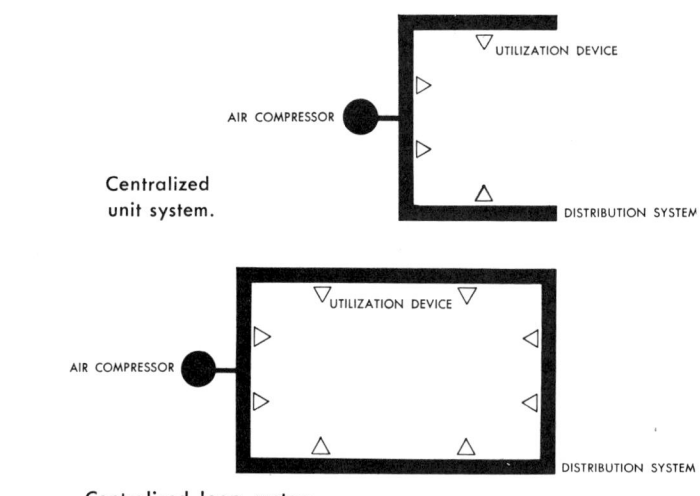

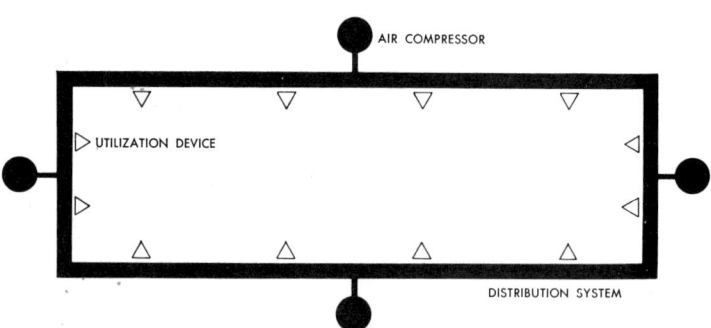

in a distribution system should be slightly pitched from the compressor or main storage tank to the utilization devices to ensure that drainage is across the water legs.

Three types of compressed air distribution systems are in use. They are the centralized unit, centralized loop, and decentralized loop systems (see Fig. 9.15).[5] A centralized unit system includes one compressor–main storage tank unit that serves all utilization devices. A centralized loop system also makes use of one compressor and main storage tank, but the pipes form a complete loop around the area served. Air flows in two directions and pressure is more nearly equal in all parts of the system. A decentralized loop system utilizes two or more compressor–main storage tank units — one for every major work area. However, each compressor-tank unit serves the entire system. Pressure equalization is excellent, and peak demands can be handled with ease. A decentralized loop system is, in fact, two or more centralized loop systems connected to form one large loop.

A decentralized loop system is recommended where a compressed air system must serve a very large area, such as an entire school. Both loop systems operate with less compressor action and consequently consume less electricity than a centralized unit system. Pipes that serve as cross-connectors should be installed approximately every one hundred feet. They add to the effectiveness of a loop system by permitting air to flow more freely in two directions.

Centralized loop systems are recommended for single- and multiple-laboratory facilities. If a system is to function well:

1. The compressor–main storage tank unit should be installed in a cool, dry, well ventilated, soundproof room located near the center of the loop but not in any laboratory.
2. Ample working space should be provided around the compressor-tank unit. It should be at least thirty-six inches from walls and partitions. The flywheel should face a wall or partition.
3. A cut-off valve should be placed in the pipe just beyond the main storage tank to facilitate maintenance procedures.
4. Each laboratory should have its own master cut-off valve located inside the laboratory in an easily reached place.
5. Cut-off valves should be installed just beyond the takeoffs in lead lines that serve the various utilization devices.
6. Utilization devices should be controlled by pressure

[5]Ibid.

indicator-regulators wherever necessary. Spray guns and hard soldering torches require regulators because air pressure is a critical factor. Certain other devices, such as spark plug testers, have their own built-in pressure indicator-regulators. Blow guns are not usually regulated except in situations in which full line pressure is too high for delicate cleaning jobs.

7. Oil and moisture extractors must be installed in lines supplying utilization devices that require unusually clean, dry air. Extractors should have replaceable cartridge elements capable of trapping minute quantities of oil and water as well as solid particles of microscopic size.

A compressed air system is more complex than it seems. All parts of it — compression equipment, control devices, the distribution system, and utilization devices — must be properly designed, and the system must be constructed with care if it is to perform satisfactorily. Maintenance is important and more extensive in nature than it is for any other utility service system. Periodically, it is necessary to drain accumulated water from the storage tank, change filter cartridges, examine the system for leakage, adjust drive belt tension, check the compressor oil level, calibrate control and indicating devices, and inspect the hoses. Major overhaul of the compressor will eventually become necessary. Finally, utilization devices must be kept clean and in good repair.

FOR FURTHER READING

Air Power Division, Joy Manufacturing Co. *Joy Twistair Screw Compressor Model TA-030*. Operator's Manual and Parts List. Michigan City, Ind.: Joy Manufacturing Co.

Air Power Division, Joy Manufacturing Co. *WG Series Joy Air Compressors*. Michigan City, Ind.: Joy Manufacturing Co.

Champion Pneumatic Machinery Co. *Compressors, Pumps and Hi-pressure Washers*. Princeton, Ill.: Champion Pneumatic Machinery Co.

Champion Pneumatic Machinery Co. *Selecting Your Compressor*. Princeton, Ill.: Champion Pneumatic Machinery Co.

General Electric. *Aluminum Plug-in Flex-a-power Busways*. Plainville, Conn.: General Electric.

General Electric. *Armor-clad Feeder Busway*. Plainville, Conn.: General Electric.

General Electric. *High Resistance Current-limiting Busways*. Plainville, Conn.: General Electric.

McGuinness, William J., and Stein, Benjamin. *Building Technology: Mechanical and Electrical Systems*. New York: John Wiley & Sons, 1977.

McPartland, J. *Constructing Electrical Systems*. New York: McGraw-Hill, 1964.

National Association of Plumbing-heating-cooling Contractors and American Society of Plumbing Engineers. *National Standard Plumbing Code*.

National Fire Protection Association. *National Electrical Code*. Boston: National Fire Protection Association.

Palumbo, Anthony. "Brainstorming Shop Flexibility." *School Shop*, April 1976, p. 60.

Ramsey, Charles G., and Sleeper, Harold R. *Architectural Graphic Standards*. 6th ed. rev. New York: John Wiley & Sons, 1970.

Snyder, James F., and Hales, James A. "Trailblazing to 2016 in Shop Planning." *School Shop*, April 1976, p. 80.

Sumption, Merle R., and Landes, Jack L. *Planning Functional School Buildings*. New York: Harper and Brothers Publishers, 1957.

White, Mark. "Portable Power Center." *Industrial Arts and Vocational Education*, March 1972, p. 56.

10
Acquisition of Equipment, Materials, and Contractual Services

INTRODUCTION

Early in the second part of the planning process, as noted in Chapter 2, it is necessary to take steps to acquire items and services for the projected program. Equipment for construction activities, test procedures, teaching, and laboratory maintenance must be purchased. Materials to be used in project construction, instructional media, and maintenance and services essential to the proper installation of equipment and preparation of the laboratory also must be obtained.

Wise selection of equipment, materials, and services helps to ensure smooth laboratory operation and to eliminate program-disrupting equipment breakdowns and equipment and supply shortages. It increases the probability that the laboratory will be one in which students will like to work and the teacher will enjoy teaching. In addition, it will make the work environment much safer and make possible a satisfactory range of work.

Poor selection, on the other hand, is likely to result in the creation of a laboratory that permits only a rather limited program and provides a work environment that is neither very safe nor very satisfying.

The only valid basis for choosing *types* of equipment, materials, and services is the nature and scope of the educational program being planned. The educational philosophy of the industrial teacher should have a great effect on the choices made because he or she will have the most to do with operating the program. For example, if a teacher who is responsible for planning a general crafts laboratory believes that centrifugal casting is an activity that will help to meet the goals of the program, the appropriate equipment and materials should be acquired. If not, the money should be spent on items that offer greater learning potential. The choice-making process is as simple as that — and as demanding. The practice of equipping a laboratory with nearly everything available, regardless of need, has never been defensible.

Once the decision has been made to purchase a particular type of item, the selection process begins. In most cases, cost should be a minor selection criterion. No one can argue seriously that reasonable standards of safety, durability, accuracy, operating convenience, appearance, and versatility should be compromised to save money. But high quality and high cost should not be equated. The difference in cost between a piece of equipment that is well designed and soundly constructed and one that is not may be slight or nonexistent. An inferior item may even be sold at a price higher than that of an item of good quality. The old saying "the customer gets what he pays for" is generally true, but there are many exceptions to it. Consumer information publications exist to point this out.

Four selection practices should be avoided, because they are not effective. The first is to allow the offerings of a single general supplier to determine the types and brands of equipment and the materials ordered. As reliable as most are, such companies do not carry all types of products or all competing brands; consequently the planner's alternatives are fewer and costs may be increased. Even worse, some companies feature lines of equipment that are distinctly inferior to but not necessarily cheaper than competing lines that they do not handle.

It is equally erroneous to consider only the best-advertised "name" brands. Frequently, less-known makes offer greater value.

Nor is it wise for a teacher to select certain types and brands of equipment simply because they were present in the teacher education laboratories in which he or she was a student. Such equipment may or may not have been well selected, and it might have been in use for a variety of reasons, not all of them good. Some pieces acquired through surplus sales, for example, might have been intended for temporary service only.

Finally, it is a mistake to equip a laboratory with a great many brands of equipment in order to achieve brand variety or to purchase very few brands in an attempt to promote some sort of uniformity or to make it easier to obtain repair parts and services. The best of a particular type of equipment should always be sought without regard to brands already selected.

EQUIPMENT SELECTION

Broadly speaking, the three best guides to proper equipment selection are function, manufacturer's services, and appearance. Industrial designers view a valid design as one that presents a fine blend of functional qualities and appearance and can be sold at a reasonable price. The role of appearance as a contributor to good teaching/learning environments should not be underestimated. Function, however, is paramount. Manufacturers' services are important in helping to provide *continuing* good function.

An accurate comparison of the functional and aesthetic qualities of competing brands of equipment can be made if the industrial teacher begins by identifying features that are essential. Next, a comprehensive checklist of such features should be developed and used to construct a profile of each brand. Finally, the profiles of the several brands must be compared. Sometimes, one brand will be obviously superior. If competing brands exhibit similar strengths and weaknesses, however, evaluations made by impartial testing organizations and the past experience of the teacher can be helpful in making decisions.

The expression "functional validity," as it applies to a piece of equipment, implies possession of a number of qualities that relate both to its physical construction and to its appropriateness in a teaching-learning situation. Equipment is placed in laboratories to assist in the educative process. By using and studying it, students learn operating techniques, work procedures, and applications of scientific principles. They also become skilled performers and develop certain desirable attitudes and appreciations. Function, therefore, must be evaluated in terms of potential for student development and not solely as an aid to production processes.

A piece of equipment that is educationally worthwhile makes its operating principle evident. Automatic operating devices that hide function should not be included unless safety or accuracy requires them. Such devices can even inhibit the development of craftsmanship by making operations obscure and impersonal, thereby preventing the development of the bond that often exists between a skilled person and his or her equipment. The design of each piece of equipment should make it as easy as possible for the teacher to explain what really happens during its operation.

A functional item of equipment is capable of doing the job it was designed to do. Its potential accuracy is high; good craftsmanship and interest in creative work are not often developed using inferior tools, such as ripping fences that cannot be correctly aligned, indexing mechanisms that do not lock securely, dials that cannot be calibrated for absolute accuracy, machine tables that are too small, and pyrometers that do not indicate temperatures precisely. Functional excellence means also that the piece is well matched to the age, size, strength, sex, handedness, and degree of muscular coordination of those who will use it. Students must be able to work safely and accurately within a suitably wide range of activities. They must be able to make necessary operating adjustments conveniently, exactly, and without danger of accident.

Ostensibly similar units of equipment often vary widely with respect to ease and accuracy of operation, and competent selection requires answers to the following questions:

1. Are handles, grips, levers, electrical switches, and other controls large enough and shaped to fit the hand (or foot, if foot-operated)? Are they corrosionproof? Are nonslip surface textures used wherever necessary? Are operating devices placed to facilitate their use and to make accidental operation all but impossible? Is a left-handed model available at the same price?
2. Can the piece of equipment be operated smoothly? Do operating devices work easily and accurately? For example, are screw threads, hinges, latches, lever locks, and set screws well fitted?
3. Are dials, gauges, and scales conveniently positioned? Do their graphic designs make them easy to read?
4. Are adjustments for basic accuracy made by built-in devices, instead of detachable tools? If detachable tools are used, are they furnished at no extra cost?
5. What degree of accuracy is possible in making adjustments for the various operations?
6. Is the work surface sufficiently large to allow accurate work without hampering the efforts of smaller students?

EQUIPMENT SELECTION

7. Are smaller dimensions, such as lower bench surface heights, available without sacrifice of quality or functional features?
8. Are cabinet bases and mechanism housings designed so that they do not interfere with operators' movements?
9. Is the breadth of operation sufficient to meet classroom needs? Can all normal operations and all, or most, special operations be performed?
10. Are effective guards and housings furnished as standard equipment? If not, are they available as options?

In choosing equipment for a school laboratory, safety is a prime consideration. Increasingly demanding legal interpretations of liability are forcing school districts to examine all phases of their operations. More important, the physical and emotional damage that can result from an accident must be avoided wherever possible. No one wants a student to suffer permanent injury. Good equipment selection plays a vital part in promoting safety.

It is evident that most pieces of equipment, because of their purposes and because they will be used by human beings, can never be entirely free of hazards, but there *are* important differences in design that make some pieces safer than others for student use. To the extent that safety is based on equipment design, the same expenditure of money can produce a relatively safe working environment or build danger into it.

Guards and housings are used to protect operators from mechanisms and from injuries suffered at points of operation. They enclose gears, belts, pulleys, and shafts, and they partially or fully enclose cutting edges and abrasive surfaces. Most pieces of equipment provide adequate protection from their mechanisms; fewer are effective in protecting against injury at the point of operation. Unfortunately, machines such as drill presses and lathes cannot be fully guarded at the point of operation without making efficient operation inordinately difficult or even impossible.

It is highly desirable that guards be supplied as integral parts of pieces of equipment. If the installation of a guard is made optional by a manufacturer, it will not always be purchased, and it will seldom function as well as a guard that is planned as an important part of the total design.

A well designed guard is durable, simple in construction, readily adjustable, easily activated, and positive in action. It adjusts automatically to the work and causes no real interference with production or machine maintenance. A protective device that requires extensive adjustment each time it is used (or each time the nature of the work

Figure 10.1 *Effective machinery guards prevent many injuries.* (Oliver Machinery Company)

changes during a period of continuous operation) should be avoided. It will afford little protection because it will quickly fall into disuse. The guard on the typical jointer is an example of excellent design that meets all of the criteria listed. The usual table saw guard, on the other hand, meets few of these qualifications.

The way in which a piece of equipment is designed and built electrically is of great concern to the safety-minded industrial teacher. Reputable manufacturers usually do well in this regard and, in fact, welcome new ways of making electrical systems safer. These qualities are indicative of good electrical design:

1. Power options that permit operation in any electrical distribution system and ensure satisfactory operation throughout the equipment's rated capacity
2. Heavy-duty, rubber-covered power cords
3. Three-conductor power cords equipped with three-prong,

EQUIPMENT SELECTION

grounding-type plugs (removal of ground prongs or the use of adaptors that bypass ground prongs should be avoided)
4. Electrical plugs constructed of heavy rubber or durable, high-impact-strength plastic (all connections must be strongly made)
5. Power cords and other wires protected from abrasion by accurate adjustment of length, proper location, and the use of plastic or rubber grommets where wires pass through metal surfaces
6. Power-cord storage devices that do not damage cords
7. Wiring that can carry peak loads for reasonable periods of time
8. Circuit breakers incorporated in the designs of electric motors or switches
9. Consuming devices, such as electric motors, insulated from equipment housings and frames
10. Electric motors and other heat-producing devices adequately ventilated (where necessary, mechanical ventilation should be provided)
11. Shielded electrical connections
12. High-impact-strength plastic housings (where they can be used to advantage) that eliminate danger of shock

The care that a manufacturer exercises in the construction of equipment also has a direct and noticeable effect on safety. Quality control that eliminates sharp edges, sharply pointed corners, burrs, rough welds, improperly conditioned cutting edges, overtightness, overlooseness, splintery wood surfaces, and other defects in materials and workmanship can do much to decrease the accident potential of equipment. All moving parts should be designed so that they are smooth and free of projections. Set screws, bolt heads, sharp edges, and corners that protrude from moving parts can inflict painful and sometimes serious injuries.

Wear begins the first time a piece of equipment is used, but good design includes an effective lubrication system that retards the rate of deterioration. The best systems make maximum use of sealed lubricant reservoirs and self-lubricating materials. The number of points needing periodic lubrication is kept to a minimum. Such systems also make provision for convenient lubrication of points that cannot be permanently lubricated at the factory. Common means of doing this include grease fittings and grease cups, felt wicks that store large quantities of oil, adequate oil sump sizes, simple methods of determining lubricant level (especially the visible level method), snap caps to keep foreign materials out of lubricant reservoirs, properly designed oil slingers and oil pumps, large, easily-reached lubricant filler holes, and lubricant drains that can be opened easily and closed tightly.

A prospective purchaser should check pieces of equipment carefully for lubricant leaks. Seepage present in demonstration or display equipment may be indicative of design faults that will be difficult to correct.

Design features that facilitate laboratory cleanup and the maintenance of equipment are important in perpetuating good function. Each unit of equipment should be planned so that it eliminates or minimizes accumulations of waste materials at critical points and so that normal wear and minor damage can be easily compensated by adjustment. Repair procedures for equipment that is worn beyond the point of adjustment should be simple, effective, and inexpensive. Affirmative answers to these questions are furnished by a valid equipment design:

1. Is the base enclosed to the floor to make cleanup easy?
2. Is the major housing designed for attachment to a central or portable waste collection system? If the equipment is portable, is a waste collection system furnished as an integral part?
3. Does the base house the electric motor so that it remains clean yet fully accessible for service, adjustment, and lubrication? Do mechanism housings meet this qualification?
4. Can interior spaces, such as the base cabinet of a table saw, be cleaned without difficulty?
5. Can accuracy be maintained by adjustment wherever necessary? For example, can dials, gauges, and scales be accurately calibrated with a minimum of effort? Can excessive clearance in adjusting threads be easily removed?
6. Can parts be readily removed without resort to special tools? Are disassembly and reassembly easy? Are the spaces in which hands will work while making adjustments and repairs large enough?
7. Can worn parts be replaced as units so that the major repair procedures involve removal and installation rather than reconstruction?
8. If necessary, will basic overhaul — including remachining — be feasible?
9. Is an easily operated leveling device included?

Each piece of equipment should have the virtue of simplicity of mechanical design. At the same time, it must be complex enough to be entirely satisfactory with regard to its basic construction and operational qualities. Unnecessary complexity, however, is of no advantage in laboratory equipment. It does not contribute to good function, and it leads directly to higher manufacturing and maintenance costs. Certain of the manifestations of mechanical simplicity can be set forth as follows: little or no overfunction (the piece of equipment should not include elaborate provision for performing operations it will seldom, if ever, be called upon to perform); few basic parts; a minimum of levers, knobs, gauges, clamps, and other operating and installation devices; and simply made parts.

Most often, the advantages of unit design outweigh those of multiple-function design. If a manufacturer has combined functions skillfully in order to improve the versatility of a product, it may prove beneficial to laboratory programs. But if additional functions have been added to increase sales by making it possible to claim rather illusory advantages, there is little gain. A combination knife–screwdriver–corkscrew–leather awl–bottle opener may be convenient at times, but it is overly complex and it performs the function of each separate tool in an inferior way.

Many pieces of equipment must be designed to perform more than one operation of the same general type and/or more than one size of the same operation. For example, a table saw must be able to crosscut, rip, dado, and do other sawing jobs, while a mortiser must be capable of cutting several sizes of mortises. Switching such a machine from one operation to another or from one size of operation to another frequently requires an operator to make changes in sleeves, collets, spindles, holders, and other parts. It should be possible to do so easily and without danger to the machine, the parts, or the person.

In some types of equipment, portability is a distinct advantage. Where it is, casters, elevating devices, brakes, and leveling mechanisms should be incorporated as standard equipment by manufacturers. Carrying cases for smaller pieces often maximize the benefits of portability. Cases should store their contents safely and be capable of being loaded and unloaded easily. Durability and the inclusion of a strong lock are other functional qualities of a satisfactory carrying case.

Materials utilized in equipment for school programs must be capable of withstanding intensive and protracted service. They should meet industrial quality standards. Aluminum should not be used where the properties of cast iron are needed. Aluminum is generally not suitable for use in machine tables, fences, and ways; hand plane beds; most screw threads; and other applications where normal abrasion will cause rapid wear. Equipment constructed of less expensive and inherently less durable materials should not be rejected out-of-hand, however. In some instances it is possible to achieve substantially the same function at less cost by means of materials substitution. Galvanized steel, for example, is much less expensive than stainless steel but may be adequately serviceable where it will not come in contact with corrosive or abrasive agents.

Components should be considered to be construction materials and evaluated as such. A manufacturer's use of standardized parts — threads, bearings, keys, electric motors, etc. — purchased from outstanding makers contributes to good design by improving function and assisting teachers in obtaining repair parts.

Not easily recognized, but nonetheless important to good design, is the degree to which a manufacturer has succeeded in removing useless weight from a product. Little is gained by incorporating more material than the structural needs of a piece demand. Among contemporary manufacturers, there is a noticeable trend in the direction of developing pieces of equipment that are lighter, more compact, more functional, better looking, and occasionally less expensive than previous models.

Figure 10.2 *Standardized parts improve designs.* (Clausing Corporation, Machine Tool Group)

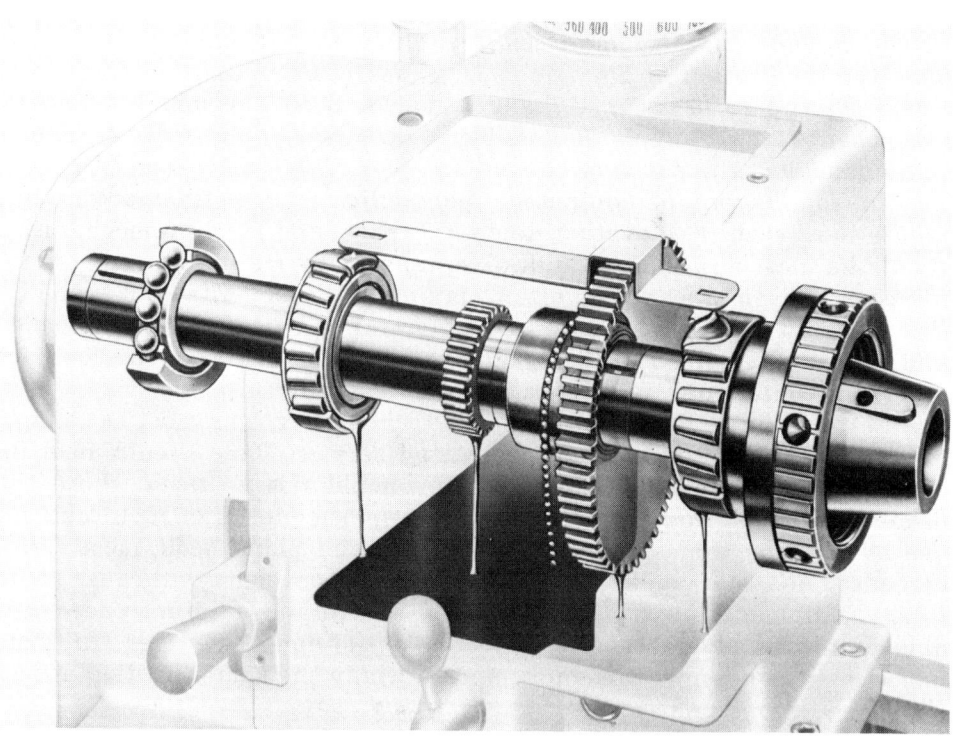

Weight removal requires astute design work. An unusual amount of vibration or a high noise level may reveal that a manufacturer has not used enough material. Other indications of this shortcoming are the impossibility of really tight assembly (as in the case of a housing that lacks sufficient fasteners), unwanted flexibility of parts, and undersize work surfaces that do not permit accurate work.

Acoustic design is an important part of mechanical design. Excessive noise and/or vibration can be distracting, even injurious to hearing; and it can lead to inaccurate work and accidents. A short period of operation, especially under normal work conditions, is the best way of determining whether or not a piece of equipment runs quietly.

A builder — beginning with a base of good theoretical design — must produce accurate parts and assemble and finish them carefully to ensure satisfactory function. The way in which a manufactured product is executed at the factory can be an accurate indicator of its functional validity. Evidence of carelessness in some aspect of its construction should cause the person who is selecting equipment to examine *all* aspects with great care.

General conditions that signify good manufacture should be kept in mind by the prospective buyer, and each piece of equipment being considered for purchase should be closely inspected to determine the level of skill that went into its manufacture. Good workmanship speaks of the pride that a company takes in its products. It indicates an interest not only in sales but also in the welfare of the consumer, and it is apparent in many visible conditions, such as:

1. Exact alignment of mating parts and maintenance of close tolerances
2. Work surfaces that are ground smoothly and accurately
3. An absence of blowholes in castings, unremoved casting flash, disfiguring tool marks, spoiled threads, damage to surfaces and finishes caused by careless assembly, and other surface imperfections
4. Tight assembly
5. Complete assembly in which no fasteners or other parts have been omitted through carelessness
6. Finish well applied: no runs, voids, or other defects
7. Parts properly lubricated at the factory
8. Adequate preparation for immediate operation

Ideally, items intended for school use should have highly durable finishes that are pleasing in appearance, easily cleaned, and low in light reflectance.

A high quality semigloss enamel, applied in several thin coats over a well-cleaned and suitably primed surface and baked for hardness and wear resistance, provides a good finish for any piece of equipment. The available colors should fit recognized coordinated color systems. Such color coding improves both function and appearance, and avoiding the need to repaint newly acquired items of equipment in order to fit them into laboratory color systems means great savings of time and money and less disruption of classes.

Appearance. There is no reason for an item of laboratory equipment to be unattractive and out-of-touch with contemporary design standards. A competent designer does not perceive a problem of design as a choice between function and appearance. Therefore the manufacturer whose product seems functional but makes a poor appearance may have been careless in other ways as well. At the very least, the company has not availed itself of the services of an industrial designer. The laboratory planner should be aware that the equipment may not be, on balance, as good as it should be.

It is not a purpose of this discussion to examine in detail all aesthetic qualities that are a part of good design, since it seems unlikely that they will soon be emphasized in laboratory equipment to the extent they are in consumer products. Greatly increased competition for sales of equipment to schools and for home workshops is, however, forcing manufacturers to face the problem. Even such utilitarian products as radial arm saws and claw hammers now have refreshing appearances.

A basic quality that a piece of equipment should have is eye appeal. Appearance is the element of design that is the most affected by subjective judgment. It is certainly an element that causes much controversy among both laymen and professional designers. Nonetheless, it is possible to judge the aesthetic quality of a piece by examining it carefully and evaluating it in terms of each important determinant of appearance: proportion, aesthetic balance, color, proper use of materials, simplicity, expression of function, and craftsmanship.

A piece of equipment that is well designed with respect to proportion exhibits pleasing ratios of height to width, depth to width, and depth to height (see Fig. 10.3). A proportion of $1:\sqrt{u}$—that is, one to the square root of any number that does not have a whole number as its square root — is considered good. Thus the proportions $1:\sqrt{2}$, $1:\sqrt{3}$, and $1:\sqrt{5}$ are pleasing. Conversely, the proportions $1:\sqrt{4}$, $1:\sqrt{9}$, $1:\sqrt{16}$, and $1:\sqrt{25}$ are much less attractive. A square is too complete and incapable of modification to hold real interest.

Ancient Greek architects who developed these proportion principles believed also that the proportion of $1:1.618+$ was ideal, and they called it the golden section. From a practical standpoint, the difficulty in applying

Figure 10.3 *Laboratory equipment should exhibit good aesthetic design.* (Rockwell International, Power Tool Division)

these guidelines lies in the fact that the eye always sees an object in perspective, not as it really is. Its proportions, therefore, may appear distorted and in need of modification even though they are theoretically excellent. In such cases, the human eye — especially the trained and experienced one — is the only instrument capable of determining what changes should be made.

Aesthetic balance is a related consideration. A piece of equipment should give the impression that it is stable and at rest. It should possess either symmetrical or asymmetrical balance around each of the three visual axes—the vertical, the horizontal, and the profile.

Skillful use of color is essential to good design. The base color of a piece of equipment must be restful yet attractive. Vivid colors should be chiefly employed to call attention to points of operation and danger areas. For maximum effect, they must be used with restraint. The total color scheme should use relatively few colors, preferably no more than three.

The appearance of a piece of equipment should be honest with respect to the materials used in its construction. Most materials have beauty and need not be disguised to resemble more expensive materials. There are many exceptions to this point, but it has validity.

Simplicity contributes greatly to good appearance. Clean, smooth, straight (or interestingly curved) lines that blend materials and colors into integrated wholes and give convincing evidence of function help to eliminate superficiality. Decoration should be applied sparingly. Streamlining, in its functional sense, is out of place in laboratory equipment. But the "rounding off" that is done in order to provide good function and to eliminate safety hazards is entirely appropriate.

Competent workmanship enhances the aesthetic quality of any manufactured product. Everyone is attracted to appearances generated by well made pieces. Good appearance cannot exist without skillful execution.

Manufacturer's services. The dependable manufacturer provides services that help the industrial teacher to establish and maintain a smoothly running laboratory and to get the most out of equipment. In an effort to make wise choices of equipment, the laboratory planner should become familiar with the various manufacturers' services. The following questions should be asked in measuring a manufacturer's performance:

1. Does the guarantee provide satisfactorily inclusive no-cost protection to the purchaser?
2. Is the guarantee unequivocal?
3. Does the guarantee cover an adequate period of time?
4. Who will make repairs and replacements covered by the guarantee?
5. Will repairs and replacements be made on site, at the dealer's place of business, or at the factory?
6. Is operating and service literature furnished?
7. Are detailed installation instructions furnished with each unit sold?
8. Is expert assistance readily available, free-of-charge, where it is needed for proper installation and to familiarize the teacher with the operation and maintenance of the equipment?
9. Are repair parts easily obtainable? Does the manufacturer make available a full line of repair parts at reasonable cost, or must large components be replaced to correct operating difficulties?
10. Will repair parts be available during the expected life of the equipment?

MATERIALS SELECTION

11. Does the factory maintain a nearby service center where low-cost, competent repair work can be obtained?
12. Does the manufacturer make modifications available to purchasers of earlier models so that equipment can be kept up-to-date?
13. Are enough attachments furnished and options offered to permit the broadest possible use of the equipment?
14. Does the manufacturer offer (free-of-charge or at minimal cost) instructional media that assist the teacher in explaining the use of the equipment?
15. Does the manufacturer make available various kinds of literature that will be helpful to students?

It is rather unusual to discover a piece of equipment possessing *all* desirable design qualities. In many cases, however, competing brands are comparable with regard to necessary features. The prospective purchaser must decide which make has the fewest objectionable features and, especially, the fewest design defects that cannot be corrected. In fact, the possibilities for after-purchase modification should be studied very carefully during the selection process. The best designs make it possible to add features that manufacturers cannot afford to provide at standard selling prices. Lack of local lighting, an unfortunate choice of color, poor electrical switch placement, and the use of detachable adjusting wrenches are examples of weaknesses that can be remedied. Lack of a left-handed model, inadequate fence length, and a high sound level are examples of drawbacks that usually cannot be corrected and must be weighted more heavily in the selection process.

Industrial teachers should not miss opportunities to serve themselves and equipment manufacturers by calling attention to design deficiencies and poor quality control wherever they exist. Reactions of users can provide an extremely valuable foundation upon which to base product design improvements. Manufacturers are well aware of this fact, and many actively seek information from consumers and potential consumers.

In sum, the best available combination of key features, the smallest number of uncorrectable design faults, and tight quality control should be sought in each piece of equipment purchased for a school laboratory.

MATERIALS SELECTION

Every laboratory must be well supplied with construction materials and supporting materials. Construction materials are used to create the basic structures of projects. Supporting materials contribute to design details, make certain operations and construction procedures possible, and are important to laboratory maintenance. Walnut, acrylic plastic, copper, paper, and aluminum are examples of construction materials. Supporting materials include adhesives, fasteners, finishing materials, abrasives, lubricants, fuels, solvents, hardware, and chemicals.

Since the aggregate of materials purchased for a laboratory can be very large, it is necessary to limit both types and quantities so that the inventory can be kept at a reasonable size. There is seldom reason to stock more than a two-year supply of any material. In the case of a material that has a specified "shelf" life, it is necessary to keep the supply closely matched to consumption in order to avoid serious loss due to aging.

In effect, good local sources of supply increase a laboratory's materials storage capacity and inventory without increasing its materials budget. Except where it is possible to achieve significant cost reductions through quantity buying, it is worthwhile to make students responsible for acquiring certain of the materials they will use. Special pieces of hardware, unusual sheet metal forms, upholstery fabrics, repair parts (such as piston ring sets), and a host of other materials cannot be stocked in the varieties and quantities needed without an undue increase in inventory size. They should be purchased, as required, by students. Teachers can often make arrangements whereby students can purchase at discount from local vendors. This procedure has the additional benefits of acquainting students with retail sources of supply and giving them experiences as consumers.

The process of purchasing any material represents a search for *the most reliable sources of supply, appropriate quality, reasonable price,* and *good dealer service*. It is difficult to arrange these factors in order of importance; however, the emphasis must always be on quality.

Availability is the factor that first concerns industrial teachers. They must know where to obtain essential materials. In the years immediately following entry into teaching, it is well to develop a comprehensive list of sources of materials because it is unwise to depend entirely on a few general suppliers. General suppliers, of course, should appear on the list; their usefulness will be determined largely by the extent and quality of their offerings. Each should stock a wide variety of standard items, certain of the more exotic materials, many special sizes and shapes, and a satisfactory range of widths, depths, thicknesses, weights, and brands. But specialty concerns should be listed also, because the materials they stock can add immensely to the total number of types available. For example, a company that specializes in wood veneers invariably offers a much wider selection — and often lower prices — than a general supplier of equipment and materials.

A material that is not high enough in quality can negate an entire design. On the other hand, a material that provides an unnecessarily high degree of durability or a needlessly fine appearance can have the same effect if it makes a project too expensive to construct. Materials specifications must be written so that they conform to class needs. In the case of plywood, sheets that are good on one side (G1S) will often serve as well as sheets that are good on both sides (G2S). Less than the best grades of other materials may also be wise purchases at times.

Frequently, however, the top grades of materials should be ordered so that designs and craftsmanship will not be degraded by such things as poor natural color, inferior grain structure, and visible flaws. Removal of defects from a lower-grade material — with the attendant loss of stock and loss of utility in portions that are left undersize — can easily raise its true cost to a level higher than that of the best grade. Moreover, constructing smaller projects of top quality materials usually increases costs by insignificant amounts.

If processing is an important determinant of the quality of a material, as kiln drying is in the case of lumber, the best processing method should always be specified in a purchase request.

A list of supply sources must be revised from time-to-time in the light of experiences with the various suppliers. Materials may be advertised as conforming to an accepted set of quality standards, such as hardwood grading rules drafted by the National Hardwood Lumber Association, but some suppliers adhere to standards more closely than others. The industrial teacher's concern, therefore, is that *advertised* quality and *delivered* quality be similar.

The prices of materials are important for four reasons: first, no industrial teacher wants to see the costs of taking laboratory courses played beyond the financial ability of many students; second, school districts often pay for some of the materials consumed, and they are interested in reducing costs as much as possible; third, sound financial procedures require that the values of inventories be kept relatively low; and finally, the value of each completed project should exceed its cost.

Frequently vendors of a given materials advertise list prices that are substantially the same, but this factor should not lead a teacher to cut short the search for lower prices. Discounts vary, and some vendors offer additional price reductions in the form of waived transportation charges, free shipping insurance, and special operations (such as surfacing) performed at no extra charge.

Good dealer service is indispensable. As one of many services, a reputable dealer searches widely for new materials, interesting variations of existing materials, and less expensive sources of supply in order to be able to offer customers the best in choice, quality, and price. Each sale carries a written guarantee giving the purchaser absolute protection against material defects due to poor quality, inadequate processing, or careless handling. Most important, the dealer backs such a guarantee with a prompt response to every complaint so that purchasers never suffer losses.

Other dealer services that are helpful to schools and industrial teachers include:

1. Immediate answers to inquiries
2. Prompt submission of bids
3. Maintenance of adequate inventories so that back-ordering and substituting are rarely necessary
4. Business procedures that eliminate shipping errors
5. Accurate inspection to prevent shipment of defective materials
6. Skillful packing for shipment and proper choice of carrier
7. Rapid shipment, once an order has been placed
8. Business procedures that facilitate the return of defective or unwanted materials
9. Business policies that allow schools to make payment in accordance with their own established practices without loss of discounts
10. Provision of area representatives who can advise teachers, make occasional class presentations, and improve lines of communication between teachers and the company
11. Free, periodically-revised catalogs and other descriptive literature
12. Free, professionally-written and illustrated technical literature describing the properties and utilization of materials

SELECTION OF CONTRACTUAL SERVICES

Many services are necessary in the creation of a school laboratory. The step from the completed physical plant to a functioning laboratory is a long one, made possible only by the application of many kinds of skilled labor. Some tasks — such as unpacking, assembling, and degreasing equipment and placing it on the floor — are chiefly manual and can be satisfactorily performed by a school's custodial and/or maintenance staff or by a moving company. Some of the work can be done best by the industrial teacher. Tool panel design; adjustment and testing of machines; final conditioning of certain cutting edges; construction of jigs, fixtures, and holders; and preparation of instructional media are his or her province. Other jobs — for example, electrical, water, gas, and compressed air hookups made during the installation of equipment; tool panel construction; the painting of equipment; and dust collection system installation and testing — should be performed by private business firms on a contractual service basis.

A number of services must be performed periodically to ensure the efficient operation of a laboratory. Services that should be contracted to private firms fall in the general areas of modification of utility service systems, redecorating, building remodeling, major equipment overhaul, and maintenance tasks that are excessively time-consuming or that require equipment not usually present in laboratories — for example, handsaw filing and shaper-cutter grinding. Routine lubrication, adjustment, and tool conditioning are most often performed by teachers as part of their jobs.

To obtain contractual services that are satisfactory and reasonable in cost it is often necessary to deal with firms outside the community, and every school district should be prepared to do so. As a general rule, districts prefer to expend funds locally. This approach strengthens tax sources and maintains goodwill. These are not inconsiderable advantages. However, costs may be increased by patronizing local services that are comparatively expensive or not as good as they should be. In certain highly technical areas, reliable companies that operate throughout a state, a region, or the nation almost always provide better service than local firms.

Over the years, industrial teachers and their schools' administrative staffs should compile a list of sources of skilled services. Qualifications of listed firms can be based on reputation, recommendations of other schools, and personal experience. Each service purchased should be evaluated upon completion, and in no case should the district continue to engage a firm that gave unsatisfactory service.

It is a standard business procedure for a school district to contract for a service on the basis of bids submitted by interested firms. Local and/or state statutes often require that an invitation to bid be published in a news medium that serves the entire district. In addition, the invitation should be extended to reliable firms that operate more widely. Each firm must bid on exactly the same specifications for the work to be done, and the district must be the sole judge of any proposed equivalencies. In addition, the district should have the option of not accepting the lowest bid, even though this privilege can open the door to favoritism. It is, perhaps, a sound compromise to permit awarding a contract to either of the two lowest bidders so that the district, if it desires, can apply its judgment regarding differences in the reputations or past performances of the firms involved or in extra services offered.

The contract signed by the school district and the successful bidder should include all items listed in the bid, as well as the agreed-upon price and the date by which the work must be completed. It should also specify that all changes be approved in writing by both parties and that the district has the right to reject any and all work that, in its sole judgment, does not conform to the specifications. The district, for its part, must exercise such a contractual right with equity and discretion.

Certain circumstances (such as a strike in a supplying industry) that are beyond the control of the contractor may constitute valid reasons for making contractual changes. Errors made when a bid is prepared are rarely excusable because allowing cost increases might well turn the successful low bidder into a high bidder to the disadvantage of firms that submitted legitimately lower bids. The school and the other interested contractors should not suffer because of careless or unscrupulous bidding on the part of the successful bidder.

DEVELOPMENT OF PURCHASE REQUESTS

Invitations for vendors' bids to supply equipment and materials are formulated, usually, from purchase requests prepared by teachers. Some purchasing systems permit listing suppliers' names, catalog numbers, brand names, and trademarks on purchase requests. Others do not. Many systems make it possible to specify brands only if they are followed by the words "or equivalent," so that charges of favoritism or collusion cannot be made.

Where brand names either cannot be specified or must be qualified by the phrase "or equivalent," the task of developing specifications is much more difficult. If a particular brand is desired, it is necessary to list the features of that brand so exactly that it alone can qualify for purchase. Obviously, this step should be taken because the selection process followed by a teacher before writing a purchase request will have resulted in a choice from among the available brands. It certainly does not follow that this choice should, in effect, be disallowed by a purchasing agent to whom brands that are not really equal appear to be so.

Construction materials, types of finishes, colors, surface treatments, dimensions, functional features, horsepower ratings, manufacturing techniques, and all other specifications should be listed in order to identify a desired piece of equipment on a purchase request. Brand names and suppliers' catalog numbers should be included, if permissible. It is not possible to overemphasize the importance of complete and accurate specifications. Equipment placed in a laboratory is expected to perform well for a long period of time. Undesirable items often require early replacement or they may handicap the instructional program for many years. The same meticulous care must be exercised in preparing purchase requests for materials. Each material must be specified so completely that there can be no doubt as to what is wanted.

In preparation for the purchase of a service, a school district should develop exact specifications covering its requirements. The specifications should contain the date by which bids are to be submitted, a description of the work to be performed, a list of the materials to be used, a statement concerning the level of skill demanded, and the dates by which the work is to be started and completed. Regarding the work to be performed, specifications should require the submission of drawings for approval and describe in detail all bases upon which the work will be evaluated when finished.

If a standard school form is not available, a department should

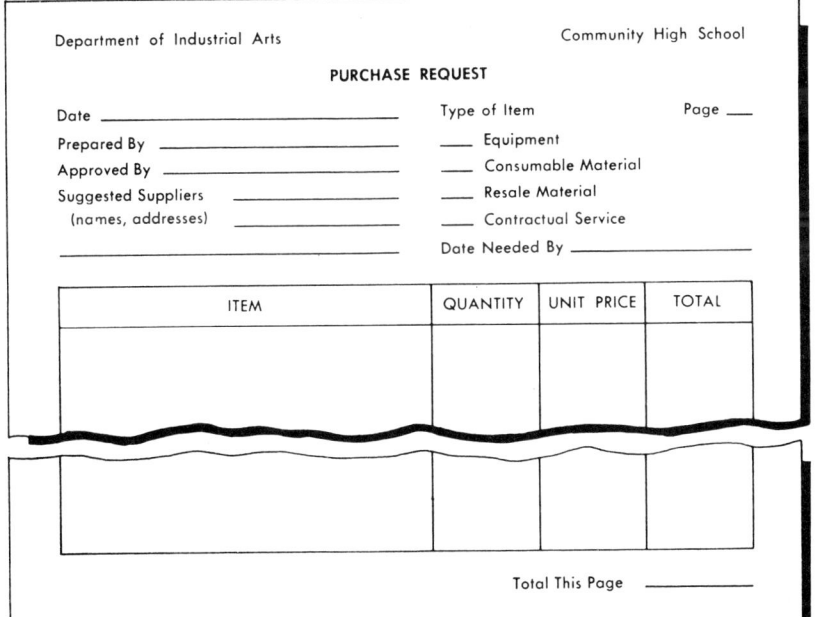

Figure 10.4 *Purchase request form.*

design its own purchase request form, preferably a simple one. Such a form will make it convenient for the teacher to identify recommended purchases. It will ease the task of the purchasing department if the form is similar to bid request and purchase order forms and provides all information necessary for their preparation. There is no reason that the three forms cannot be essentially the same. The purchase request form shown in Fig. 10.4[1] is presented as a guide to departments in developing forms that meet their own particular needs.

Certain pieces of equipment, materials, and contractual services are purchased frequently. Exact specifications for these should be kept on file as a means of saving time when purchase requests are prepared. Periodic revisions, incorporating technological advances, changing needs of programs, and fluctuations in price, of course, will be necessary.

FOR FURTHER READING

American Council on Industrial Arts Teacher Education. *Planning Industrial Arts Facilities.* 8th yearbook. Bloomington, Ill.: McKnight Publishing Co., 1959.

Baker, Gus E. "Controlled Purchase System for Greater Efficiency." *Industrial Education,* December 1975, p. 25.

Coverdill, Ernest J. "Specification Writing for ... Equipment Procurement." *Industrial Arts and Vocational Education,* March 1965, p. 70.

Feirer, John L. "Purchasing Is One of the Teacher's Major Responsibilities." *Industrial Education,* March 1974, p. 31.

Finsterbach, Fred C., and McNeice, William C. *Creative Facilities Planning for Occupational Education.* Berkeley Heights, N. J.: Educaré Associates, 1969.

Irvin, Daniel W. "Suggestions for Effective Ways to Specify Industrial Arts Equipment You Want." *Journal of Industrial Arts Education,* May-June 1964, p. 42.

Peterson, Sterling, and Buttschau, Ray. "Innovations in Purchasing Industrial Arts Supplies." *Industrial Education,* December 1975, p. 35.

Rowlett, John D. "Set Your Drafting Equipment and Materials Standards Above the Minimum." *Industrial Arts and Vocational Education,* April 1964, p. 41.

Stallsmith, Douglas. "Equipment Planning for IE Facilities." *School Shop,* April 1976, p. 69.

---

[1]Developed by the Department of Industry and Technology, Northern Illinois University.

11
Principles of Laboratory Organization

INTRODUCTION

The designs of an industrial education facility and the laboratories it houses are begun and largely completed in part one, phase 2 of the planning procedure. A building, wing, or industrial education area should be planned by an entire industrial education staff, but for efficiency, a small committee of faculty members — preferably no more than three — should take the lead in preparing alternative layouts and suggesting construction specifications. After this step has been completed, the whole group should react to the committee's work. The final design should reflect the philosophy of each faculty member and have the enthusiastic approval of all.

Individual laboratories should be designed by the teachers who will use them. However, everyone who plans a laboratory should seek the guidance and assistance of other faculty members whenever necessary.

INDUSTRIAL EDUCATION WING DESIGN

Wings can be arranged in H, I, L, T, and other shapes. Each shape can be effective, but in a specific planning situation, the shape of a wing will be determined mainly by the number and types of laboratories it is to include. Nine characteristics of a well-designed wing are:

1. Efficient use of land
2. Adequate physical separation from the main school building but not isolation
3. Attachment to the main school building in a way that creates an efficient traffic flow between the two units
4. A relatively small amount of floor space taken up by corridors, but minimal corridor congestion and easy access to all rooms
5. Laboratory accessibility to evening class students without their having to pass through the main school building
6. Laboratories arranged in order of increasing noise and waste production, beginning at the point of attachment to the main school building
7. Efficient handling and storage of incoming equipment and materials provided for
8. Centrally located faculty area, display facilities, and rest rooms
9. Representative of the best techniques of physical plant design and construction

The industrial arts wing shown in Fig. 11.1 satisfies the preceding design criteria. It is intended to serve the needs of a senior high school having an enrollment of approximately 1600 students. All industrial arts areas are represented, and each has been assigned enough floor space to meet its needs. Individual laboratories can be designed so that vocational-technical courses can be offered in the eleventh and twelfth grades. It is assumed that the program would enroll both boys and girls.

The cross-shaped primary corridor makes possible a very efficient flow of traffic between laboratories, between the wing and the parking lot, and between the wing and the main school building. The corridor is twelve feet wide. It has a terrazzo floor and a suspended ceiling. Corridor partitions are constructed of eight-inch, lightweight, two-core stretcher block laid in running-bond form. The block is glazed on both sides with a satin glaze. Recessed student lockers extend from near floor level to the seventy-two-inch level on both sides of the corridor, except along the faculty area and rest rooms. Lighted bulletin boards line partition surfaces that bound the faculty area. Fluorescent luminaires provide thirty footcandles of illumination. A refrigerated drinking fountain is recessed in the woods laboratory partition opposite the display case. The second-

INDUSTRIAL EDUCATION WING DESIGN

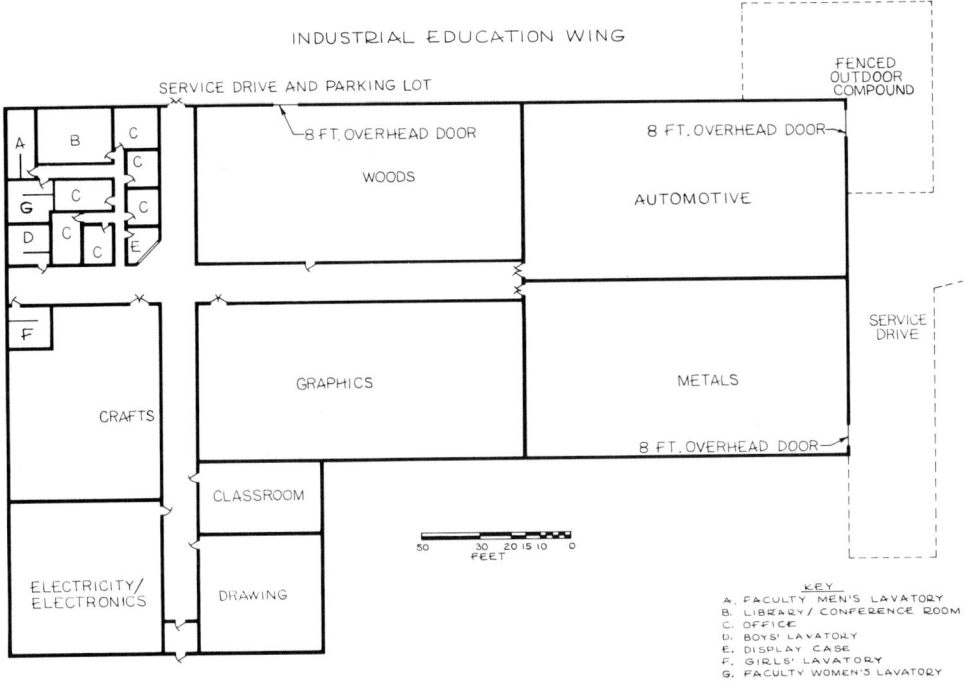

Figure 11.1 *L-shaped building wing for industrial education.*

ary corridor that serves the faculty area is four feet wide. Its construction is similar to that of the primary corridor, except that the floor is carpeted.

The entrance on the north side of the wing provides access for evening classes and makes it unnecessary to open the rest of the building when only classes in industrial education are in session. During the day, the north entrance serves as an effective emergency exit because it can be quickly reached from all rooms in the wing. The south entrance leads to the main school building at the point of attachment.

Doors opening into the primary corridor are staggered to minimize the congestion that can develop immediately before and after class periods. Laboratories that need exterior exits are equipped with 9 × 9-foot overhead doors or double 3-foot hinged doors. The doors are all served by a single service drive that borders the north and east sides of the wing. A fenced compound extends along portions of the east and north walls of the automotive laboratory. The compound permits outdoor work during good weather, as well as temporary storage of large units that will not suffer damage from exposure to the weather.

The faculty area adds greatly to the professional quality of the wing. This area provides a convenient location for rooms devoted to out-of-class teacher activities. Every office is close to all other offices and to the laboratories, but it affords the privacy and quiet needed for study and for teacher-student conferences. Each office is 12 × 12 feet or larger. Continuous glass extends from the 9-foot level to the ceiling along both corridor partitions. The floors are carpeted, and office walls, partitions, and ceilings are surfaced with sound-absorbent plaster. Fluorescent luminaires provide 150 footcandles of illumination. The basic equipment of each office includes a desk, a swivel-type arm chair, a flexible-arm fluorescent desk lamp, a side chair, a bookcase, a wardrobe-type storage cabinet, a regular storage cabinet, a four-drawer filing cabinet, a drafting table, a drafting machine, a drafting chair, a typing table, a typewriter, a typing chair, a wall clock, a pencil sharpener, a memo-type desk calendar, a transparent tape dispenser, a stapler, and a telephone.

The library/conference room measures approximately 17 × 26 feet. It is large enough to serve the needs of a staff of six teachers. A tinted, laminated safety-plate-glass window section extends vertically from the 9-foot level to the ceiling and laterally the entire length of the north wall. Additional protection from sun glare is afforded by the substantial overhang of the roof. Fluorescent luminaires provide 150 footcandles of illumination. The floor, wall, partitions, and ceiling are surfaced in the same manner as those in the offices. Built-in book shelves line the east partition between the 3-foot and 7-foot levels, and a chalkboard and pull-down projection screen are installed on the west partition. Room equipment includes a conference table designed to seat eight in comfort, eight arm chairs, window drapes, a four-drawer filing cabinet, a countertop-mounted stainless steel bowl equipped with a single-lever faucet, a recessed, refrigerated drinking fountain, a wall clock, and a pencil sharpener. With minor additions of equipment, the room also could serve as a faculty lounge.

The display case is located so that it will be seen by all who enter the wing. It has a variety of movable shelves and shelf supports that facilitate the arrangement of displays of all kinds. Numerous lighting effects can be created by the equipment provided. The case is loaded and locked from the rear. It is mechanically cooled and ventilated.

Each faculty rest room is designed for simultaneous use by a maximum of three people. Sound-absorbent partitions separate these rooms from the adjacent library/conference room, office, and boys' rest room. Fluorescent luminaires provide thirty footcandles of illumination. The floors are surfaced with terrazzo and equipped with four-inch drains. Partitions are constructed in the same way as corridor partitions. Suspended ceilings are installed in the two rooms. Each room's equipment is fabricated of highly durable materials, such as vitreous-glazed china, stainless steel, chrome-plated bronze, and aluminum. The equipment includes an enclosed, wall-hung toilet, a toilet tissue dispenser, two urinals (men's rest room only), a wall-hung lavatory equipped with a single-lever faucet, a powdered soap dispenser, a linen roll towel dispenser, a paper towel dispenser, a waste receptacle, a large plate glass mirror, and a wall shelf. Mechanical ventilation is provided.

Student rest rooms are constructed and equipped in the same way, except that each is designed for simultaneous use by no more than six persons, and paper towel dispensers are not provided.

One separate classroom makes it possible to schedule presentations for groups as large as twenty-four persons. The room has comfortable, stepped seating so that everyone can see and hear well. The fiberglass seats have folding writing surfaces and book storage space. Other items of room equipment include a demonstration bench, a chalkboard that extends the length of the west partition, a pull-down projection screen, a variety of audio-visual equipment, a steel storage cabinet, and a wall clock. Glazed stretcher block furnishes the desired wall and partition surface qualities, the ceiling is suspended, and the floor is finished with vinyl tile. Fluorescent luminaires provide 150 footcandles of illumination.

The woods and automotive laboratories have high-level window sections that begin at the nine-foot level, extend to ceiling height, and run the length of the north wall, except in storage areas. The graphic arts and metals laboratories have similar window sections set in their south walls. East and west walls are windowless. The overhang of the roof helps control sun glare.

The air environment in all rooms is controlled by a central plant, which provides mechanical ventilation, heat, and refrigerated cooling. Compressed air is piped to each laboratory from compressing equipment installed in a central location outside the wing.

Solid-core, flush oak doors are used throughout. Each is two inches thick and finished with a clear, semigloss finishing material. Colors used in corridors, rest rooms, the library/conference room, offices, the display case, and the separate classroom provide interest, variety, and optimum light reflectances.

LABORATORY DESIGN

Designing the floor plan of an industrial education laboratory is an activity that both precedes and follows construction of the physical plant. Work continues through all steps of planning and is not complete until the last piece of equipment has been installed and everything is ready for classes to begin.

Initially, it is necessary to select equipment and plan its organization so that auxiliary areas, distribution points for utility service systems, and exhaust system ducts can be included in the construction of the physical plant. It is apparent that such tasks as installing exhaust ducts in an automotive laboratory cannot be completed until an equipment layout is available.

The job of arranging machines, benches, tool panels, and other pieces of equipment on the floor of a laboratory remains after the physical plant has been built. Changes in the original floor plan invariably will suggest themselves, and a sensitive approach to planning at this point can greatly increase the likelihood of obtaining an outstanding program.

Three fundamental objectives must be met by any equipment arrangement. First, equipment must be placed so that its arrangement facilitates instruction. It must assist, not hamper, the instructor in teaching effectively. Second, equipment must be arranged to promote safety. To prevent accidents completely, it would be necessary to remove much of the equipment from a laboratory and halt many important activities having elements of danger that could not be entirely eliminated. But laboratories can be made satisfactorily safe, in part, through wise equipment organization. Finally, equipment must be placed in such a way that it aids the teacher in administering the laboratory and program. Many administrative problems — such as issuance of materials, record keeping, machine maintenance, laboratory cleanup, and inventory control — are immeasurably aided by good equipment organization. Poor lumber storage practices, for example, result in stock spoilage and unsatisfactory inventory control.

Normal student movements through a laboratory should influence the arrangement of equipment. Students must be able to enter a laboratory and move easily to all areas without having to avoid poorly placed pieces of equipment. Distinct traffic lanes should be established between areas of heavy use, such as tool panels, groups of machines, project storage rooms, and finishing rooms. In some instances, it is desirable to denote traffic lanes by painting four-inch-wide white lines on the floors.

Traffic lane width is an important consideration. In most laboratories there should be four feet or more of space between pieces of equipment in places where students will be walking or where cleanup and maintenance will be necessary. Longitudinal traffic lanes in drawing laboratories should be at least three feet wide, and lateral lanes should be no less than two feet in width.

Unfortunately, an efficient flow of traffic is not a feature found in all industrial education laboratories. Poor placement of benches, so that students must pass around or between them in moving from a main entrance to a locker area, is an often noted violation of traffic lane design. Frequently equipment stands in the way of doors or bulletin boards and chalkboards. Through the years, as a laboratory's inventory grows, the temptation to encroach on traffic lanes increases, but it must be resisted in order to preserve the integrity of the original plan.

Most manufacturing and service industries localize machinery, hand tools, attachments, jigs, fixtures, and other pieces of equipment. Any good, comprehensive automobile service center illustrates the practice of localizing equipment. In these facilities, the usual procedure is to group equipment pertaining to automatic transmission work, wheel balancing and alignment, lubrication, electrical service, and other types of repair and maintenance in separate parts of the service area. Certain industrial education laboratories lend themselves to this kind of organizational pattern. Crafts laboratories, for example, can be compartmented in accordance with the main instructional areas — plastics, leatherwork, art metalwork, ceramics, lapidary, and wood sculpture. Metals, automotive, graphic arts, and general laboratories can be organized in much the same way. Localizing equipment lends efficiency to the process of putting tools in the hands of those who will use them.

Machines must be arranged in such a way as to hold student travel to a minimum and to eliminate the need to carry large and heavy pieces of stock around the laboratory. Power hacksaws, paper cutters, squaring shears, and similar machines are often permanently located in materials storage rooms. This arrangement makes it unnecessary to carry materials out and return unused pieces. Certain other machines, including radial arm saws, jointers, planers, and table saws, also should be placed as close as possible to materials storage rooms.

Many machines should be located to serve specific parts of main work areas. In a woods laboratory, for example, drill presses, vertical belt sanders, shapers, and several other machines that are frequently used in conjunction with bench work should be adjacent to the bench area. The aim is to put each machine in the most convenient place.

An entire laboratory can and should be organized to promote efficient movement of materials. There should be a smooth flow from storage room to finished product, with as little backtracking as possible. In a woods laboratory, heavy production machines should be grouped near the major storage room in an area containing a substantial amount of free floor space. The arrangement of these machines should enable a student to move stock on a roller track from storage to the radial arm saw, cut it to rough length, and then carry it short distances to the jointer, planer, table saw (and back to the jointer and planer, if necessary), bench area, and other machines. At no time during the sequence of operations should the student be obliged to walk very far or walk around machines in the group. Obviously movements of lumber will not always take place in precisely the order suggested. Nevertheless such an organization of equipment facilitates mass production projects, and it helps to conserve students' time in all activities.

It is often worthwhile to group duplicate pieces of equipment and similar types of equipment. As an example, all of a woods laboratory's scroll saws should be in a single area that serves the bench area. A band saw that will not be extensively used for resawing should be in the same group. In a senior high school laboratory, it is frequently desirable to include a twenty-inch band saw in the planer–jointer–table saw–radial arm saw group but to place a fourteen-inch band saw with the scroll saws. Thus the larger machine will be available for resawing and heavy work and the smaller saw will perform much of the day-to-day sawing. Sanders, metal lathes, milling machines, platen presses, hydraulic hoists, ceramic kilns, and many other pieces of equipment should be grouped in a similar manner.

Grinders and other kinds of equipment used both in service and in production activities cannot always be handled this way. Although it is often wise to group grinding equipment, it is sometimes more useful to install grinders in different areas where grinding is a necessary activity. The area in which it is most convenient to grind tools may or may not be in the same part of a laboratory where production grinding operations can best be performed.

Safety considerations should influence any arrangement of equipment. Machines such as table saws, jointers, and planers, which are capable of violently expelling stock from their infeed sides, must be arranged so that pieces of stock will not be thrown into areas where students are likely to be working. All machines should be located so that stock will not protrude from their infeed or outfeed sides into traffic lanes, bench areas, or other machine areas. In short, the space allocated to each machine should be sufficient to allow safe and convenient movement around it whenever stock is being processed.

Work stations should be located so that interference from and with adjacent work stations and laboratory traffic will be minimal. Areas in which dangerous materials — for example, molten metals in a foundry and acids in a crafts laboratory — are handled should be removed from normal traffic and other class activities. Machines that are more than normally hazardous should also be isolated.

Metal containers equipped with foot-operated covers should be provided in finishing rooms, automotive laboratories, graphic arts laboratories, and other places where used rags and flammable wastes accumulate.

Each laboratory should have at least one fire extinguisher. Water and soda acid extinguishers are suitable for general use, but neither should be used on electrical or flammable liquid fires. Both present a shock hazard when used to extinguish electrical fires, and both will spread rather than extinguish flammable liquid fires. Electrical fires can best be extinguished by carbon dioxide, while flammable-liquid fires require the use of a smothering agent, such as chemical foam. Carbon tetrachloride produces toxic gases and is therefore not acceptable for school use. Chemical fires must be extinguished by agents that conform to the nature of the burning materials. Fire extinguishers should be simple in design, easy to use, difficult to operate accidentally, and installed where they can be quickly reached in emergencies. The best locations for fire extinguishers are in parts of laboratories where the danger of fire is greatest, for example, in woods finishing rooms and automotive fuel system service areas.

Since the successful administration of a laboratory depends, in part, upon the *ease* with which equipment can be cleaned and maintained, it is clear that housekeeping and maintenance considerations must play a part in determining equipment arrangement. Consequently machines and other pieces of equipment should be placed twelve inches or more away from walls and partitions. This guideline, together with suggestions concerning traffic lane widths and clearances around machines, will ensure adequate working room around each piece of equipment.

Generally, tool storage repositories in industrial education laboratories include three kinds of facilities: the tool storage room, the comprehensive open tool panel or locking tool cabinet (installed in a main work area), and the tool panel or cabinet series system, which localizes tool storage. The oldest storage method is to equip a separate tool storage room with one or more tool panels or cabinets. Such a room offers maximum security, especially if locking tool cabinets are used. Inconvenience, inefficient use of floor space, and potential waste of student time combine to make the tool room the least desirable of the three methods. Nonetheless, it may be the most workable choice if security is a problem.

The most effective method of tool storage makes use of one or more

Figure 11.2 *Proper tool storage contributes to efficient laboratory utilization.* (San Diego State University, Department of Industrial Studies)

open panels or locking cabinets strategically placed near bench areas and machines and in some auxiliary areas. Attachments, jigs, fixtures, and adjusting tools belonging to particular machines should be stored on special panels (or in locking cabinets) near where they will be needed.

Tools are put in laboratories to be used, not hidden. Thus the best tool storage systems are those that make it the most convenient for students to obtain the tools they need for construction or service activities (Fig. 11.2). Security is important, and it can be had by putting everything under lock and key, as is sometimes necessary. Ideally, however, education that stresses development of pride and responsibility offers the best protection against tool loss.

Tool storage facilities should be as nearly self-administering as possible. Dispensing, replacing, and checking tools should require very little teacher and student time. Parenthetically, with respect to its self-administering qualities, an open tool panel is far superior to any other storage method.

LABORATORY DESIGN

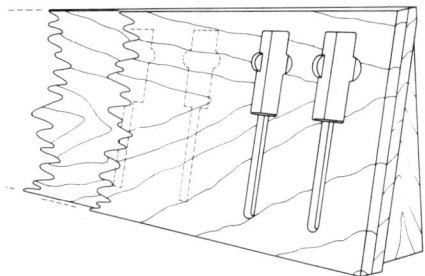

Figure 11.3 *Routed tool holder-silhouettes.* (George Sullivan)

A special holding device that holds only one type and size of tool should be provided for each tool stored on a panel. A holding device must grasp a tool without damaging it and in a manner that makes the tool easy to remove and replace.

Each tool should be silhouetted on its panel. Silhouettes can be painted on a panel as solid areas of color or in solid outline or dashed outline form. They may also be cut from thin sheet material—for example, 3/32-inch plywood—painted, and fastened to panels with small wire nails or brass escutcheon pins. One company offers adhesive-backed, black paper silhouettes of a number of common hand woodworking tools. If time allows, it is desirable to construct tool holder/silhouettes for many of the tools by routing their shapes in blocks of wood. The faces of routed holders must slope so that tools remain in place (Fig. 11.3).

A silhouette should match only one type and size of tool (duplicate tools are exceptions) and should be painted a bright color that contrasts sharply with the color of the panel. Red, orange, blue, and black are effective silhouette colors. The panel should either have a natural wood finish or be painted a tint or shade of the color of the wall on which it is mounted.

In a laboratory that has more than one tool panel, each tool should be assigned to a specific panel. Screwdrivers, pliers, and the like may be stored on several panels; and a system of color coding will help to ensure that tools do not "float" between the panels.

Color coding may consist of painting a spot or band of the silhouette color on each tool in an easily seen place where the paint will not wear off or interfere with the proper functioning of the tool. It is neither necessary nor desirable to color-code entire handles or other large areas of tools. For example, a one-half-inch band painted around the shank of a screwdriver near the handle is sufficient for identification. The paint used for color coding should be a durable, semigloss metal enamel.

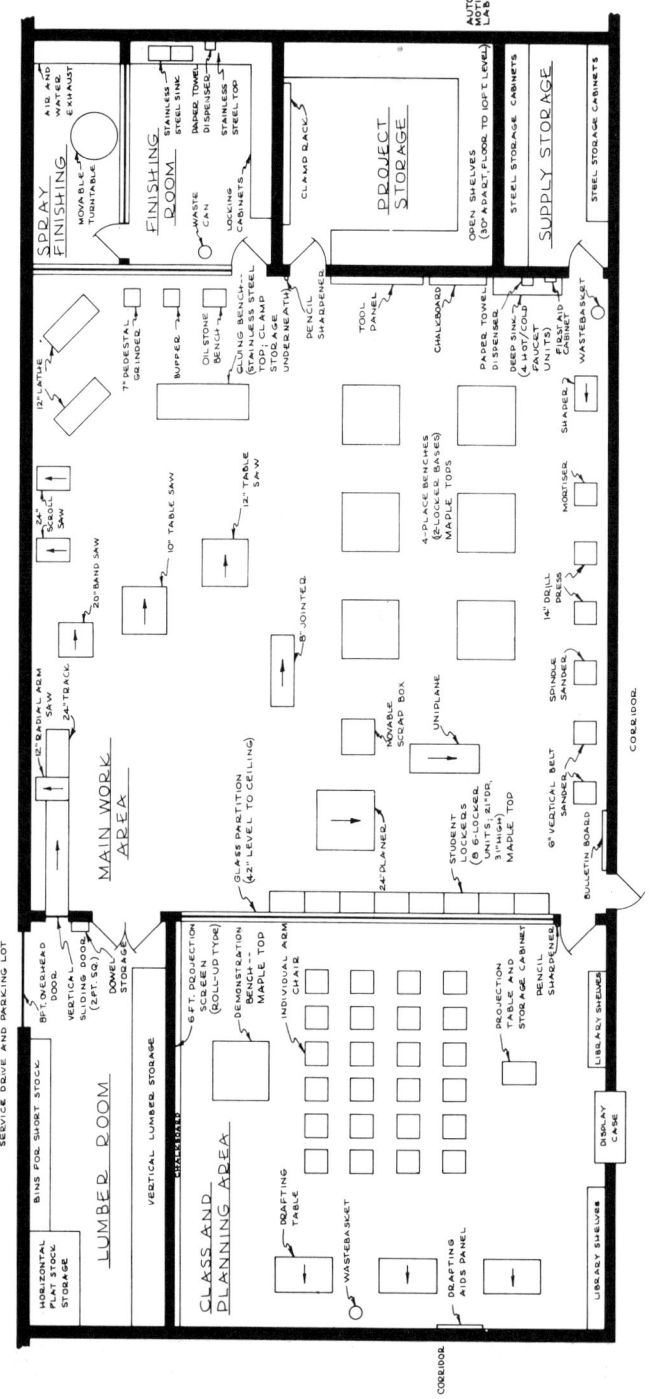

Figure 11.4 Woods laboratory for senior high school.

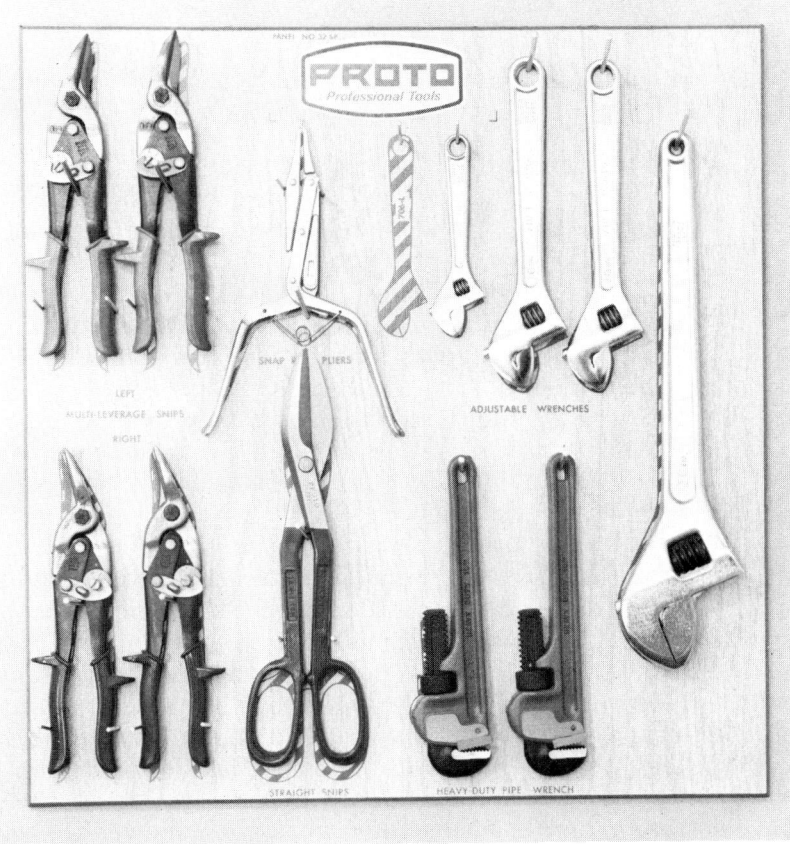

Figure 11.5 *Silhouettes aid in tool panel administration.* (Proto Tools)

Arranging tools on a panel is somewhat a matter of expedience and personal preference. However, there are a number of important general guides to tool panel design, and anyone who plans a panel should be familiar with them. The most significant are the following:

1. The appearance of a panel should be neat and attractive.
2. Duplicate tools and duplicate sizes of tools should be grouped.
3. Smaller, lighter, and infrequently used tools should be placed near the top of a panel and in other less accessible places.
4. Larger, heavier, and frequently used tools should be placed in the most reachable areas — usually near the bottom and in the center.
5. Tools that are included in large numbers (wood chisels, hand

planes, files, etc.) should be located in places that are easy to reach.

6. Each tool should be held in a position that prevents hand injuries and damage to the tool as it is removed from its holder or replaced in it. There must be no sharp edges to grasp, and it should be impossible for the tool to come in contact with another tool.

7. Tools should never be crowded on a panel. Space should not be wasted, however. Practices such as mounting hand saws flat make it impossible to utilize space efficiently and should be avoided.

8. Space for additional tools must be provided, but no extra tool holders or silhouettes should be installed on a panel.

9. All tool holders should be fastened to the panel from the front.

Tools that are frequently employed in performing routine operations might well be distributed to students in kit form. This procedure is especially useful in metals, automotive, and other laboratories in which a number of tools, including lathe dogs, wrenches, cutter bits, and micrometers, are used in precisely this way. Kits can be checked out to students at the beginning of a school term and returned at the close of the term. Convenience is a major advantage of the use of tool kits. The cost of providing the necessary additional tools is its chief limitation.

The senior high school woods laboratory shown in Fig. 11.4 is one valid organization of equipment that was developed for the space allocated to woodwork in the industrial arts wing shown in Fig. 11.1. Other good arrangements are possible.

The starting point in designing this laboratory was the belief that courses taught there should strive to develop in each student:

1. The ability to use and maintain a variety of pieces of woodworking equipment
2. An understanding of safety principles and the ability to apply them in laboratory activities
3. A substantial depth of knowledge about lumber, plywood, adhesives, abrasives, fasteners, joinery, finishing, design, and other common materials and technical processes
4. An interest in creative work with wood and the ability to plan and construct well-designed wood products
5. An understanding of his or her interests and abilities regarding work with wood

LABORATORY DESIGN

6. The ability to recognize quality of design and craftsmanship in products manufactured by woods industries
7. An understanding of the design and productive functions of modern woods industries
8. A knowledge of career opportunities offered by woods industries

A statement of laboratory activities that would be useful in achieving these objectives was prepared. Included were furniture design, cabinetmaking, lamination, bending, sculpture, inlay, turning, finishing, upholstery, carpentry, boat building, and equipment maintenance.

Finally, the statement of activities was used as the basis for compiling a list of fundamental equipment and materials that should be provided (Table 11.1). Quantities were determined by assuming that the laboratory would be used by five classes per day and that each class would enroll a maximum of twenty-four students. It was estimated that the suggested amounts of materials would be sufficient to operate the program for at least one year. Materials that students would normally purchase for themselves, such as upholstery fabrics and cabinet hardware, were not included. Pieces of equipment shown on the floor plan, as well as pieces that could not be shown, were listed. It should be noted that the classification of equipment is, in a sense, theoretical. Certain of the items included are classified as materials by many school business offices. Complete specifications for all items would need to be drafted before purchase requests could be written.

Undoubtedly, other pieces of equipment and other types of materials would be purchased from time-to-time, either as additions to the initial inventory or as replacements. It is not assumed that the list presented in Table 11.1 contains all of the things that ultimately might be needed. Quite often, course improvements are possible only if a laboratory's inventory can be modified appropriately.

A main work area and eight auxiliary areas (classroom/design center/library, display facilities, student locker areas, a project storage room, major and minor storage rooms, a project assembly area, and a wash area) constitute the complete laboratory. The classroom is separated from the main work area by a glass partition that allows the teacher to work anywhere in the laboratory without losing visual contact with students. Lightproof draw drapes make it possible to darken the room when audiovisual materials are to be used. Placement of the classroom door near the door leading from the corridor to the main work area enables students to go directly into the classroom without passing through any other part of the laboratory. Twenty-four folding chairs with

Table 11.1 EQUIPMENT AND MATERIALS LIST PREPARED FOR A SENIOR HIGH SCHOOL WOODS LABORATORY

Materials Quantity	Item
3	Orbital sander
1	Belt sander, portable, complete
2	Vertical belt sander, 6 in., complete
1	Oscillating spindle sander
1	Band sander, complete
1	Buffer, 7 in., pedestal-type, complete
1	Grinder, 7 in., pedestal-type, complete
2	Lathe, 12 in., complete
1	Jointer, 8 in., with one extra knife set
1	Planer, 24 in., complete, with one extra knife set
1	Miter box, 26 in. saw
1	Miter machine
2	Scroll saw, 24 in., complete, with assorted blades
1	Sabre saw, complete
1	Band saw, 20 in., complete, with assorted blades
1	Radial arm saw, 12 in., complete
1	Table saw, 12 in., complete
1	Table saw, 10 in., complete
1	Circular saw, 7 in., portable, complete
1	Uniplane, complete
3	Drill, ¼ in., portable electric
1	Drill, ⅜ in., portable electric
2	Drill press, 14 in., complete
1	Mortiser, 14 in., complete
1	Router-shaper, portable electric, complete
1	Spindle shaper, complete
1 unit	Spray-painting equipment (air regulator-filter, with gauge; 2 spray guns; 1 air-dusting gun; 2 feed cups, complete; 2 10-ft. air hoses with connections)
3	Fire extinguisher, carbon dioxide–type
7	Work bench, 4 stations, complete with 12-locker base
1	Projection table, cabinet-type with casters
1	Turntable, movable, steel, for spray finishing
1	Drawing table, individual
1	Finishing bench, wall-type with stainless steel top and locking door cabinet base, approximately 25 ft. in length
11	Steel storage cabinet, swinging door–type, 36 × 24 × 78 in.

LABORATORY DESIGN

Materials Quantity	Item
1	Gluing bench, 6 ft., with stainless steel top
8	Bench, wall-type with 6-locker base and 2¼-in. maple top
1	Bench with 24 × 24 in. stainless steel top
1	Wall projection screen, 6 ft., white matte
1	Finishing room exhaust system, air-water, complete
16 ft.	Roller track, 24 in., complete with stand
12	Stool, tubular steel, adjustable 24 in. to 35 in.
1	Spirit level, 24 in.
1	Line level
1	Plumb
3	Drafting machine, 16 in.
3 sets	Drawing instruments
1	Beam compass
3	Circle template
1	Ellipse template
1	Irregular curve
3	Draftsman's brush
3	Scissors, 8 in.
12	Half-round cabinet wood file
6	Flat wood file
3	Mill file, bastard
3	Mill file, second cut
3	Mill file, smooth
2	Saw file, slim taper
2	Saw file, extra slim taper
3	Rattail file, bastard
2	Auger bit file
1 set	Needle file
3	File card
36	File handle, Skroo-Zon, assorted sizes
1	Foreplane
6	Jack plane
3	Smooth plane
3	Block plane
1	Router plane
2	Spokeshave, 10 in.
1	Draw knife, 8 in.
3	Cabinet scraper 3 × 5 in., flat
16	Wood chisel, assorted sizes

Table 11.1 EQUIPMENT AND MATERIALS LIST PREPARED FOR A SENIOR HIGH SCHOOL WOODS LABORATORY

Materials Quantity	Item
12	Carving tool, assorted types and sizes
6	Gouge, outside bevel, assorted sizes
3	Gouge, inside bevel, assorted sizes
4	Sloyd knife, No. 13
1	X-Acto set, complete
2	Hand saw, rip, 20 in., 5½ point
4	Hand saw, crosscut, 20 in., 10 point
3	Back saw, 12 in.
2	Dovetail saw, 10 in.
4	Coping saw frame, 6½ in. blade
2	Jeweler's saw frame, 5 in. blade
1	Hack saw frame, 12 in.
2	Hand drill, ¼ in.
2	Auger brace, 12 in., ratchet-type
1	Drill grinding attachment
2 each size	Twist drill, H.S., $1/16$ in. through ½ in. by 64ths
1 each size	Auger bit, No. 4 through No. 16
1 each size	Power bit, ⅜ in. through 1 in., Millers Falls Dyn-O-Mite
1 each size	Multispur machine bit
1 each size	Forstner bit, machine, No. 4 through No. 16
2	Expansion bit, ⅝ in. to 1½ in.
1 each size	Forstner bit, brace, No. 4 through No. 16
3	Countersink, ¼ in., round shank
2	Brace countersink, ¾ in.
2	Doweling jig, complete
2	Bit gauge
1 each size	Plug cutter, ⅜ in., ½ in., ⅝ in., round shank
1	Circle cutter, ½ in., round shank
1	Tap and die set, N.C., standard
4	Wood threading kit, assorted sizes
1 set	Screw extractor
25	Woodworker's vise, 12 in. jaw opening
2	Machinist's vise, 4 in. jaw width
1	Drill press vise, 2⅜ in. jaw width
3	Miter vise
1	V-block and clamp
12	C-clamp, 4 in.
12	C-clamp, 6 in.
24	C-clamp, 8 in.

LABORATORY DESIGN

Materials Quantity	Item
12	C-clamp, 10 in.
12	C-clamp, 12 in.
6	Hand screw, 5/0
6	Hand screw, 4/0
6	Hand screw, 3/0
12	Hand screw, 2/0
12	Hand screw, 0
24	Hand screw, 1
12	Hand screw, 2
6	Hand screw, 3
12	I-bar clamp, 2 ft.
12	I-bar clamp, 3 ft.
24	I-bar clamp, 4 ft.
12	I-bar clamp, 5 ft.
12	I-bar clamp, 6 ft.
2	Screwdriver, 4 in.
3	Screwdriver, 6 in.
3	Screwdriver, 8 in.
3	Phillips screwdriver, points 1, 2, and 3
1	Spiral screwdriver, complete
4	Offset screwdriver, assorted lengths
1	Screwdriver bit, ¼ in.
1	Screwdriver bit, ⅜ in.
6	Bench rule, 1 ft., steel
6	Bench rule, 2 ft., steel
3	Bench rule, 3 ft., steel
1	Tape rule, 8 ft.
8	Try square, 8 in.
2	Framing square, 24 in., stainless steel
2	Machinist's combination square, complete
3	Protractor, 6 in., steel
3	Outside caliper, 8 in.
2	Inside caliper, 8 in.
4	Claw hammer, 16 oz.
2	Ball peen hammer, 13 oz.
2	Upholsterer's hammer, 7 oz.
1	Soft face hammer, 8 oz.
6	Mallet, 3 × 6 in., wood
3	Center punch, assorted sizes
3	Pin punch, assorted sizes

Table 11.1 EQUIPMENT AND MATERIALS LIST PREPARED FOR A SENIOR HIGH SCHOOL WOODS LABORATORY

Materials Quantity	Item
6	Nail set, assorted sizes
2	Cold chisel, ½ in.
4	Combination pliers, assorted sizes
2	Side cutting pliers, 7 in.
2	Diagonal cutting pliers, 6 in.
2	Needle nose pliers, 6 in.
1	Carpenter's pincer, 8 in.
1 set	Allen wrench
4	Crescent wrench, 6 in., 8 in., 10 in., 12 in.
1 set	Open end wrench, ¼ in. through 1 in. by 16ths
1 set	Box wrench, ¼ in. through 1 in. by 16ths
2	Pipe wrench, 12 in.
3	Scratch awl, 6 in.
2	Wing divider, 8 in.
1	Sliding T-bevel, 8 in.
1 pair	Trammel points
1	Burnisher
3	Oilstone, combination
1 each grit	Gouge slip, medium and fine
1 set	Carving tool slip
18	Paintbrush, nylon bristles, assorted sizes
2	Wire brush
8	Glue brush, ¾ in. diameter
24	Bench brush
3	Push broom, 16 in.
1 set	Propane torch
1	Soldering copper, electric, 200 W.
1	Sparklighter
6	Monogoggle
1	Wrecking bar, 24 in.
1	Grinding wheel dresser
3	Hydraulic pump oiler
1	Grease gun, lever-type
1	Tubing cutter, capacity ⅛ in. to 1 in.
3	Putty knife
3	Glass cutter
1	Bench anvil, 9 lb.
2	Compound lever snips, 8 in.
3	Molders bellow, 10 in.
2	Asbestos, hard, ¼ in. × 2 ft. × 2 ft. sheet

LABORATORY DESIGN

Materials Quantity	*Item*
1	First aid kit, complete
5	Powdered soap dispenser
2	Paper towel dispenser
24	Armchair, folding, tubular steel with laminated plastic-faced writing surface
2	Pencil sharpener, self-feeding type
2	Wastebasket, steel
1	Waste can, steel, foot-operated cover

Materials Quantity	*Item*
10 lb.	Finishing nail, assorted sizes
10 lb.	Common nail, assorted sizes
3 lb.	Wire brad, assorted sizes
25 gross	Wood screw, flat head, steel, assorted numbers and lengths
10 gross	Wood screw, flat head, brass, assorted numbers and lengths
10 gross	Wood screw, round head, steel, assorted numbers and lengths
10 gross	Wood screw, round head, brass, assorted numbers and lengths
25 gross	Wood screw, flat Phillips head, steel, assorted numbers and lengths
1 gross	Rivet, soft iron, round head, $1/8 \times 3/8$ in.
1 gross	Rivet, soft iron, flat head, $1/8 \times 3/8$ in.
100	Miter joint fastener
100	Corrugated fastener
1 gross	Desk top clip
3 gal.	Polyvinyl resin glue
25 lb	Urea resin glue
6 tubes	Epoxy cement
2 gal.	Contact cement
5 lb.	Solder, rosin core wire, 40% lead–60% tin
8 oz.	Silver solder
1 lb.	Soldering paste
1 lb.	Boraxo
24 pt.	Enamel, assorted colors

Table 11.1 EQUIPMENT AND MATERIALS LIST PREPARED FOR A SENIOR HIGH SCHOOL WOODS LABORATORY

Materials Quantity	Item
4 pt.	Brushing lacquer, flat black
40 qt.	Spraying lacquer, clear gloss
12 qt.	Spraying lacquer, assorted colors
40 qt.	Sanding sealer, clear
4 qt.	White shellac, 4 lb. cut
42 pt.	Wipe-on finish, Sealacell
20 gal.	Lacquer thinner
5 gal.	Paint thinner
2 gal.	Linseed oil, boiled
5 gal.	Alcohol, denatured
6 qt.	Paste wood filler, assorted colors
6 qt.	Oil stain, penetrating, assorted colors
6 lb.	Water stain, assorted colors
12 tubes	Colors-in-oil, assorted colors
2 qt.	Paint and varnish remover
4 lb.	Paste wax
2 lb.	Cup grease
4 qt.	Motor oil, SAE 10, nondetergent
1 pt.	Penetrating oil
2 gal.	Kerosene
250 sheets each	Abrasive paper, aluminum oxide; grades 9/0, 6/0, 4/0, 2/0, 0, 1/2
200 sheets each	Abrasive paper, silicon carbide, waterproof; 200, 400, 600 grit
18 pkg.	Steel wool pad, 3/0
2 lb.	Pumice, FFF
2 lb.	Rottenstone
1 lb.	Tripoli
1 lb.	Jeweler's rouge
1 qt.	Metal polish
1 gal.	Cutting oil
3 doz.	Stick shellac, assorted colors
2 lb.	Plastic Wood, assorted colors
1 pt.	Plastic Wood solvent
4 rolls	Masking tape, ¾ in.
100 lb.	Wiping cloth, white
2 rolls	Wrapping paper, 36 in., brown
	Upholsterer's supplies, assorted
450 B.F.	Basswood, 1¼ in., rough
300 B.F.	Yellow poplar, 1¼ in., rough

LABORATORY DESIGN

Materials *Quantity*	Item
750 B.F.	Cherry, 1¼ in., rough
1500 B.F.	Philippine mahogany, 1¼ in., rough
750 B.F.	Hard maple, 1¼ in., rough
500 B.F.	Sugar pine, 1¼ in., rough
750 B.F.	Black walnut, 1¼ in., rough
300 B.F.	Ash, 1¼ in., rough
750 B.F.	Mahogany, 1¼ in., rough
75 lin. ft.	Square stock, cherry, 2 × 2 in.
75 lin. ft.	Square stock, hard maple, 2 × 2 in.
75 lin. ft.	Square stock, mahogany, 2 × 2 in.
75 lin. ft.	Square stock, black walnut, 2 × 2 in.
3 panels	Plywood, fir, ¼ in., GIS, 4 × 8 ft.
3 panels	Plywood, fir, ⅜ in., GIS, 4 × 8 ft.
3 panels	Plywood, fir, ½ in., GIS, 4 × 8 ft.
2 panels	Plywood, fir, ¾ in., GIS, 4 × 8 ft.
2 panels	Plywood, birch, ¼ in., 4 × 8 ft.
24 each size	Dowel rod, birch, ⅛ in., ¼ in., ⅜ in., ½ in., ⅝ in., ¾ in.
2 panels	Hardboard, ⅛ in., 4 × 8 ft.
4 panels	Hardboard, ¼ in., 4 × 8 ft.
8 sheets	Laminated plastic, 2 × 4 ft., assorted solid colors
300 sheets	Vellum, 12 × 18 in.

writing surfaces provide good seating. They are arranged so that each affords a clear view of the projection screen and chalkboard. All seats are placed within an area extending 30° on both sides of a line that is perpendicular to the center of the screen. Side fadeout of projected images is minimized by the use of a matte screen. No seat is less than two screen widths from the screen, and none is more than six screen widths from it.

The demonstration bench at the front of the classroom is equipped with a woodworker's vise and a machinist's vise. Floor-mounted convenience outlets provide 115 v. single-phase electrical current at two opposite corners. Chalkboard aids include a large wooden 30–60° triangle, a three-foot straightedge graduated in inches and eighths, and a gravity protractor. All are stored on the wall below the chalkboard. A combination portable projection table–storage cabinet is located at the rear of the room. The cabinet provides storage space for a 16 mm. motion picture projector, a 35 mm. slide projector, and other audiovisual equipment.

Three large drawing tables face the west side of the classroom. Each table is equipped with a drafting machine. A drafting aids panel is mounted on the wall close at hand.

One bulletin board is located on the west partition of the classroom, and a second board is placed on the left side of the door from the main work area to the corridor. Display facilities also include a large, lighted display case at the rear of the classroom. The case is extended into the classroom for depth. It can be loaded only from the classroom side.

Locker space for 120 students is provided in the main work area. Seventy-two individual lockers are located in the work bench bases, and 48 lockers are contained in locker base units placed against the partition that separates the main work area from the classroom. The locker base units are bolted together and used to support a 2¼ in. maple top. When locker assignments are made, each class can be divided into two groups in order to reduce congestion at the lockers at the beginning and end of each class period.

The major storage room is equipped with a six-foot double door. Lumber, plywood, and other materials can be unloaded directly into the room from delivery vehicles parked in the service drive. A double door between the major storage room and the main work area offers easy passage for full-size sheets of plywood and hardboard. Lumber can be moved to the radial arm saw on a twenty-four-inch roller track supported at the same height as the saw table.

The minor storage room, project storage room, and finishing rooms are placed between the main work area and the automotive laboratory as a means of reducing noise transmission in both directions.

Locking steel storage cabinets are installed in the minor storage room, and whole cabinets or portions of cabinets can be assigned to the storage of such items as duplicate tools, spare parts, nails, screws, adhesives, abrasives, and finishing materials. Each cabinet has hinged doors, four adjustable shelves, and the basic dimensions 21 × 36 × 78 inches. The minor storage room thus possesses the two fundamental attributes of a good storage facility: supplies can be kept in order and adequate security can be maintained.

The doors to the project storage room and the finishing room are located side by side in order to improve the traffic flow from one room to the other. By means of open shelves and free floor space, the project storage room provides adequate storage for both large and small projects.

Glass partitions separate the finishing area from the main work area and divide it into two rooms — one for hand finishing and the other for spray finishing.

A compressed air outlet is installed on the mullion in the spray finishing room. Blow gun operation is permitted by a second air outlet mounted on the classroom partition next to the door to the major storage room.

Four separate wash spaces are provided in the main work area. All include a dual temperature–flow control faucet and a powdered soap dispenser. One paper towel holder serves all four wash spaces.

A wet pipe automatic sprinkler system furnishes protection against damage and injuries from fire. Carbon dioxide fire extinguishers are installed in the finishing rooms and in the main work area on the right side of the door to the finishing room.

Machines are arranged for efficiency of production and in a pattern that prevents stock from being kicked back into places where students would normally work. An adequate amount of free floor space is allocated around each machine. The jointer is placed at the right and rear of the table saws to permit freedom of movement between the three machines when alternate sawing and jointing operations are in progress.

A Uniplane installed near the bench area provides additional capacity during periods of unusually heavy jointer use.

Arranging the belt sanders, spindle sander, drill presses, mortiser, and shaper in a straight row allows each machine to serve the bench area. The row is planned so that alternate and sequential operations can be efficiently performed. Similarly, the scroll saws and band saw are grouped to make it possible to produce all types of curved cuts in one area of the laboratory. The grinder, buffer, and oilstone bench are between the bench area and the lathes.

A special gluing bench stores C-clamps and hand screws. Bar clamps are kept nearby in the project storage room. The gluing bench is close to the bench area, project storage room, and finishing room. A generous area of free floor space surrounds it so that large projects can be assembled on the floor. Stock also can be glued on the work benches, provided newspapers are used to protect the bench tops.

A panel that stores lathe tools and attachments is secured to the wall on the right side of each lathe in order to create a self-contained work station in which all common turning activities can be carried on. Both panels are constructed of three-quarter-inch birch plywood and finished with a clear finish. Similar panels are installed on or near the scroll saws, table saws, spindle sander, drill presses, mortiser, and shaper. Each panel's silhouettes are painted a different color and are applied in dashed outline form. All tools are color-coded accordingly.

The main tool panel is mounted on the project storage room partition near the bench area. A locking tool cabinet encloses it. Each tool is silhouetted with a dashed black outline on a clear finished birch background.

A wall-mounted chalkboard serves the bench area. It is placed so that it can be seen from standing and sitting positions in all parts of the area.

Each machine is supported by a cabinet base that is enclosed to the floor. The cabinets rest on vibration-absorbent pads, and the insides of sheet metal enclosures are coated with sound-absorbent materials. No machine is installed less than twelve inches away from a wall or partition.

All pieces of laboratory equipment are painted in accordance with PPG Industries Color Dynamics system. Durable, semigloss enamels were used for this purpose.

The traffic lane widths are adequate throughout the laboratory. No lane is narrower than thirty-six inches, and most are forty-eight or sixty inches wide. Diagonal placement of lathes conserves traffic lane space.

The north wall of the main work area is a cavity wall. The backing wall is constructed of six-inch, lightweight, two-core stretcher block laid in running bond form. The block is glazed with a medium green satin glaze having a light reflectance value of 35 per cent. Partitions are similarly constructed of eight-inch stretcher block glazed on both sides.

All ceilings are suspended fourteen feet above floor level. The ceiling panels are finished in an off-white color.

The concrete slab floor is faced with solid maple parquet blocks. The blocks are finished with a clear, semigloss floor seal.

Fluorescent luminaires provide adequate general illumination of the following intensities:

1. Classroom — 150 footcandles
2. Finishing rooms — 150 footcandles
3. Main work area — 150 footcandles
4. Project storage room — 50 footcandles
5. Major storage room — 30 footcandles
6. Minor storage room — 50 footcandles.

In addition, the drill presses, mortiser, shaper, grinder, band saw, scroll saws, and lathes have built-in local lighting systems. Arcproof switches and vaporproof fluorescent luminaires are installed in both finishing rooms.

The laboratory's air environment is controlled by the school's central heating and air-conditioning plant. During the cold weather, the plant maintains a steady temperature of 68°F. at seventy-two inches above floor level and a relative humidity of 40 to 60 per cent. It provides a steady flow of filtered air of a velocity sufficient to introduce approximately one and one-quarter complete changes of air per hour. Temperature variation between the floor and the seventy-two-inch level is 2°F. or less. In warm weather, a temperature of 70–80°F. (depending on the outdoor temperature) and the same conditions of relative humidity and air movement are maintained.

The dust collection system can serve two floor sweeps and the radial arm saw, band saw, table saws, jointer, Uniplane, planer, belt sanders, spindle sander, shaper, scroll saws, and lathes in simultaneous operation. The finishing room is equipped with a simple through-the-wall exhaust fan, while a comprehensive water and air exhaust system removes waste materials from the spray-finishing room.

A busway distributes 115 v., single-phase current and 230 v., three-phase current to the machines. Convenience outlets for both voltage/phase combinations are installed on the walls and partitions of all rooms except storage rooms. In addition, each work bench has a duplex 115 v., single-phase outlet suspended above it. The busway and convenience outlet circuits are controlled at a locking switch panel located on the partition on the right side of the door to the major storage room. The switch panel is equipped with a master switch that controls electrical service to all consuming devices and convenience outlets except the lights. An additional master switch is centrally located on the north wall and on each of the other two partitions. Every machine has its own switch box containing a manual external switch that mechanically breaks the motor circuit.

CONCLUSION

Change that retains proven values makes teaching a rewarding experience. On the other hand, sameness in laboratories and learning activities can erode the interest of teachers and students.

Obviously, industrial education must be improved in order to exploit fully its true potential as a part of our educational system. But few teachers are better than their laboratories permit them to be; therefore it is axiomatic that competent laboratory planning must help lead the way to improved programs.

Some pieces of equipment and materials that will be in common use within a decade are not now in existence, and their development will probably suggest new course content and better methods of laboratory organization. Certainly our proficiencies in the critically important planning areas of lighting, acoustics, and air environment control will increase.

FOR FURTHER READING

American Council on Industrial Arts Teacher Education. *A Guide to the Planning of Industrial Arts Facilities.* 24th yearbook. Bloomington, Ill.: McKnight Publishing Co., 1975.

American Council on Industrial Arts Teacher Education. *Planning Industrial Arts Facilities.* 8th yearbook. Bloomington, Ill.: McKnight Publishing Co., 1959.

Ashton, Denis. "Mobile Tool Cabinets for the Auto Shop." *Industrial Education,* March 1975, p. 77.

Campbell, Edward A. "Strike Down Haphazard Junior High Planning." *Industrial Education,* March 1973, p. 27.

Finsterbach, Fred C., and McNeice, William C. *Creative Facilities Planning for Occupational Education."* Berkeley Heights, N. J.: Educaré Associates, 1969.

Gallington, Ralph O. "A Unit Metals Shop for the Senior High School." *Industrial Arts and Vocational Education,* March 1965, p. 40.

Palumbo, Anthony. "Brainstorming Shop Flexibility." *School Shop,* April 1976, p. 60.

Pinelli, Thomas E., and Curtis, Myron W. "Build a Mobile Tool Panel." *School Shop,* November 1976, p. 38.

Pinelli, Thomas E., and Curtis, Myron W. "Individualize Tool Storage with Under-the-Bench-Kits." *Industrial Education,* March 1974, p. 70.

Schmitt, Marshall L., and Taylor, James L. *Planning and Designing Functional Facilities for Industrial Arts Education.* Washington, D. C.: U. S. Department of Health, Education, and Welfare, 1968.

Shemick, John M. "Clamp Racks You Can Build." *Industrial Education,* March 1975, p. 70.

Zook, Wayne H., and Collins, Dwight. "Storage/Work/Demonstration Units Update Shop." *Industrial Education,* March 1974, p. 49.

12

Administration of Programs and Facilities

INTRODUCTION

Each of the preceding chapters deals with a major segment of facilities planning that is at least partly administrative in nature. Thus, the entire planning process is substantially an administrative undertaking, and its importance transcends that of most other administrative activities. A number of significant administrative tasks, however, are related to the *operation* of instructional programs and laboratories. These tasks should be well understood by industrial teachers because it is they who will perform them.

Administrative procedures are intended to help set the stage for learning. As Homer J. Smith believed, they have been developed as ways of getting all things ready for those who will teach.[1] Instruction is the primary purpose of a school, and administrative procedures exist as support services designed to increase the effectiveness of teachers. Industrial teachers administer their laboratories and programs so that the stage *is* set for learning whenever a class is in session — but without

[1] Homer J. Smith, *Industrial Education — Administration and Supervision* (New York: Appleton-Century Co., 1927), p. 87.

attaching undue importance to administration, as such, or allowing it to consume more than a reasonable amount of time.

Administrative tasks that must be completed in order for a program and laboratory to operate effectively include:

1. Selection, organization, and improvement of course content
2. Acquisition of instructional media
3. Utilization of external resources
4. Promotion of laboratory safety
5. Development of a public relations program
6. Design of evening programs
7. Maintenance of records
8. Operation of a personnel system
9. Provision of laboratory maintenance services
10. Issuance of materials and equipment
11. Preparation of budgets

To be efficient administrators, industrial teachers must understand the importance of good administration and be able to apply many abilities to the solution of administrative problems. They should possess the fundamental qualities of good teachers — mental and physical health, intelligence, high moral character, pedagogical skill, knowledge of subject matter, interest in education, initiative, ambition, leadership abilities, and good judgment. In addition, it is necessary for them to have certain administrative competencies, such as an understanding of fundamental business procedures and the ability to tolerate a moderate amount of repetitious work. In short, a teacher must be able to manage as well as instruct.

SELECTION, ORGANIZATION, AND IMPROVEMENT OF COURSE CONTENT

A course of study should be viewed as a guide to teaching and learning. It directs instruction toward certain clearly defined educational goals, just as a road map charts the direction of a journey from one geographic location to another.

A course of study should be written by the teacher who will use it. If multiple sections of a course are to be taught by two or more teachers, similarity of content is desirable. This can be achieved through a list of content prepared by a committee of the teachers who will teach the course. It is not necessary, however, for emphases, teaching materials, and methods of approach to be the same in all sections. In fact, the opposite should be true. Individual teachers should be encouraged to teach the course in the manner that their intelligence, education, experience, capabilities, and philosophy indicate it should be taught. Therein, after all, lies the essence of academic freedom; but it exacts its price in the form of two burdens it imposes on teachers. The first requirement is that they must know about and be able to apply the best in philosophy, content, and pedagogy. The second is that each course must be planned so that it fits the realities of the situation in which the teacher must work — the amount of financial support, special needs of the community, the abilities of students who take the course, and other pertinent conditions.

The need for continuity of instruction is a factor that complicates course organization. As much as possible, the overlap of courses offered at various school levels must be eliminated so that students can make normal progress from one level of instruction to another. At the same time, the needs of transfer students who often have diverse educational backgrounds must be met. A logical solution is to expand the course offerings of industrial education departments so that introductory courses can be offered at all educational levels above the junior high school level. Then the introductory courses or previously taken "basic courses" would be strictly prerequisite to advanced courses. This approach makes necessary a coordinated program-structuring effort on the part of a school district's teachers, and it offers the likelihood of a much more meaningful total program.

In writing a course of study, a teacher must state objectives, list teaching resources, set forth a workable method of approach, and specify appropriate means of evaluation. The completed course should, in effect, say to the teacher and students, "This is where we are going. These are things that will help us get there. This is the route we will take. And these are devices that will be used to check our progress as we go along and, at the end of the term, to see how close to our destination we have come."

Objectives should be teacher objectives stated in terms of desired student behavior — new or enhanced skills, knowledge, understandings, attitudes, and appreciations. Objectives must be valid, understandable to the teacher and students, practical in the sense that they are attainable with the teaching resources at hand, and visionary in the sense that they encourage excellence.

Teaching resources include teachers' capabilities; laboratory facilities, equipment, and materials; instructional media; and external resources, such as industrial plants. They should be carefully selected so that course objectives can be achieved in the least amount of time.

A method of approach must be flexible enough to permit students of varying abilities to achieve all they are capable of achieving. Laboratory courses can, and do, excel at providing for individual differences, but this potential is not always fully exploited. Too few teachers understand that the practice of forcing everyone in a class to construct the same required projects — even with minor variations — does relatively little to encourage real personal development. The informational content of a course is highly important because it furnishes bases for planning and manipulative activities. But substantial emphasis should be placed on problem-solving, hands-on experiences, and the application of scientific and design principles in a variety of practical situations.

Common methods of evaluation include pencil-and-paper tests, performance tests, analyses of projects and other completed assignments, formal and informal teacher/student discussions, and observation periods that give a teacher the opportunity of evaluating students' attitudes, use of equipment, adherence to safety practices, and general progress in meeting course goals. Student achievement in every course should be carefully measured.

One important result of a teacher's efforts at course construction should be the preparation of a course outline to be distributed to students. If the outline clearly states the goals of the course, activities to be undertaken, assignments to be completed, means by which students' work will be evaluated, and standards by which the work will be judged, it can be a valuable teaching tool.

ACQUISITION OF INSTRUCTIONAL MEDIA

An instructional medium is any device or procedure that can be used to help make a lesson more meaningful to students. The major types of media include assigned readings; demonstrations; three-dimensional aids such as models, mock-ups, objects, and specimens; the chalkboard; graphic materials such as instruction sheets, drawings, photographs, diagrams, charts, and graphs; projects; displays; field trips; radio; television; and programmed instructional materials. In general, the more complex the material to be learned and/or the less able the learner, the greater the need for instructional media.

Potentially, all instructional media are helpful, but in order to be of maximum use in a given situation, a particular medium must be simple enough to be understandable to all members of the class. Its design, construction, and physical condition must be good, and its use must be timed to produce the greatest possible impact (Fig. 12.1).

In most cases, removing a student from actual participation in an experience makes it much less easy for him or her to understand what is

Figure 12.1 *35mm transparencies assist in mastering study materials.* (Eastman Kodak Company)

happening. However, comprehension is also a product of the student's mental and physical capabilities, educational development, and level of maturity. For example, a series of 35 mm. slides that show the procedures to be followed in performing operations on a metal lathe is inherently more abstract than a demonstration of the use of the machine, especially if the demonstration if followed by a practice period. At the same time, obtaining information from transparencies is a less abstract experience for some students than for others. Therefore, a teacher must be able to choose the instructional media that will be the most effective in each teaching/learning situation. It is a serious pedagogical error to depend too heavily on the most common media — assigned readings, the chalkboard, and motion pictures — because they are too abstract for many students.

The level of craftsmanship employed in preparing an instructional medium should be appropriate to its nature and to the way in which it will be used. A large, teacher-made, wood model of hand saw teeth, for instance, should be well constructed, but it need not exhibit the fine workmanship desirable in a piece of living room furniture. Nevertheless it does exemplify the expertise of the teacher and should require no apology. It is well to remember that teacher-made media of various kinds provide numerous examples of the technical competence of a teacher and that the correct impression should be given to students.

Instructional media must be kept up to date through modification and replacement. It is particularly necessary that instruction sheets, such as operation sheets, information sheets, process sheets, job assignment sheets, and activity assignment sheets, be periodically revised. Information that they present concerning materials and processes must always be as current as possible. An instruction sheet that assigns a project needs frequent revision so that, over the years, parents will not be presented with several copies of a project that may or may not be well designed. In this regard, an activity assignment sheet is the most useful, because it requires students to be creative within a specified activity; consequently it is more or less self-revising.

Preparing instructional media can be a time-consuming and expensive activity. It is true that some very good media are available free of charge from businesses, industries, governmental units, and other sources; but time is required to locate, obtain, and — in some cases — modify them so that they meet classroom needs. Since the acquisition of instructional media is one of an industrial teacher's important tasks, he or she must have free time in which to do it. In addition, every teacher needs a budget that permits purchasing commercially prepared media, materials to be used in making media, and storage devices — such as slide trays, storage cabinets, and flat drawer files — that keep aids properly classified, in good condition, and readily available for use.

Much of the desired effect of an instructional medium can be lost if its use is not well timed. Good timing is especially necessary where projected materials are to be shown. Consequently a teacher's schedule of class periods (prepared for the whole term) and daily lesson plans should indicate the days on which specific media will be used.

UTILIZATION OF EXTERNAL RESOURCES

External resources can be defined as anything outside the school environment — people, services, equipment, materials, facilities, or geographic features — that can be used to supplement the work of a teacher and make classroom instruction more meaningful. Examples of external resources are professional workers, industrial plants, mines, museums, libraries, and sources of scrap materials. These and many other external resources can be used to enrich industrial education courses and increase students' enjoyment of their work. Indirectly, resource persons from public schools, state departments of education, colleges, and universities can increase students' achievement by helping to improve facilities, courses of study, instructional materials, administrative procedures, and teachers' preparation.

External resources can also be of considerable value in establishing and maintaining good relations between a school and the district it serves. Many people take pride in working with schools and welcome opportunities to serve them. In fact, the more lay people who can be involved in contributing to the work of a school, the broader its base of support and goodwill becomes.

Every industrial teacher should make a continuous effort to identify useful external resources. A card file of these resources, periodically reviewed and edited, can provide an effective means of storing information so that it is readily available.

Usually it is best for a teacher to make the greatest use of external resources that can be brought into the laboratory and to minimize the number of field trips. There is little doubt that a field trip can be a valuable teaching tool, and it is the only way in which students can experience the sights, sounds, smells, heat, and orderly confusion of industry. But it is an abstract kind of experience for many students, as judged by the amount of learning that actually takes place. It is also time-consuming. Therefore field trips should be used sparingly to achieve clear-cut goals that cannot be reached by other, more efficient means.

To have real educational value, a field trip must be skillfully administered. Contacts should be initiated at an early date and arrangements concerning the time, place, number of students to be accommodated, and other details determined so that all parties clearly understand what will be done and what obligations will be incurred. Final confirmation several days prior to the visit is always wise. All necessary arrangements for transportation, meals, and lodging must be made in advance and confirmed prior to departure. Students must be instructed as to what to look for. They should also be informed of the need, if any, for written parental permission, acceptable standards of dress, the time and place of departure, expected behavior, and the financial arrangements. As soon as possible after a visit, all bills should be paid and expressions of appreciation extended to those who arranged or conducted the trip. The experience should be followed by discussions, reports, tests, and other activities that help to recall and explain what was experienced.

PROMOTION OF LABORATORY SAFETY

The word "accident" is widely used, but it is not an accurate term because it suggests that an event that has resulted in injury and/or property damage has occurred by chance. A few laboratory accidents may be chance happenings, but nearly all accidents are caused by identifiable, unsafe acts or conditions and are, therefore, avoidable. Major causes of accidents in industrial education laboratories include:

1. Too little laboratory space
2. Unfavorable environmental conditions, such as ineffectual lighting and poor ventilation
3. Unsafe electrical systems
4. Lack of or improper types of fire extinguishers
5. Insufficient storage space for materials
6. Unwise selection of equipment
7. Ineffective laboratory organization
8. Unsatisfactory laboratory maintenance
9. Machine guards that are missing, defective, or poorly designed
10. Lack of safety glasses, safety shoes, face shields, and other safety devices
11. Inadequate means of handling flammable materials and wastes
12. Classes that are too large
13. Courses of study requiring activities that are beyond the capabilities of some students
14. Inadequate safety instruction
15. Teacher's careless work habits
16. Safety rules not enforced
17. Poor attitudes toward safety
18. Lack of effective class discipline
19. Lack of skill
20. Fear of equipment
21. Physical defects, such as poor eyesight and hearing loss
22. Unsafe clothing worn by students (long ties, long sleeves, rings, etc.)

Consideration of these causes makes three conclusions inescapable: first, each is a condition that can be prevented or offset; second, unless a teacher makes a purposeful effort to achieve satisfactory laboratory safety, accidents probably will occur; and third, the most important means of promoting safety are skillful laboratory planning, proper laboratory maintenance, and good teaching.

The necessity of planning for safety in an industrial education laboratory has been discussed in the preceding chapters. The remaining

PROMOTION OF LABORATORY SAFETY

question is this: How can a laboratory and program be administered so that accidents are avoided?

Course organization is the logical starting point. Courses must be

Figure 12.2 *Lists of safety rules help to teach accident prevention.*

SAFETY RULES FOR THE CIRCULAR SAW

The possibility of having an accident with a circular saw is ever-present. However, it can be operated in perfect safety, if the operator knows and practices the rules of safe usage. There are no dangerous machines — only dangerous operators.

1. Keep your machine in good condition: keep it clean, lubricate it regularly, and be sure that the blades are sharp and properly set. Poorly conditioned blades are dangerous!
2. Keep tools and materials off the saw table whenever the machine is in use.
3. Keep the floor around the saw clean.
4. Check the setup for your job carefully before turning on the power.
5. Stock must lay flat on the saw table. Do not saw badly cupped stock. If it is cupped slightly, it can be sawed safely, if it is held with the concave side down. Never attempt to saw stock that is in wind.
6. Roll up your sleeves, tuck in your tie and NEVER wear gloves.
7. Adjust the saw blade so that it projects approximately $1/8''$ above the stock.
8. Whenever possible, use the blade guard and other safety devices.
9. Always use the ripping fence or mitre gauge. Freehand sawing increases the risk of serious accident.
10. Use a clearance block when cutting duplicate pieces to length against the ripping fence.
11. Stand slightly to the left of the saw blade, never directly in line with it.
12. When ripping stock, feed with the right hand and guide with the left. The left hand should seldom go beyond the front edge of the saw table.
13. REMEMBER, the minimum safe width for ripping without the use of a pusher is three inches.
14. Make no adjustments to the machine while it is running.
15. Keep your mind and eyes on the job. Talk to no one while operating the circular saw, and allow no one to talk to you.
16. Stop the saw before reaching for scrap pieces laying on the table.

BE A SAFE OPERATOR

designed to interest and challenge students at their own levels of capability so that no one is handicapped by course content that presents too great a challenge or represents no real challenge at all. Boredom and irritation caused by lack of purpose can result in accidents. Consequently the often stated ideal that courses should provide for individual differences must represent conviction rather than mere verbalism.

As a course progresses, students should receive instruction in the safe use of each piece of equipment before being permitted to operate it. In class demonstrations and work, the teacher should serve as an example of the best in safe work habits.

At the conclusion of demonstrations covering the use of more hazardous machines — table saws, jointers, shapers, band saws, grinders, and lathes — comprehensive lists of safety rules should be distributed to students (see Fig. 12.2). A condensed list of safety rules should be posted at each machine.

Unit safety tests covering the use of hazardous machines should be given, and students should be required to pass each test with a perfect score before operating the equipment. Each unit test should also require students to sign a statement saying that they have been given safety instruction pertaining to that piece of equipment.

Minors cannot, of course, sign their legal rights away; but such a

Figure 12.3 *Parents' permission form.*

```
                    PARENTS' PERMISSION FORM

_____ has our permission to
              (student's name)

operate the equipment in the _____ laboratory.
It is understood that instruction in safe operation will be given before
he is allowed to use any piece of equipment and that he will be
supervised properly at all times.
      In case of accident, we prefer that he be given treatment by
Dr. _____
Our home phone number is _____
Date _____
                                            _____
                                                    (father)
                                            _____
                                                    (mother)
                                            _____
                                                (legal guardian)
```

statement is an indication to all concerned that the students know that safe operating practices have been taught. It may also be a wise policy to ask parents and legal guardians to give students written permission to use laboratory equipment after instruction in safe usage has been given. Again, a minor's legal rights cannot be signed away, but a signed permission form similar to the one shown in Fig. 12.3 provides evidence that the parent understands that hazards exist and has approved the student's use of the equipment.

For their part, industrial teachers must understand all federal, state, and local safety statutes; give adequate safety instruction; avoid making students afraid of equipment; and provide proper supervision whenever a class is in session. Teachers must never be absent from a laboratory when students are using power tools and should always be alert to detect unsafe acts or conditions. Teachers should also watch for evidence of physical defects, poor physical health, or poor mental health in students. If any of these conditions is discovered, it should be brought to the attention of the appropriate school administrative officer, and the student should not be allowed to operate power tools until the problem has been resolved.

A second important means of promoting safety in an industrial education laboratory is a maintenance program designed to ensure that each piece of equipment will be in its best operating condition at all times. Dull cutting edges, worn parts, lack of lubrication, improper adjustment, damage, absence or improper functioning of protective devices, unsafe storage of equipment, and other deficiencies should be corrected as soon as they have been discovered, even if it is necessary to remove pieces of equipment from service for short periods of time. Routine safety inspections offer the best way of determining the need for maintenance. A chart–check sheet that shows periodic lubrication needs — time intervals, types of lubricants, and amounts of lubricants required — and provides space in which to record the dates on which lubrication jobs were performed is always useful in making preventive maintenance procedures more efficient and less time-consuming.

Finally, every industrial teacher must make a determined effort to minimize the seriousness and effects of accidents that *do* occur. Each accident should be carefully analyzed so that its causes can be discovered and steps can be taken to prevent a recurrence. This is scant comfort to a student who has sustained an injury but of great benefit to those who might otherwise be injured in the same way. A well-designed, comprehensive accident report form can be instrumental in determining causes of accidents (see Fig. 12.4).

Each laboratory should be equipped with a first aid kit, and, ideally,

```
                        ACCIDENT REPORT FORM

Name of person injured _____ Date _____
Type of injury _____
Laboratory in which accident occurred _____
Did accident take place during regularly scheduled class period? _____
Name of teacher in charge _____ Was teacher present? _____
Action taken to administer first aid/or obtain medical assistance _____
_____
_____
_____
_____

Circumstances under which accident occurred and the cause of injury _____
_____
_____
_____
_____
_____
_____

Action taken or recommended to prevent recurrence _____
_____
_____
_____
_____

Comments _____
_____
_____
```

Figure 12.4 *Accident report form.*

industrial teachers should be trained in basic first aid procedures. Statutes, however, severely limit what a lay person can do in giving medical assistance to an accident victim, and perhaps rightly so; but they can make it very difficult to aid someone who must have help quickly. Therefore an industrial teacher should plan and rehearse the procedure to be followed in obtaining medical assistance in the event of an accident. Such a procedure should specify the actions of both the teacher and students during an emergency.

School districts should seriously consider the desirability of providing accident insurance benefits for industrial teachers and students. Moreover, it seems evident that teachers should be protected at district expense by liability insurance. No district, in good conscience, can force persons who are injured while taking part in educational programs to pay for their own medical treatment, and legal judgments against teachers must not be allowed to damage professional careers and family financial structures.

DEVELOPMENT OF A PUBLIC RELATIONS PROGRAM

Because the public pays the cost of operating public schools, it is entitled to know how well the schools are educating its children. Given the knowledge that the job is being done, that expenditures of tax money are, in fact, purchasing quality education, the public will usually support any worthwhile program that a school proposes. Therefore schools must do everything in their power to promote harmonious public relations and keep the residents of a district fully informed as to the educational progress being made. Special efforts must be made to reach public officials, news media, parents, taxpayers' organizations, fraternal organizations, and civic, religious, business, industrial, labor, and professional groups, all of which are important sources of support for education. A good public relations program keeps all members of a community informed of the progress and needs of their schools, and it does so in an interesting, thought-provoking, factual way.

Support for an industrial arts or vocational-technical program must come from the groups just listed, as well as from school administrative officers, teachers, and students who enroll in the various laboratory courses. Good public relations are especially important to industrial arts teachers, because the per-student costs of industrial arts classes are much higher than those of most other subject matter areas and, therefore, in need of careful justification. No industrial arts teacher can afford to assume that having a well-equipped laboratory signifies that the program has universal acceptance in the community.

Publicity can be formal or informal. Informal publicity results from observations of school administrators, teachers, parents, and other people. It comes from comments by students who have taken laboratory courses and from impressions created by projects that are taken home or put on display. Favorable informal publicity is the result of:

1. Friendly, competent industrial teachers who have broad interests and a deep respect for other curriculum areas
2. Valid courses of study that provide for individual differences by means of interesting and educationally valuable activities
3. Fair and consistent class discipline
4. Laboratory personnel systems that serve their purposes without exploiting students
5. High course standards that encourage excellent scholarship
6. Well planned and well maintained laboratory facilities

Of course there can be no better publicity than that generated by a top quality program.

Formal publicity can be obtained from articles published in newspapers, professional journals, and other periodicals; speeches, panel discussions, and demonstrations presented to various groups; and exhibits that show projects, laboratory equipment, industrial processes, and instructional media. Publicity also can be gained through field trips and visits to businesses, industries, and other community resources; visiting days or nights that bring the community into industrial education laboratories; and the development of clubs and fraternities for industrial education students. All of these approaches are potentially effective.

Visiting nights have some unique advantages. They allow parents and others to see industrial education laboratories in operation and give them the opportunity to ask questions of teachers and students, learn more about the work of individual classes, and develop an understanding of the scope of the total program. Student guides, written explanatory materials, and small displays can make visiting nights more meaningful.

A project exhibit makes it possible for an industrial education department to acquaint members of the community with the finest work done during a school term. It gives the department the opportunity to put its best foot forward in a way that is invariably interesting. The chief limitation of exhibits, especially those that are presented periodically, is that they can influence the program in an unfortunate way if they determine the nature of projects undertaken and/or make it necessary for teachers to neglect weaker students whose work will not be suitable for display.

It is difficult for industrial teachers to fully develop their programs unless they can establish good professional rapport with other teachers. Lack of understanding of the goals and values of industrial education can lead to friction that is detrimental to program development. To project a satisfactory image, industrial teachers must be convinced that their profession is worthwhile and that the courses taught are vital to the total school program. There is no room for feelings of professional inferiority if other teachers are to respect their competence. Industrial teachers must be articulate about the values of their subject area and knowledgeable about the values of other areas. Finding ways to correlate industrial education courses with other courses by identifying educational undertakings in which there can be cooperation can result in improved teaching and greatly enhanced intraschool relations.

Industrial education classes should not do production work that should be contracted to private firms. However, certain jobs — if they can be worked into courses of study without making it more difficult to achieve course objectives — can be undertaken as a service to other teachers and school administrators, thereby creating goodwill for an industrial education department. The reverse is also true. An industrial teacher can build goodwill by accepting the help of other teachers.

In general, it is wise for industrial teachers to prohibit unauthorized use of laboratories and to make certain that it does not take place. Loss of materials and damage to tools and equipment can generate serious misunderstandings. On the other hand, an uncooperative attitude can be harmful to professional relationships. Therefore it is often helpful to open a laboratory to other teachers at regular intervals for supervised work, provided it does not hamper the industrial teacher's activities or the operation of classes.

DESIGN OF EVENING PROGRAMS

An evening class program offers a fine way to render important services to members of a community and, at the same time, to publicize a school district's industrial education program. If the industrial education program is reasonably comprehensive, it will be possible to offer types of evening courses that appeal to large numbers of people. It is usually wise to offer both beginning and advanced courses each term. Industrial teachers who have conducted evening classes have discovered that they provide a welcome change of pace, new challenges, the opportunity of working with adults, and a chance to develop additional professional competence.

Most evening classes are designed to serve specific purposes. The basic types of courses offered include:

1. Avocational classes
2. Home maintenance classes
3. Training classes for local industries
4. In-service classes for teachers

5. Supervised work periods for teachers
6. Classes for handicapped students

Of these, the first three have been and probably will continue to be the most popular.

It can be argued that because many industrial arts teachers lack extensive industrial experience and are not certified as vocational/technical teachers, they should not teach training courses for industries. No doubt there are instances when this is true. However, in a number of technical areas, lack of a vocational certificate is not a real handicap. For example, an experienced industrial arts teacher who has substantial expertise in the area of drafting — and there are many such teachers — can do an excellent job of teaching drawing principles and practices to evening class students from industry. The teacher may not be familiar with all of the drafting standards of each industry in the community, but students can acquire this knowledge on the job. It is not suggested that industrial arts teachers take part in comprehensive vocational/technical training programs. But where certified vocational/technical teachers are not available, industrial arts teachers can be of service in upgrading industrial workers.

Work with equipment and materials interests many teachers, regardless of subject specialty. Consequently, evening classes especially for teachers can be very effective means of helping them to develop and pursue avocational activities, prepare instructional media, and acquire useful skills and knowledge. Supervised work periods can be equally valuable to teachers who have already developed proficiencies in laboratory work.

Persons who have physical handicaps of various kinds often can benefit from laboratory work. The therapeutic values of laboratory activities in rebuilding strength, muscular coordination, interests, and emotional balance are well known. Evening classes for handicapped persons have never been widely offered, yet the potential for significant service is there, as professionals in the field of special education have discovered. School districts should welcome such opportunities to be of service.

An evening class program must be well publicized in order to be successful. Information concerning the content of each course, as well as the starting date, length, admission requirements, cost, and time and place of class meetings should be sent to people most likely to be interested in enrolling in evening classes. Newspaper advertisements, radio and television announcements, posters, telephone calls, and personal contacts by industrial teachers and school administrators can be used to acquaint possible students with educational opportunities the school will make available. One of the most productive ways of providing information is to distribute an illustrated brochure — or even a brief printed notice — to teachers, to students, and to the rest of the community. Usually, a comprehensive approach that includes several means of reaching the prospective clientele is best. And the values of postcourse publicity that describes and gives credit for work done should not be overlooked.

Evening classes should be scheduled so that, as much as possible, they will be taught during the free time of potential students. It is not possible to meet the needs of everyone, but church nights, nights when other well-established programs are offered, and other times when regularly scheduled activities take place should be avoided.

The amount of instructional time provided by an evening class should be sufficient to cover the content of the course but not enough to cause students' interest to wane. It is well to reach the end of a course and find that students wish it was not over. Some courses should be one semester in length, while others may need more (or less) time. It may be comfortable to administer a program in which all courses are the same length, but this approach may be much less productive.

Evening classes are often organized as short unit courses, such as wood finishing, that stress parts of larger areas of instruction. Evening students, as a rule, begin courses with quite definite goals in mind and are unhappy if they cannot achieve them. Consequently, course organization must satisfy students' needs as they perceive them but not necessarily as the instructor sees them. For example, a person who enrolls in a course in architectural drawing in order to make working drawings of a home he or she intends to build does not wish to be unduly harassed with course requirements. The necessary study of architectural design, house construction, and drawing practices is certainly of interest, but above all, the goal is to complete the needed plans.

Instruction sheets of various kinds can be used to provide for individual differences, provided they allow students to choose their own projects within specified limits.

Evaluation is not an important factor in the conduct of many evening classes. Usually, students do not enroll to earn grades. They want to receive the professional approval of the teacher and acquire useful skills and information.

MAINTENANCE OF RECORDS

School records are written statements that preserve knowledge of school events. They make it possible for a school to evaluate its performance in achieving its objectives, to provide certain services for students, and to manage its business affairs. In many cases, the effectiveness of administrative procedures is dependent on the kinds of records kept and on their accuracy.

Every industrial teacher must maintain two types of records: those that the school's administrative officers require be kept and those that make possible a good teaching performance. Usually, attendance records provide the basis upon which a significant portion of a school's financial support rests, since state aid monies are often allocated according to average daily attendance. Attendance records are, therefore, highly important. Most schools require teachers to keep accurate daily counts of students who are present and absent.

Teachers also must prepare records that can be used in writing recommendations for students when they apply for employment, admission to colleges and other types of schools, and enlistment in the armed services. Such records include final course grades, attendance, and, sometimes, anecdotal accounts containing information about attitudes, interests, abilities, and achievement that help depict a student's total school

Figure 12.5 *Equipment inventory card.*

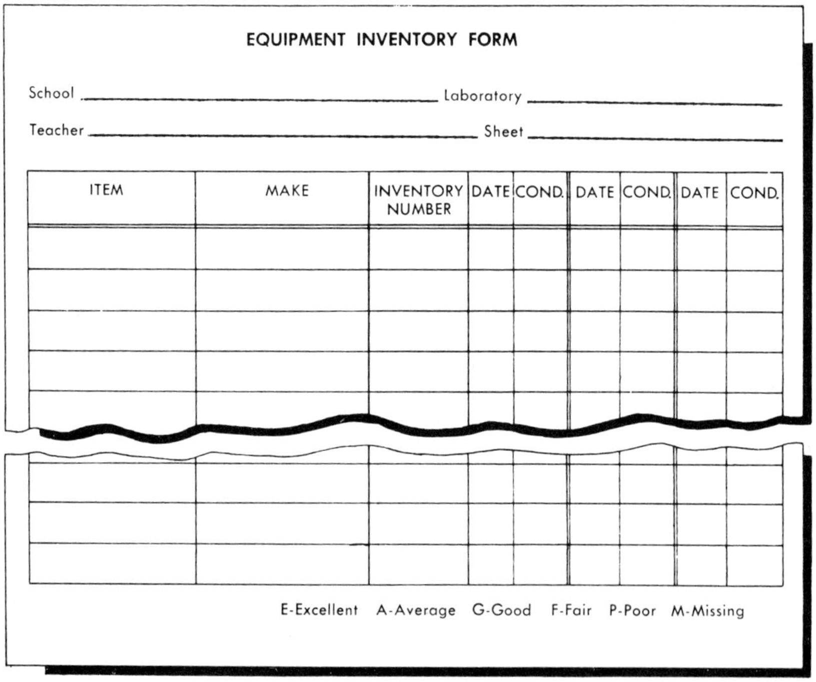

EQUIPMENT INVENTORY FORM

School ____________ Laboratory ____________

Teacher ____________ Sheet ____________

ITEM	MAKE	INVENTORY NUMBER	DATE	COND.	DATE	COND.	DATE	COND.

E-Excellent A-Average G-Good F-Fair P-Poor M-Missing

MAINTENANCE OF RECORDS

performance. Well-kept records make it more likely that recommendations will be helpful to students and to those who request information about them.

As is necessary for any commercial enterprise, a school must manage its assets well. Accurate inventories of equipment and materials should be maintained at all times. Each piece of equipment should be assigned a school inventory number that is permanently marked on it, and it should be identified by number and type on an inventory sheet that also lists its brand name and location (Fig. 12.5).

Inventories should be carefully checked each year and whenever teachers are replaced. Before being relieved, an outgoing teacher should be required to list missing items and justify the absence of each. The incoming teacher should check the inventory and, before assuming control of it, note all discrepancies between items listed and those present in the laboratory.

It is convenient to keep a running inventory of materials by means of a card file in which each addition and withdrawal is accurately recorded. Cards should be filed within logical categories. In the case of a crafts laboratory, for example, material categories include metals, plastics, leather, and other general types of materials, depending on the scope of the program. Every category should contain one card for each different material stocked. Each card should list the name of the material and the quantity on hand (Fig. 12.6).

Figure 12.6 *Materials inventory card.*

A reliable corps of substitute teachers is essential to the efficient operation of a school. School administrative officers should require regular teachers to prepare a written plan for each class session a week or more in advance of the day on which it will be held. This plan will help substitute teachers to assume responsibility for classes and carry on the instruction.

Lesson plans for an industrial education class should be accompanied by additional sheets listing the location of keys, equipment, materials, and electrical distribution system controls; basic safety rules; and standards of laboratory operation. A substitute teacher should be treated as a professional who has come to do what can be a difficult job, not as someone who cannot be trusted to get out materials, use the equipment, and conduct classes in the normal way.

Optional records that an industrial teacher may find it desirable to keep (or require students to keep) include the following:

1. A list of equipment and materials that students must purchase outside the school. Names of items, quantities, and other needed information should be given. Each student should have a copy of the list (Fig. 12.7).
2. Records that assist students in completing assignments and

Figure 12.7 *Parts list for small engine repair.*

	PARTS LIST — SMALL ENGINE REPAIR		
ENGINE MAKE	MODEL NO.	TYPE NO.	SERIAL NO.
QUANTITY	PART NEEDED	MANUFACTURER'S NO.	COST
1	crankshaft magneto oil seal		
1	crankshaft P.T.O. oil seal		
1	engine gasket set		
1	piston ring set		
1	breaker point set		
1	crankshaft magneto key		
1	crankshaft P.T.O. key		
1	oil slinger bracket		

MAINTENANCE OF RECORDS 293

WEAR CHECKPOINTS — SMALL ENGINE REPAIR					
ENGINE MAKE	MODEL NO.	TYPE NO.		SERIAL NO.	
CHECKPOINT		GAUGE NO.	LIMIT	MY ENGINE	ACTION
cylinder dia., max.					
cylinder out-of-round, max.					
piston: piston pin bearing dia., max.					
piston pin dia., min.					
connecting rod: pin bearing dia., max.					
valve guide dia., max.					
oil slinger bracket shaft dia., min.					
breaker point plunger, length					

Figure 12.8 *Engine evaluation form—small engine repair.*

evaluating their laboratory work — for example, bills of materials, plans of procedure, project evaluation forms (Fig. 12.8), and data sheets on which to record facts pertinent to the performance of tasks.

3. A progress chart on which to keep a running account of each student's completion of tests, projects, and other assignments (Fig. 12.9). If grades or scores are recorded, they should be listed opposite students' code numbers in order to ensure privacy.

4. Records that provide protection against charges of malpractice. An example of this type of record is a form on which a student certifies that he or she has been taught the safety rules pertaining to a certain machine.

5. A running account of the teacher's progress during a course, as well as a schedule of class periods that makes it possible to check off demonstrations given, assignments made and collected, and tests administered.

6. A list of all industrial education courses offered in the program. Each entry should include the course number (if any), the course title, and a brief description of content.

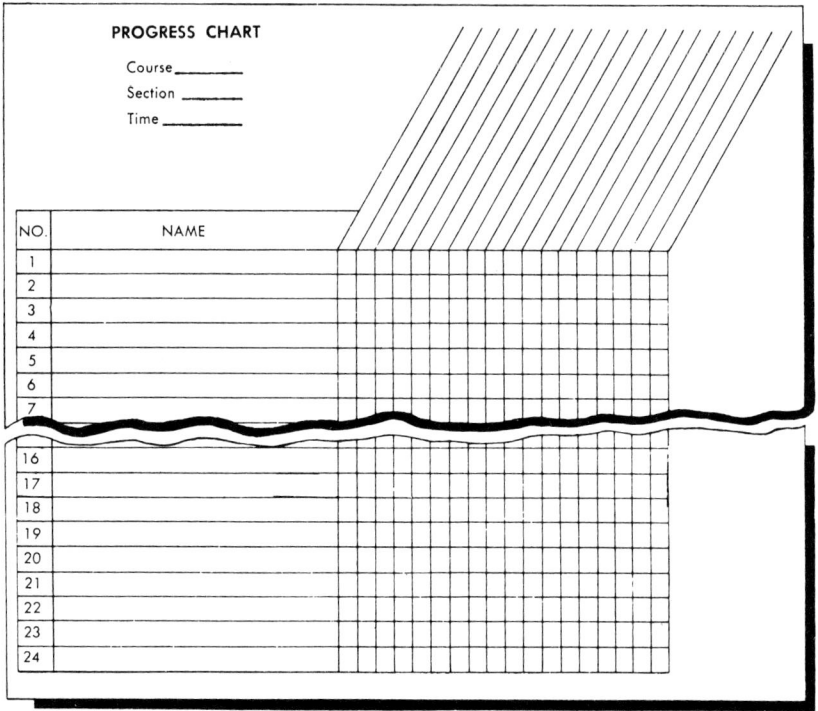

Figure 12.9 *Progress chart.*

7. Records that chart the progress of the industrial education department and provide information that will be useful in answering questions about the program — for example, a year-by-year list of courses offered, the number of students enrolled in each course, and new equipment purchased.
8. Records (such as receipt forms) designed to keep the industrial education department's financial affairs on a businesslike basis and to prevent errors in monetary transactions.
9. A card file record of locker or drawer keys issued. The cards should contain blank spaces in which the teacher can mark the key deposit paid or returned to the student and spaces in which the course title and section number, date, number of the key, and student's name can be recorded (Fig. 12.10). The amount of a key deposit should be several times the replace-

MAINTENANCE OF RECORDS

ment cost of the key so that a student will have an incentive to find a key that has been misplaced. Keys not issued should hang on hooks in a locking key cabinet. The number of each key — which should be the same as the number of the locker or the desk and drawer it fits — should be marked on the key panel above its hook. At least one duplicate of each key must be kept in the cabinet, and the teacher should have a master key.

10. A list that matches each locker or drawer key's laboratory number with its manufacturer's number. (The manufacturer's number will be stamped on the lock it operates.)
11. A card file of library books and a book card system that facilitates lending books to students.

In order for records to meet the needs of a department and a teacher, a good filing system is essential. As has been suggested, card files are useful for storing several kinds of records. Other records should be kept in standard file folders in four-drawer filing cabinets. Consequently, every industrial education laboratory should be equipped with at least three four-drawer filing cabinets and as many card files as necessary.

Record forms are not difficult to design. Each should be planned for a specific purpose, and it should be simple and easy to use. An important point to remember is that records are not ends in themselves. They should not be used to retain useless information. The best system is one that includes only essential records.

Figure 12.10 *Record cards are essential to laboratory key security.*

```
                    KEY DEPOSIT CARD

Course Title _____ Course No. _____ Section No. _____

Student's Name _____ Key No. _____

Deposit Paid _____ Date _____
                        (teacher)

Deposit Returned _____ Date _____
                        (teacher)
```

OPERATION OF A PERSONNEL SYSTEM

The personnel system used in an industrial educational laboratory can achieve at least three objectives. It can acquaint students with the nature and operation of industrial plant personnel systems and it can provide some valuable team experiences. The primary function of any personnel system, however, is to ensure that necessary laboratory cleanup and maintenance work is done. Such a system should not be needlessly encumbered with tasks that cannot be performed well or that are unnecessary.

A personnel system must be as simple as possible. Its operation should require only a small amount of teacher and student time because it has relatively little intrinsic value. Each student should be assigned to perform a specific task or to serve as an alternate who takes the place of someone who is absent. Two or three alternates are usually sufficient. Tasks should be planned so that students have roughly equal amounts of work to do, and the required standards of performance must be made clear. Job rotation at regular intervals is desirable because it lends impressions of equity. Job titles, such as "tool foreman," may carry a little prestige, but students are seldom led to believe that titles represent anything more than routine work to be done. Therefore the important thing is to convince students that by keeping laboratories clean and in good operating condition, they are serving their own best interests.

Grades that are arbitrarily selected fractions of project grades can be assigned in order to increase the thoroughness with which each cleanup task is performed. But this procedure is workable only if the performance of each student is evaluated at the end of each class period. Such evaluations need not be time-consuming, but they must be thorough.

A personnel system can be designed so that the teacher is in direct control of its operation or so that he or she acts as the general manager. The first type of organization requires the teacher to supervise the work of all students and to keep the necessary records. The second type is designed to permit the teacher to work through a student superintendent to whom student workers are responsible. Variations of the two systems are presented in Fig. 12.11. Jobs can be filled by appointment, election, or initial appointment or election followed by periodic rotation. The first and third methods are recommended because they conserve class time and are effective. A sheet describing the duties of each job should be distributed to every student. A copy of the sheet should also be posted in a conspicuous place near the personnel chart.

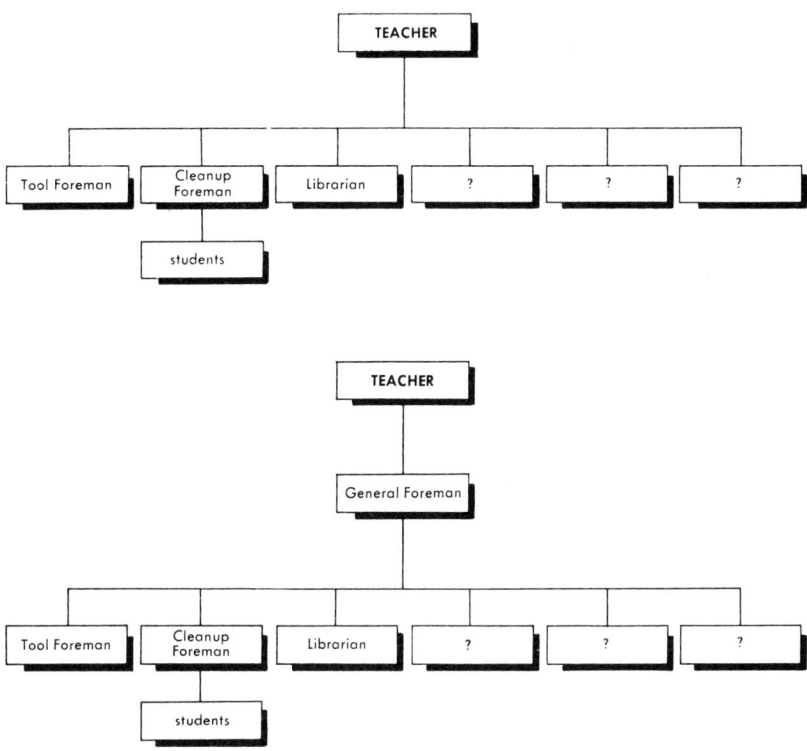

Figure 12.11 *Two types of personnel systems for industrial education laboratories.*

PROVISION OF LABORATORY MAINTENANCE SERVICES

Unless a laboratory is well cared for, courses cannot be taught with maximum effectiveness, and it is difficult to maintain adequate standards of safety and discipline. Hand tools, power tools, laboratory furniture, and instructional media must be kept clean, tight, properly lubricated, in good adjustment, free of rust, and well finished. Worn and broken parts should be promptly replaced, and cutting edges must be kept sharp. Care of materials should also be considered a maintenance problem. They must be kept in good condition by means of appropriate storage procedures and devices and accurate control of temperature and humidity.

Whether or not a laboratory is properly maintained depends on the industrial teacher's concept of the value of good maintenance, as well as on skill, knowledge, efficiency, and initiative in identifying and meeting maintenance needs. Teachers who are convinced of the importance of good maintenance, have the required skill and knowledge, and are willing to make the necessary effort, will have laboratories that are always in satisfactory condition. Otherwise a laboratory will seldom be fully ready for teaching and learning.

Good maintenance begins with the development of a list of standards. The list should include lubrication intervals, types of lubricants, amounts of lubricants, adjustment specifications, sharpening specifications, and part tolerances for each piece of laboratory equipment.

Inspections and minor maintenance services can often be performed during class periods, but the bulk of the work must be undertaken during free periods, after school hours, on Saturdays, and during vacation periods. Maintenance jobs such as grinding metal lathe cutter bits, honing plane irons, and calibrating meters of various kinds can be performed by students. But the educational values to be derived from time spent maintaining equipment must be carefully weighed against the benefits of time devoted to other types of class activities. Maintenance tasks that require considerable skill and/or are unusually time-consuming should be performed by industrial teachers or contracted to private firms.

Improvement of laboratory appearance should be considered an important element of any maintenance program. Teachers should not be entirely responsible for the appearances of laboratories but their requests for certain contractual services and their administration of personnel systems have much to do with creating and perpetuating satisfactory appearances.

At the end of each class period, students should clean all pieces of equipment that have been used. There is little question that this is a legitimate class requirement. However, it may not be as justifiable to assign students to sweep laboratory floors after class periods. It can be argued that this is a custodial function and that it represents exploitation of students. But the fact that some industrial education laboratories have unique cleanup requirements should not be forgotten. Each class adds to the quantity of waste materials present on a laboratory's floors, and if they are swept only at the end of the day by a custodian, every class after the first one inherits floors that are unsightly and dangerous. Moreover, the problem grows steadily worse as the day wears on.

Floor cleanup is seldom necessary during the day in drawing and electricity/electronics laboratories. Littered floors in graphic arts, crafts, automotive, metals, and general laboratories can be a handicap, however, and in woods laboratories, they are almost always a serious problem.

PROVISION OF LABORATORY MAINTENANCE SERVICES

STUDENT	DUTY	DESCRIPTION
	LABORATORY CLEANUP CHART	
	GENERAL FOREMAN	1. Check at the beginning of each class period to see that all members of the cleanup crew are present. 2. Assign alternates in case of absences. 3. Supervise the cleanup period. 4. Report to the teacher each instance in which a duty has been done poorly or left undone.
	MACHINE CLEANUP drill press pedestal grinder hydraulic press valve refacer	1. Remove oil, dust, and scrap materials. 2. See that all tools and attachments are in place.
	MACHINE CLEANUP distributor tester motor analy…	1. Remove oil.
	ALTERNATE	1. Perform the duties of all cleanup crew members who are absent. The first listed alternate always functions, if one cleanup crew member is absent. The second alternate functions in case of need.

every student	WORK STATION CLEANUP	1. Make sure that your own work station is in order by:
		  a. removing waste materials and rags and placing them in the designated containers.
		  b. arranging parts, mechanisms, and materials in good order on the bench top.
		  c. storing large units in the base cabinets.
		  d. storing pieces of literature and personal tools in the base cabinet.
		  e. hanging laboratory aprons in the storage cabinet. (Note: aprons should be kept clean through biweekly laundering.)

Figure 12.12 *Laboratory cleanup charts must make specific assignments.*

Except in drawing and electricity/electronics laboratories, the best solution appears to be to require all classes other than the last one to give the floors a rapid cleaning, while depending on a custodian to clean them well at the end of the day.

In many geographic areas, rust is a major maintenance problem, because it can affect the appearance, operation, and service life of equipment. On occasion, students can help with rust removal and rust prevention procedures, but these are essentially teacher tasks. Paint is effective in preventing rust as long as surfaces are kept completely coated. Surfaces that cannot be painted should be kept lightly oiled or polished with paste wax. Wax is helpful in woods, crafts, electricity/electronics, drawing, graphic arts, and general laboratories, where the presence of oil on pieces of equipment would be detrimental to proper operation.

ISSUANCE OF MATERIALS AND EQUIPMENT

Issuance of materials and equipment is an administrative activity that is carried on in all industrial education laboratories. Materials must be dispensed, checked off the inventory (if a running inventory is kept), and billed to students. Similarly, equipment will be checked out, returned, inspected, and put back in storage. And reference materials must be issued, returned, checked, and replaced on library shelves. Usually a teacher has little choice but to utilize students as stock clerks, tool room managers, and other kinds of helpers. In order to make sure that students' time is effectively used, devices for storing supplies, tools, and library materials must be as nearly self-administering as possible, and administrative procedures should be well planned.

Three methods of issuing materials to students are:

1. *The self-service system* — Students select materials directly from stock. Help in locating needed types and sizes is pro-

Figure 12.13 *Materials requisition form.*

MATERIALS REQUISITION FORM					
MATERIAL	NUMBER OF PIECES	SIZE	NUMBER OF B.F., L.F., OR SQ.FT.	UNIT PRICE	TOTAL
				TOTAL COST	

vided by the teacher, if necessary. The teacher maintains a running inventory card for each item stocked. It increases the efficiency of the system to require students to prepare written requisitions before obtaining materials (see Fig. 12.13).

2. *The student stock clerk system* — A student stock clerk issues materials upon receipt of a verbal request or written requisition. He or she also maintains a running inventory. Students are appointed to the stock clerk position for short periods of time. A rotation system should be employed to ensure equitable use of student time.

3. *The central stock room system* — The school operates a central stock room in some convenient location and employs a paid, full-time stock clerk to issue materials to students. The clerk maintains all necessary records.

In most cases, either of the first two systems — or some variation of one of them — is employed. Both systems are somewhat wasteful of teacher and/or student time, but this drawback can be offset by limiting the time during which a stock room is open. If, for example, a stock room is open during the first twenty minutes of each class period, students quickly accustom themselves to the schedule, and it presents few, if any, problems. To be viable, such a policy must be consistently followed except in emergencies.

The chief advantages of the central stock room system are that it decreases the amount of laboratory floor space that must be allocated for storage purposes, makes precise inventory control possible, and decreases a teacher's noninstructional duties. Other than the cost of the stock clerk's salary, its limitation is that it may require students to leave the laboratory to obtain materials. This inconvenience can lead to discipline problems, as well as excessive loss of class time. Such a system works best where many items are stocked and where no material is bulky or difficult to divide into small quantities.

A materials system should be planned so that teachers need not handle money. If money handling *is* necessary, errors and misunderstandings may arise. Four systems that eliminate money handling in laboratories are:

1. *The immediate statement system* — Each time a student obtains materials, a bill is prepared in quadruplicate and the student presents it for payment in the business office as soon as possible. At the time of preparation, the teacher retains one copy. Upon payment, the original and two remaining copies are marked "paid." The original is given to the student

and the business office retains the two copies, one of which it returns to the teacher. The teacher files the receipted copy and destroys the one originally retained.

2. *The periodic statement system* — The teacher keeps a running account of materials received by each student. At regular intervals — preferably no less often than monthly — the business office prepares bills on the basis of information submitted by the teacher. Upon receipt of each bill, the student pays it in the business office.
3. *The material ticket system* — Each student purchases a materials ticket worth a specified amount in the business office (see Fig. 12.14). As materials are obtained, the costs are punched on the ticket. When the ticket has been completely punched, a new one must be purchased.
4. *The laboratory fee system* — Each student pays a fee that covers the cost of materials used in a particular class. Payment is made in the business office.

The first, second, and third systems are precise from a business standpoint but time-consuming in operation. The first has the least to commend it because it is unnecessarily wasteful of class time. Use of the laboratory fee system does not consume class time, and if fees are accurately calculated so that there is neither profit nor loss, it is poten-

Figure 12.14 *Materials ticket.*

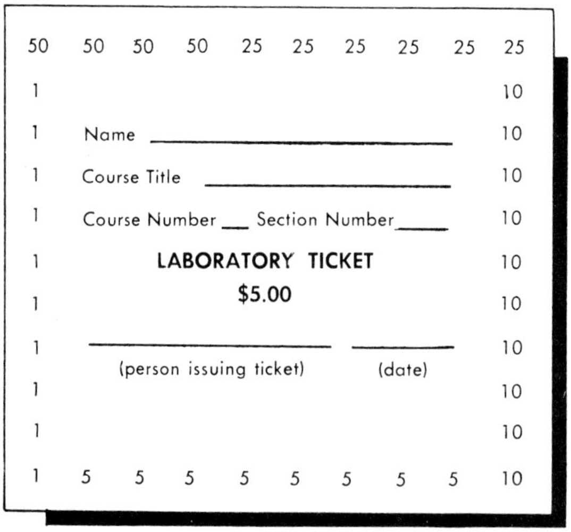
50 50 50 50 25 25 25 25 25 25
1 10
1 Name ______________ 10
1 Course Title ______________ 10
1 Course Number ___ Section Number ____ 10
1 LABORATORY TICKET 10
1 $5.00 10
1 ______________ ________ 10
(person issuing ticket) (date)
1 10
1 10
1 5 5 5 5 5 5 5 5 10

tially a satisfactory system. The limitations of the laboratory fee system are that fees can be difficult to collect and that, in effect, it forces an equal sharing of materials costs. Students' manifestly unequal consumption of materials always raises the question of equity.

One situation, perhaps the only one, in which a teacher must handle money arises when laboratory keys are issued. It is much more convenient to issue keys in a laboratory than in a business office. Money collected should be transferred to the business office as soon as the total amount has been checked against the number of keys issued, and the teacher should obtain a receipt for it.

When tools are stored in a separate tool room and issued by a student tool room manager, a record of tools issued can be maintained on requisition forms or by using student identification tags. The requisition form system makes use of a duplicated form that a student fills out and signs whenever a tool is requested. The form is kept on file in the tool room and given back to the student when the tool is returned. The time required to fill out and check requisitions reduces the efficiency of this type of system.

The identification tag system utilizes numbered tags. Each student is assigned a code number and given access to several tags — preferably six or more — bearing his or her number. A list of students' names and code numbers is posted in the tool room. Each time the student obtains a tool, a tag is exchanged for it and the tag is hung on a hook next to the tool holder. When the tool is turned in, the student's tag is returned. The tag system can work very well. Its main disadvantage is the small loss of tags that must be expected.

At least 120 tags are required for five classes of twenty-four students. Between periods, the tags should be kept in a locking cabinet. All tags of a given number should be kept together on a quick-opening key ring that is hung on a hook in the cabinet. Each hook should be marked with the code number of the tags it holds.

A self-service tool system does not require the use of requisition forms, identification tags, or any other kind of sign-out device. Students select needed tools from tool panels or cabinets and return them when the work is done. A self-service system can function satisfactorily if the teacher or a student tool manager makes a careful check at the end of each class period to be sure that all tools have been returned.

Books placed in a laboratory library should be listed by author and title in a card file that is classified according to major topics, such as machine metalwork, welding, and foundry practice. The library shelf classification system must duplicate that of the card file.

An efficient check-out procedure is needed for books and other reference materials that are loaned to students. It is important to make it convenient for students to obtain reference materials. They should be encouraged to read as widely as possible, and the ease with which materials can be checked out will certainly affect their reading habits.

If a library is small, a student should be able to check out a book by recording the date, author, title, and borrower's name on a posted sheet. Either the teacher or a student can serve as librarian. But if a book collection is extensive, a library card should be placed in a pocket inside the front cover of each book and filed in a card file when the book is checked out. The card should list the author and title of the book and provide space in which to record the date and borrower's name. Periodical and technical literature can be adequately controlled by a posted checkout sheet.

PREPARATION OF BUDGETS

An industrial education laboratory should have separate yearly budgets for equipment, materials, contractual services, and other budget line items. Funds allocated for equipment and materials should be sufficient to pay all purchase costs, including charges for shipping and insurance. Allocations should be based on teacher estimates of need. District policy governing the expenditure of approved budget monies should be flexible enough to permit modifying original allocations when such action will result in an improved program.

Budget requests should be realistic with respect to the needs of industrial education programs and the financial abilities of school districts. Industrial teachers must understand that district resources are not unlimited, and school administrators must realize that it costs substantial sums of money to establish and operate good industrial education programs. It is especially necessary that funds allocated for equipment (both purchase and maintenance) and physical plant renovation and upkeep be adequate, because laboratory safety and effective operation are dependent on it.

Materials budgets are not quite as demanding because local sources of supply are often available, and most districts require students to assume a large portion of the cost of materials. However, school districts should consider the desirability of furnishing basic materials used by students in senior high school industrial arts courses. It is true that such a policy would increase a district's yearly operating budget, but the resulting tax increase would usually be insignificant. Moreover, taxpayers must pay for the materials in one way or another. It is simply a matter of determining the method of collection.

In a junior high school program in which industrial arts is a required subject, the district should pay for most materials used. The practice of requiring students to pay for materials they consume in a course they are required to take is difficult to defend. If the school district pays for all but special materials, such as precious metals, hardware, and component parts, it is possible to avoid the unhappiness, stigma, embarrassment, and decreased educational opportunities that result when students cannot afford to pay for materials. It also lessens the amount of record keeping and other administrative work industrial arts teachers must do. A district always profits when teachers carry on a maximum of professional activity and a minimum of clerical work.

Every laboratory budget should include a contingency fund totalling 5 to 10 per cent of the total amount allocated for equipment, materials, contractual services, and the other line items. A contingency fund can make it possible to operate during an emergency caused by damage to equipment, a large increase in class sizes, or unusually heavy consumption of materials. If the use of a contingency fund is strictly controlled, flexibility of operation is gained at minimum cost, because unused funds will revert to the district at the beginning of each new fiscal year.

Budgets should be prepared at least a year in advance. Items requested should be organized in logical groups under each of the various budget line titles so that it will be easier for school administrative officers to analyze requests and make wise decisions. For example, materials requested for a crafts laboratory should include, in one group, all types, gauges, and sizes of metals; and all variations of other materials should appear in similar groups.

Budget approval should be obtained early in each new school year so that equipment and materials ordered for the following year will arrive and installations and storage arrangements can be completed prior to the start of the summer vacation period. Knowledge of what will be available when fall term classes begin is very helpful to a teacher. Moreover, checking incoming equipment and materials and reporting errors, damage, and shortages are tasks that should not be allowed to complicate the beginning of a new school year. Contractual service work should be completed during the summer months, if possible.

FOR FURTHER READING

Adams, John H. "There's More to It than Teaching." *Journal of Industrial Arts Education*, January-February 1964, p. 54.

Allen, John L. "How to Set up Sound Shop Maintenance." *Industrial Arts and Vocational Education*, March 1972, p. 39.

Cardinell, C. F. "Does the Open House Affect Our Public Relations?" *Industrial Arts and Vocational Education,* February 1964, p. 56.

Coleman, Amos D. "Closing the School Shop for the Summer." *Industrial Arts and Vocational Education,* June 1964, p. 29.

Ericson, Emanuel E., and Andrews, R. *Teaching Industrial Education: Principles and Practices.* Peoria, Ill.: Chas. A. Bennett Co., 1976.

Gardner, Leo B. "Is Your Shop Safe for a Substitute?" *Industrial Arts and Vocational Education,* September 1964, p. 28.

Griffen, Denham R. "Equipment and Lubrication Records." *Industrial Arts and Vocational Education,* March 1964, p. 83.

Lundy, Lyndall L. "After You Get It, Are You Equipped to Maintain It?" *Industrial Education,* December 1975, p. 32.

McGirr, Clint. "A Tool-check System That Works." *Industrial Arts and Vocational Education,* March 1964, p. 82.

Miller, Rex. "Methods of Public Relations." *Journal of Industrial Arts Education,* March-April 1966, p. 30.

Morrisey, Thomas J. "Why Have a Preventive Maintenance Program?" *Industrial Education,* March 1973, p. 28.

Mulski, John H. "Teacher, Don't Lock That Door Until . . ." *Industrial Education,* March 1975, p. 52.

Novak, Benjamin J., and Gessay, Roger. "The Shop Teacher and Guidance." *Industrial Arts and Vocational Education,* June 1966, p. 34.

Odell, Charles. "Vocational Guidance: An Unmet Need." *School Shop,* April 1965, p. 51.

Pelikan, Robert A., and Wolfe, Rolland C. "This Clean-up System Works." *Industrial Arts and Vocational Education,* March 1965, p. 81.

Prust, Z. A. "Attitude Development Toward Safety in Industrial Arts." *Industrial Arts and Vocational Education,* March 1966, p. 94.

Sawyer, David E. "What You Should Know About the Law and Liability." *Industrial Education,* March 1974, p. 66.

Schad, Joseph A. "How to Apply Differentiated Assignments to Industrial Arts." *Industrial Arts and Vocational Education,* February 1966, p. 23.

Silvius, G. Harold, and Bohn, Ralph C. *Planning and Organizing Instruction.* Bloomington, Ill.: McKnight Publishing Co., 1976.

Silvius, G. Harold., and Curry, Estell H. *Teaching Successfully in Industrial Education.* 2nd ed. Bloomington, Ill.: McKnight Publishing Co., 1967.

Appendixes

APPENDIX ONE

METALS LABORATORY

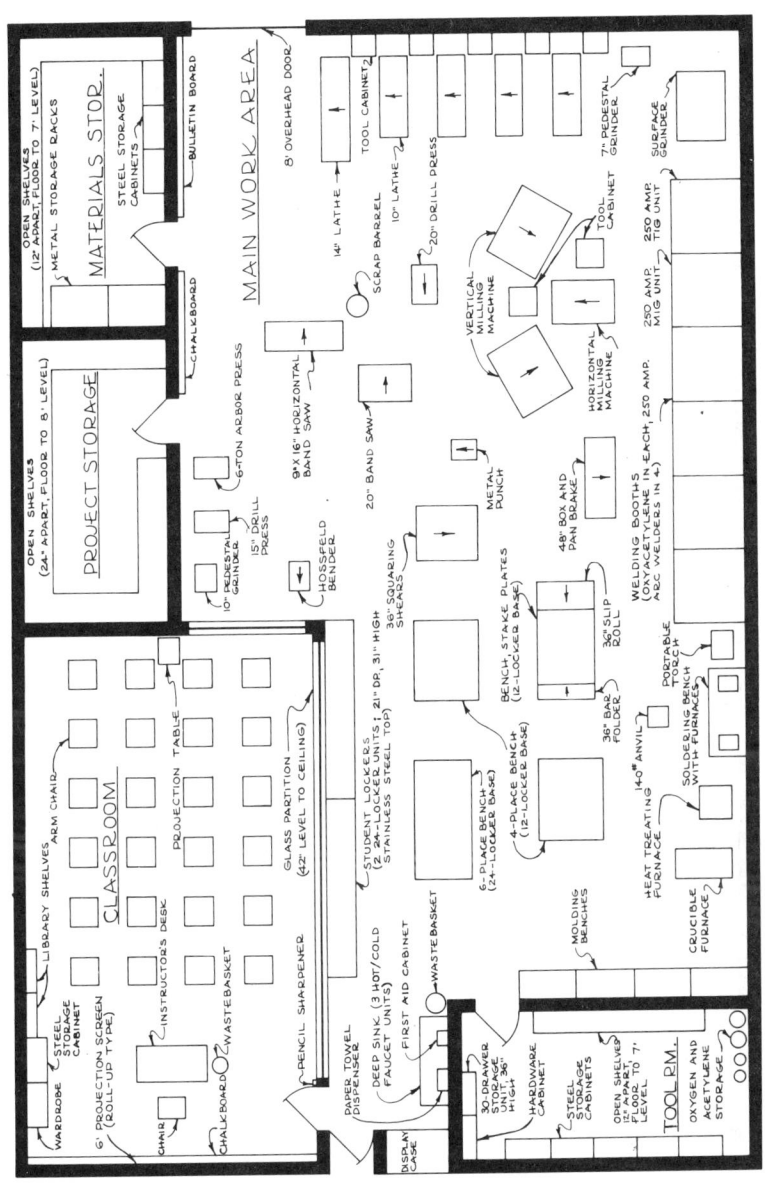

DESIGNED BY DAVID WESTEN

309

APPENDIX TWO

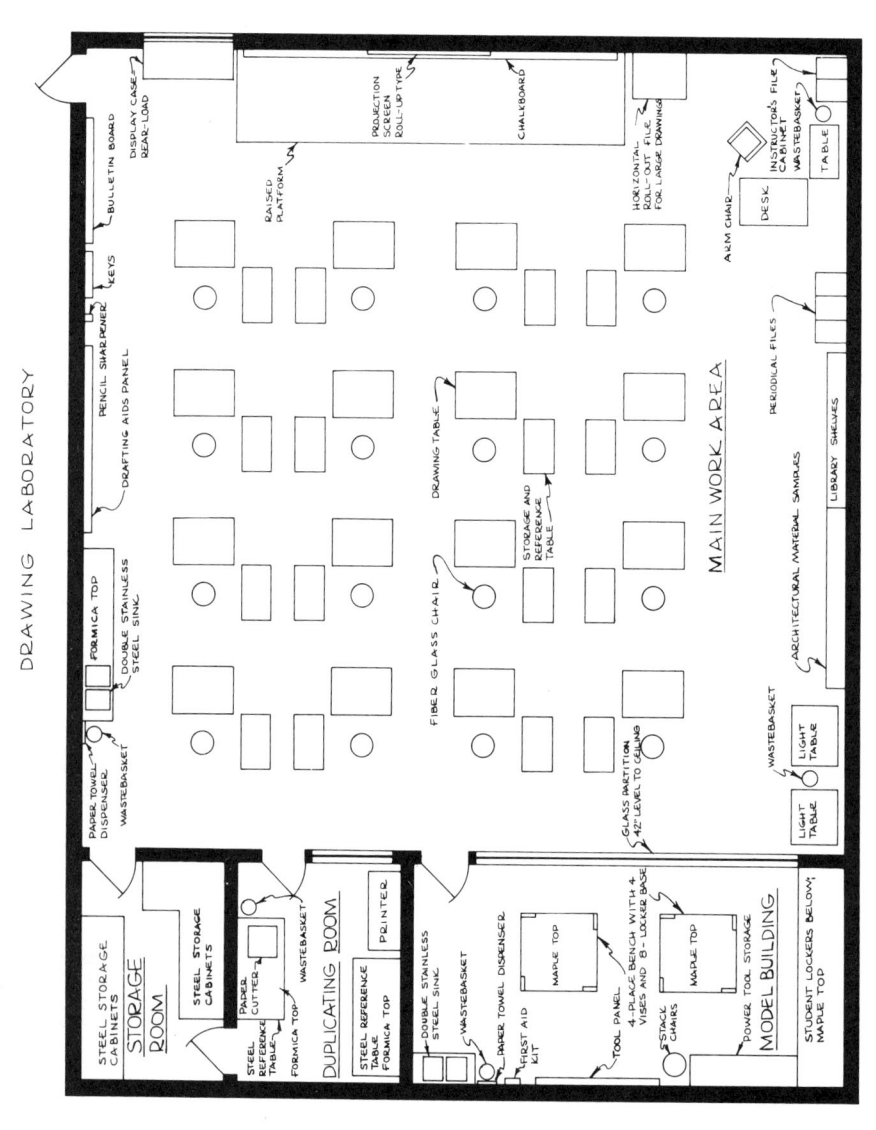

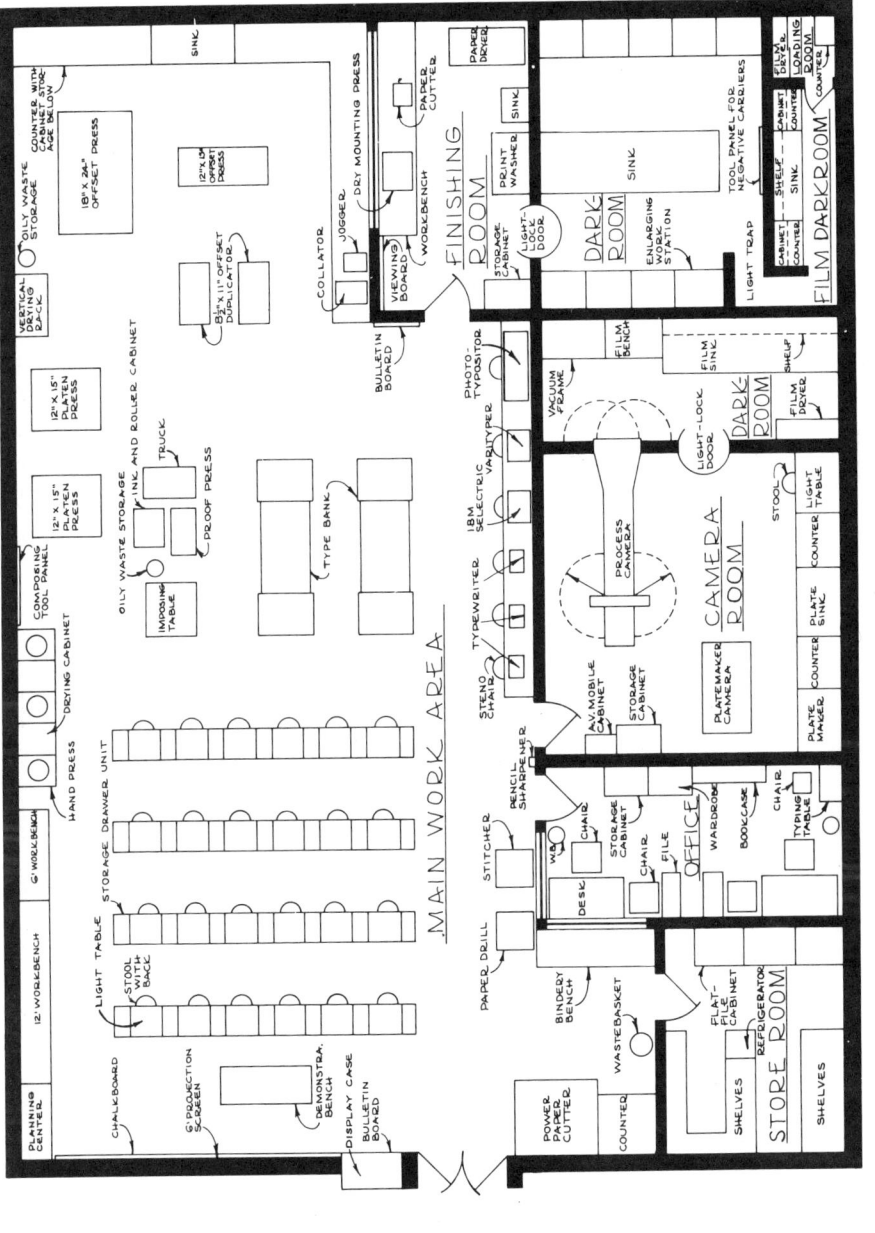

APPENDIX FOUR

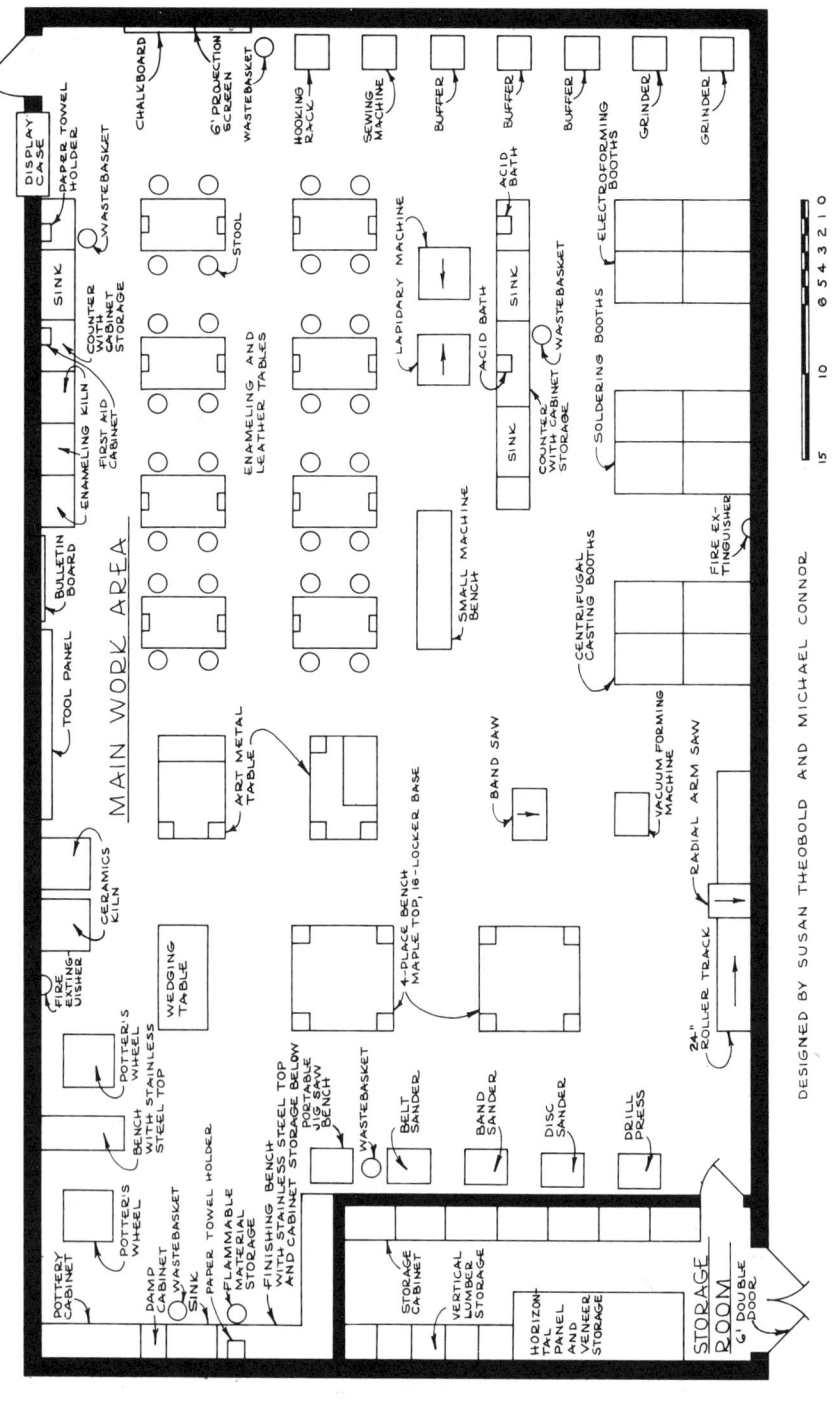

APPENDIX FIVE

313

ELECTRICITY/ELECTRONICS LABORATORY

DESIGNED BY NORMAN PAUL

FEET

314

APPENDIX SIX

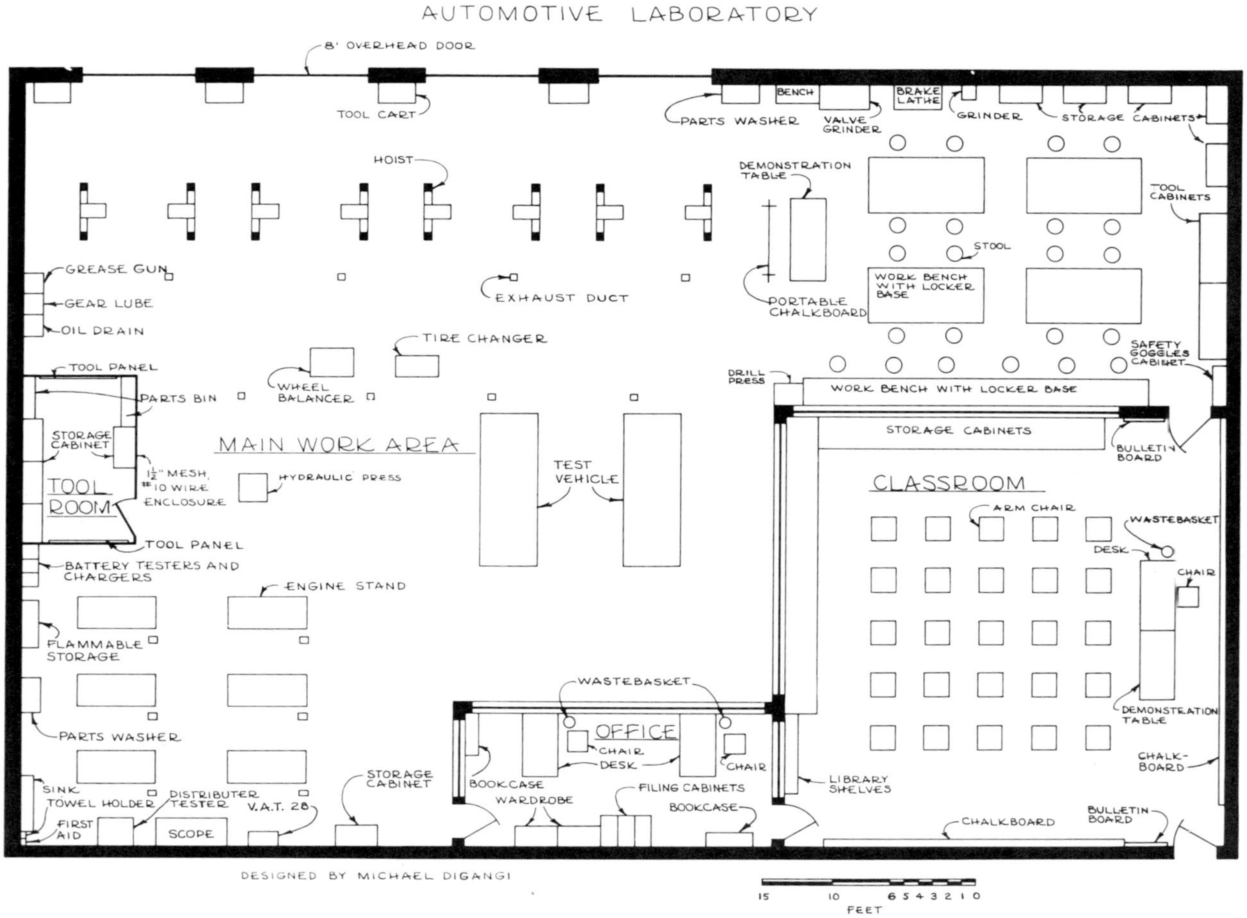

Index

Note: Numbers in italics refer to illustrations with numbers followed by a "T" indicating a table.

Acetylene, 202–204
Acoustics, 145–58. *See also* Noise
  bad in narrow laboratory, 68
  of floors, 109
  of wall facings, 98
Acrylic plastic, 102
Acquisitions, 223–44
Administration, 250, 273–306
Afterimages, 123
Air chamber, 197
Air compressors, 209–15
  controls, 212–13
  dual, *208,* 210–11, 213
  reciprocating, *208, 209,* 209–10, 213–15
  screw-type, *210, 211,* 211–12, *212*
Air conditioning, 166–68
Air environment, 159–83
  dust control, 73, 86, 161, 163, 169–82, *173, 174, 175, 176*
  exhaust systems, 149, 163, 167, 168–82
  humidity, 161, 163, 164
  temperature, 161, 162–68
  ventilation, 82, 86, 108, 160–62, 202
Air-Loc, 151

Air pressure and volume. *See* Compressed air
Aluminum
  gas pipe, 201
  machine beds, 231
Amplitude (wave), 121, *121*
Appearance (of equipment), 225, 234–36
Apprenticeship, 1–2
Attendance record, 290
Automotive laboratory, 314
Auxiliary work areas, 63, 69–92
  class area, 71–72
  demonstration area, 75
  design center, 70
  display, 75–78
  equipment storage, 85
  library, 74–75
  lockers, 78–81, *79, 80*
  materials storage, 83–84
  partitions and, 101–102
  project assembly, 85–86
  project storage, 81–82
  teacher's office, 72–74, *74*
  toilet, 86–87, *87*
  wash area, 88–91, *88, 89, 90*

Background music, 149
Balance, visual, 236
Balconies, 66–67
Beams, 94, 95
Below-grade construction, disadvantages, 62, 111
Belt drive, 151
Bennett, Charles A., 4
Bids, contractors', 241–42
Blackboard (chalkboard), 72, 75, 126, 267, 270
Branch circuit (gas), 200, 201
Brightness ratio, 134
Btu., 162
Btuh. input requirement (gas), 200
Budget, 30, 304–305. *See also* Acquisitions
Buffer zone, 154
Bulletin board, 76, 246, 268
Busway (electrical), 189, 193–94, *194*, 271

Candela, 134
Candlepower, 134
Carbon dioxide, 161–62
Cardinal Principles of Secondary Education, 9
Ceilings, 103, 105–108, 270
  and noise, 147, 149–50
  open-beam, 106
  suspended, 106–108, *107*, 148
Central heating, 164
CFR. *See* Occupational Safety and Health Act
Chalkboard, 72, 75, 126, 267, 270
Chroma, 120, 121, 123
Circuit breaker, 187, 188
Class area, 71–72, 249
Clerestories, 135
Color, 117–30
  and apparent room size, 125
  and equipment design, 236
  and warmth, 124–25
  coding, 118, 126–30, 255, 270
  complimentary, 121, 123
  display, 76
Color Conditioning, 127, 129–30
Color Dynamics, 127, 128–29
Columns, 94
Complimentary colors, 121, 123
Compressed air, 151, 185, 204–20, *204T, 206T, 208, 209, 210, 211, 212, 213T, 214, 214T, 216T, 218*, 249
Concrete, 93
  block partitions, 101
  floors, 108, *109*, 111
  prestressed, 94
  reinforced, 94–95
  slab floor, 104–105
  sunscreen, 136, *136*
Conduction, 162

Conduit (electrical), 187, 189
  flexible, *190*, 191
  rigid, 190–91
Construction materials, 237–38
Consumer information publications, 224
Contractors, selection of, 240–42
Contract Work Hours and Safety Standards Act (Construction Safety Act), 44
Convection, 162
Convenience outlet, 187, 188, 195
Copper pipe
  water, 196, 198
  gas, 201
Course content, 274–76
Crafts laboratory, 312
Cyclone, 174, *175*
Cygnaeus, 3

Darkroom, *17*
Decibel, 146–47
Decking, plank roof, 105
Delegation of authority, 296
Della Vos, 3
Demonstration area, 75, 267
Design center, 70
Diffuse reflection, 134
Diffuse transmission, 134
Direct glare, 135, 139
Discipline, 68, 153, 160
Display, 75–78, 248, 268
Doors, 99, 103, 154, 163, 247, 249, 267, 268
Drains, 198–99
Drawing, *63, 64*, 65–66, *66*, 268, *310*
Drop ceiling. *See* Ceiling, suspended
Ducts, *171, 172, 180*. *See also* Exhaust systems
Dust collectors, 172–82, *173, 174, 175, 176*
Dust control, 73, 86, 161, 163, 169–82, 188, 271. *See also* Dust collectors
Dynamic precipitation, 173–74, *174*

Ear plugs, 154
Education
  for self-realization, 8
  general, 8
Electric heating, 165
Electricity, 185, 187–95
  laboratory, *313*
Electromagnetic spectrum, *119*, 120
Electromagnetic wave theory, 118–20
Equipment
  issuance, 303
  maintenance, 151–53, 230, 253, 283
  storage, 85
Evening programs, 246, 247, 287–89
Exhaust systems, 149, 163, 167, 168–82, *170, 171, 172, 173, 174, 175, 176, 178T, 179T*

INDEX

Explosions. *See* fire prevention
External resources, 278–79

Fabric dust collector, 175, *176*
Fatigue
　and color, 123
　and lighting, 130
Fire prevention, 182, 190, 197–98, 202, 253, 269
First aid, 88, 283–85
Flammable materials. *See* Fire prevention
Floor area
　and partitions, 99
　design area, 70
　drawing area, 65–66
　library, 75
　main work area, 62–68, *67T*
　teacher's office, 72
Floors, 108–16
　materials, *114T, 115T,* 270
　sound transmission, 156
Floor sweeps, 179
Fluorescent lamp, 132, 133, 137–38, 149, 270
Footcandles, 134. *See also* Illumination
Footlambert, 135
Fountains, drinking, 197, 246
Fuels, 165, 199
Function, 225–34

Galvanized steel, 232
Gas, 185, 199–204
General lighting, 133
Girders, 94
Glass, 102
　and construction cost, 167–68
　and noise transmission, 154, 156
　diffusing, 135–36
Gloss surfaces, 126, 149
Graphic arts laboratory, *311. See also* Drawing
Greenfield. *See* Conduit, flexible
Goetze, 3
Ground-level. *See* Below-grade
Gypsum board, 101, *155*

Handicapped, 288
Hardwood flooring, 111–12
Health and safety. *See* Safety and health
Heating, 162–66
Heat loss (gain), 162
Heavy and light laboratories contrasted, 63
Hertz, 146
Hue, 120–21

Illumination, 131, 134, 141–43, *142T. See also* Light and lighting
Impact sound, 146
Incandescent lamp, 132, 133, 137

Industrial arts
　and manual training goals, 7–15, 275, 289
Insulation, 96, 155–56, *155, 156,* 165
Insurance, 285
Intensity (light). *See* Illumination
International candle, 134
Inventories, *260–67T,* 290, 291, *291, 292*
Iron pipe
　gas, 201
　water, 199
Isolation (sound), 151

Junction box, 187

Kerschensteiner, 3

Latex paint, 126
Lavatory. *See* Toilet
Lead line (gas), 200, 201
Leakage
　compressed air, 207, 216
　gas, 202
　lubricant, 230
Library, 74–75, 295, 303–04
Light and heavy laboratories contrasted, 63
Light and lighting, 130–44, 270. *See also* Luminaires
　and apparent room size, 140
　and partitions, 100
　bulletin board, 76
　ceiling reflectance, 105
　class area, 72
　color and reflectance, 122
　display, 78
　floor reflectance, 109
　fluorescent, 132, 133, 135, 137–38
　incandescent, 132–33, 135, 137
　natural, 132, 133, 136–37
　quantum theory, 119
　switches, 138
　wave theory, 118–20
Liquid propane, 199
Localizing equipment by function, 251, 269
Location of laboratories, 60–62, 147, 154
Lockers, 78–81, *79, 80,* 246, 268
Log of Occupational Injuries and Illnesses, 48–49
Longshoremen's and Harbor Workers' Compensation Act, 44
Louver, 135, 136
Lubrication, 229–30
Lumen, 134
Luminaires (lighting fixtures), 108, 133, 137, 138, 139, 140, 270
Luminous ceiling, 134

Machine noise, 149–50
Main line (gas), 200
Maintenance, 297–300, *299T*
   compressed air system, 220
   equipment, 151–53, 230, 253, 283
   manufacturers' services, 236–37
Main work area
   shape and proportions, 68–69
   size, 62–68
Manual training, 5
Massachusetts Institute of Technology, 4
Materials
   issuance, 300–303, *300, 302*
   selection, 237–40
   storage, 83–84, 251, 268
Mechanical ventilation. *See* Air environment
Media, instructional, 276–78
Metals laboratory, *309*
   materials storage, 83–84
Mechanics Institute Movement, 4
Mineral fiber, 93, 107
Mirrors, 86, 87
Motorhead drive, 150–51
Multistory buildings, 61–62, 156
Munsell hue wheel, 119–20, *119*

NACOSH. *See* Occupational Safety and Health Act
National Fire Protection Association, 187
National Standard Plumbing Code, 199
Natural gas, 199–204
Natural light, 125, 135–37
NIOSH. *See* Occupational Safety and Health Act
Noise and soundproofing, 60, 61, 145–58, 246, 270
   air compressor, 212
   and machine weight, 233
   ceilings, 106, 148, 149
   exhaust system, 177, 182
   partitions, 101, 148
   teacher's office, 73
   ventilation, 161
Nonslip flooring materials, 113, 115

Objectives, educational, 7–17, 258–59, 275, 289
Occupational illness, 48
Occupational injury, 48
Occupational Safety and Health Act (OSHA), 38–58
   and schools, 55–57
   Code of Federal Regulations (CFR), 43, 44
   definitions, 40–41
   exemptions, 40
   National Advisory Committee on Occupational Safety and Health (NACOSH), 41, 42

National Institute for Occupational Safety and Health (NIOSH), 41, 42, 47, 49
Occupational Safety and Health Review Commission, 51
Odor, 161–62
115 volt, 188, 271
Operation. *See* Administration
OSHA. *See* Occupational Safety and Health Act
Overcapacity, 67–68, 186, 206
Oxyacetylene, 202–204
Oxygen, 161–62
   and acetylene, 203–204

Panel, tool storage, 257–58, 269–70
Partitions, 99–103. *See also* Walls
   and floor area, 99
   and noise, 147, 149–50, 159
   block, *100,* 101
   masonry, 101
   movable, 99–101
   rigid, 99, 101
   steel stud, 101
Permission form, 282–83, *282*
Personnel, 296, *296T*
Pestalozzi, 3
Pigments, 120
Pipe
   compressed air, 216, *216T,* 217
   gas, 201
   water, 196–99
Planning, 17–19, 21–24, 59–92
   acoustics, 68, 98, 109, 145
   air environment, 159–83
   auxiliary areas, 69–92
   ceilings, 105–108
   color, use of, 117–30
   design procedure, 24–32, 34–35
   floors, 108–16
   laboratory layout, 250–72
   lighting, 72, 76, 78, 130–44
   location of laboratories, 60–62
   main work area, 62–69
   partitions, 99–103
   renovation, 32–34
   utility service systems, 185–221
   walls, 95–99
   wing layout, 245–49, *247*
Plexiglas domes, 135
Pollution, 169–70
Project assembly area, 85–86
Projection equipment, 71, 267
Project storage area, 81–82
Proportion, 234–35
Psychology
   air quality, 159
   color, 117, 118, 121–22, 124–25, 127, 130

INDEX

display objectives, 75–76
lighting, 141, 143
separate laboratory building, 61
temperature and humidity, 163, 166–67
Public relations, 285–87, 288
Pulley drive, 151
Purchase requests, 242–44, *243*
Purlins, 94

Quantum theory (of light), 119

Raceway (electric), 187, 189, 191–93, *192*
Radiation (heat), 162
Records, 289–95, *290, 291, 292, 293, 294, 295*
Reflectance, 134
and color, 122, 125
ceiling, 109, 126
chalkboard, 126
floor, 105, 126
wall, 125
Reflected glare, 135, 139–40
Regular transmission (of light), 134
Regulator, gas, 202–203, *203*
Repairs, 236–37
Respiration, 161
Rest room. *See* Toilet
Rheostat, 201
Roof, 103–105. *See also* Ceiling
Rubber, 150, 154
Runkle, John D., 4

Safety and Health, *8, 11, 39, 47,* 279–85, *281T, 282T, 284T*
checklist for school laboratories, 55–56
color coding, 118, 126–30
compressed air, 205, 215
doors, 103
electricity, 88, 189, 196, 228–29
emergency exits, 247
equipment workmanship, 229
fire prevention, 182, 190, 197–98, 202, 253, 269
first aid, 88, 283–85
floor plan, 250, 252, 269
gas, 201–202, 204
guards and housings, 227–28, *228*
laws, 37–55, 57
maintenance, 283
noise levels, 147
supervision, 68, 283
tool storage, 258
waste materials, 169, 182, 253
Security
display, 77
materials storage, 83, 84
project storage, 82
student lockers, 81, 294–95

teacher's office, 73
tool storage, 85, 231, 268
Separate laboratory building, 61
Services, equipment manufacturers', 225, 236–37
Shadows, 139
Shape of main work area, 68–69, 147
Shelf life, 238
Shielded frames (building), 93
Shop (laboratory), 5
Showcase (display case), 77–78, 248
Six-color system, 124
Size of main work area, 62–68, *67T*
Skylights, 135
Sloyd school, 3
Smith, Homer J., 273
Soft water, 195–96
Solenoid valve, 201, 202
Sound. *See* Acoustics; Noise
Specular reflection, 134
Sprinklers, 197–98, 269
Steel
building frame, 93–94
roof bracing, 104, *104*
stud partitions, 101, 156, *156*
suspended ceiling frames, 107
wall studs and panels, 97
Storage
materials, 83–84, 251, 268
gas, 202, 204
compressed air, 215, 217–18
tools, 253–58, *254, 255, 257,* 269–70
Strikes, 242
Student purchases, 238
Substitute teachers, 292
Sumps, gas, 201
Sun, 136, 162, 204
Supplementary lighting, 133
Supporting materials, 237–38
Switchpanel, 188–89, *189,* 271

Teacher's office, 72–74, *74,* 248
Temperature regulation, gas, 201–202
Thermocouple, 201
Titles, student job, 296
Toilet, 86–87, *87,* 197, 248–49
Tool. *See* Equipment
Traffic, 250–51, 270
Transmission factor (light), 134
Transmission of noise, 154–57
230 volt, 188, 215, 271

United States Public Health Service, 37
Unit heating, 164
Unshielded frames (building), 93
Utility service systems, 185–221, *186T*
and ceilings, 106, 108

and partitions, 100
and sound transmission, 156–57

Valves, gas, 201
Value (color), 120, 121
Ventilation. *See* Air environment
Visibility
    and color, 122
    class supervision, 68, 259
Vinyl flooring, 112–13
Vocational-technical courses
    class size, 66
    evening programs, 288
    goals, 16
    high school, 246
Von Fellenberg, 3

Walls, 95–99, 270. *See also* Partitions
    cavity, *95*, 96
    composite, 96
    curtain, *96*, 97
    design area, 70
    reinforcement, *98*
    soundproofing, 149–50, 155–56
    space, 98
    surfacing materials, 97–98
    teacher's office, 73
    ties, 97
    toilet, 87
Warrantees. *See* Services
Wash facilities, 88–91, *88, 89, 90,* 269
Waste products, 60, 89, 168–82, 246
Water, 185, 195–99
Water leg, 218–19
Wave theory (light) 118–19
Wear, equipment, 229–30
Wedgemounts, 151, *152*
Windows, 249
    and natural light, 135–37
    and partitions, 100
    and sound transmission, 156
    cost, 167–68
    exposure, 62
    ledges, 98
    size, 160
Wireway, 189, 194–95
Woods laboratory, 68, *256,* 258–300
    inventory, *260–67T*
    storage, 82, 83–84, 268
Wood stud partition, 155–56, *155*
Woodward, Calvin A., 4
Worcester Polytechnical Institute, 4
Workmanship, 233
Work station, 67, 252–53